STEPHEN O'BRIEN

'Big powers in other-worldly communication
and healing'
Irish News

'Two Worlds at his feet'
Western Mail

'Britain's renowned medium
has helped thousands of people
to contact their loved ones
through his nationwide tours'
HELLO! Magazine

'There is no doubting his sincerity
or his honesty'
Girl About Town, London

'Britain's brightest young medium...
Power seems to radiate from his fingertips.
These eyes can see beyond the grave'
Daily Star

'It's hard to be sceptical of the psychic world
when a stranger tells you precisely
what you were doing that morning,
and even days before.
I was startled, almost shocked'
Liverpool Echo

Books
by the same author:

VISIONS OF ANOTHER WORLD
The Autobiography of a Medium

VOICES FROM HEAVEN
Communion with Another World

IN TOUCH WITH ETERNITY
Contact with Another World

ANGELS BY MY SIDE
The Psychic Life of a Medium

A GIFT OF GOLDEN LIGHT
The Psychic Journeys of a Medium

THE SPIRITUAL KEYS TO THE KINGDOM
A Book of Soul-Guidance for your Life

The Spoken Word,
recordings by the same author:

Life After Death
Heal Yourself
4 Meditations
Develop your Mediumship & Psychic Powers
Develop your Healing Powers
4 Visualisations

*For details of our Worldwide Internet and
Mail Order Catalogue Service, see page 384*

Angels
By My Side

The Psychic Life of a Medium

Visionary and Poet
Stephen O'Brien

Voices

PO Box 8, Swansea, United Kingdom, SA1 1BL

'ANGELS BY MY SIDE'
A VOICES BOOK
ISBN: 0-953-6620-0-4

PRINTING HISTORY:
Bantam Books edition published 1994
Bantam Books edition reprinted 1994
Voices Books reprinted edition 1999
Voices Books Updated & Revised edition 2003

© Stephen O'Brien 1994 & 2003

All rights reserved.
No part of this book may be reproduced or utilised,
in any form or by any means, electronic or mechanical,
including photocopying, recording, or by any information
storage and retrieval system, without permission in writing
from the Publisher, Voices Books.
The right of Stephen O'Brien to be identified
as the author of this work has been asserted
in accordance with sections 77 and 78
of the Copyright, Designs and Patents Act 1988.

Conditions of Sale:
This book is sold subject to the condition
that it shall not, by way of trade or
otherwise, be lent, re-sold, hired out
or otherwise circulated in any form of binding
or cover other than that in which it is published
and without a similar condition
including this condition being imposed
on the subsequent purchaser.

Typeset by *Voices*.

Printed and bound in Great Britain
by Cox & Wyman Ltd.,
Reading, Berkshire.

*To the Freedom of your Spirit,
which is its Origin and its Destiny...*

Acknowledgements
for the 1999 and 2003 editions

I'm grateful for this opportunity to revise and
update this book in its 2003 edition, and to bring it
back into its original form
(before editors and other minds brought
their influence to bear on the text).

I'm particularly pleased to simplify and further
clarify my thoughts in the chapter titled
The Living God, which I think will now be
more easily accessible to all readers.

And I thank this God for
the life of my lovely cat, Sooty,
who passed into the Light in 1994,
shortly after the first edition of this book was
published. Her body is laid to rest
in the gardens at 'Willowtrees' cottage,
under the bluebells that she loved so much.
This edition is lovingly dedicated to my dear friend,
who brought me great joy and companionship.
I shall never forget her...

Stephen O'Brien
'Willowtrees', Wales,
April 2003.

Contents

Introduction: Angels By My Side   10

1   A Candle in the Dark   13
2   Disembodied Voices   39
3   Medium Wave   52
4   Psychic Signs and Portents   69
5   The Silver Cord   89
6   Beyond the Veil   105
7   White Owl Speaks   123
8   'O, Great White Spirit...'   145
9   Farewell to a Chocolate Soldier   151
10   Chuckle-Muscles   171
11   What Awaits Us Beyond Death   185
12   Questions and Answers   201
13   Journeys of the Soul   229
14   The Living God   233
15   Heal Yourself with Light and Colour   263
16   Ancient Wisdom   291
17   Silent Sentinels   307
18   Psychic News   324
19   'I Heard a Voice from Heaven Say...'   329
20   Psychic Atmospheres   353
21   'Willowtrees'   367

Unconditional Love
is the greatest power in the Universe.
I can't grieve for the 'dead',
for they are most certainly alive;
my heart is sad for the so-called 'living' —
those billions of people who are blindly wandering
in the deepest darkness of ignorance,
when they could be feeling utterly secure,
and living as free men,
basking in the effulgent light of spiritual truth.

Stephen O'Brien

Introduction

Angels By My Side

Though I'm but a man of flesh and bone
which soon must fade to dust and die,
   the thought of death disturbs me not,
   it simply passes by
   receiving little heed –
      for no one yet has ever died,
      and I have seen a host of angels
               standing by my side.

Whenever I pass through valleys dark and grim,
feeling so utterly lost within
that I stumble at ev'ry shaded hill,
   I need no place to sigh,
   for a secret lamp lights up my soul,
               illuminating angels
                  brighter than the sky.

And though I may not always find
   the right words to say
   to express my mind as clearly as I may,
   or loose my tongue when it is tied,
      I never fear,
         for hidden wisdom flows to me
            from invisible friends
               at my right-hand side.

And even when my actions
fail to ease another's burdens
which press them to their knees, then crucify —
   I'm never dismayed;
      instead, from deep within my soul

I beseech a Presence High:
   'Send your gentle angels
     to free the souls of those who cry.'

And when heavenly voices from eternity speak to me
  (which others cannot hear
  and therefore they deride)
  their lack of understanding grieves me not,
  for behind it — fear hides.
    But I am not afraid,
    for softly moving through my mind
    are ancient sounds which cannot be denied:
       these are the silent whisperings
         of angels glorified.

Then when my days on earth
are thankfully over and done,
and my spirit drops its body
when its course is run,
  I'll breathe a breath of pure release...

  and after your tears for me have flowed and ceased,
    in the stillness of a quiet night
    perhaps you'll hear my voice upon the breeze,
    or even sense my presence
      or my peace
    within your spirit's inner tide:

  as through the shimmering veil,
    next to your bedside,
      I'll gently kiss your forehead
        and caress your tearful eyes,
          then speak again my love for you
           to show it hasn't died —

         and I will be a Starbright Angel
           standing by your side.

1

A Candle in the Dark

The television studio was absolutely silent; you could have heard a pin drop amongst the two hundred nervous people sitting in the audience: each face was full of expectation, and everyone was waiting for me to start relaying messages from the next world...

Suddenly, the bright lights dimmed and a powerful spotlight picked me out in my armchair, as three big television cameras glided quietly into position, like silent robots.

All at once, I broke the tension with a short explanation of what I was about to attempt, conscious of my every word being recorded.

'Thank you for participating in this experiment, ladies and gentlemen,' I began warmly, 'and I hope we'll get the results we're seeking, because no medium can command anyone in the next world to communicate with us...'

Then out of the blue, somewhere deep inside my mind, I heard a young lad's indistinct spirit voice psychically speaking to me, piercing the silence of death.

'All right,' I acknowledged out loud, 'just step in,'

I suggested; and then he drew close enough for me to hear him much more clearly.

'I've got a young man with me,' I announced, 'wanting to get through to someone in our audience.' And before I could say any more, he gave me a sudden psychic glimpse of exactly how he'd met his untimely death: it was a tragic car accident.

'Yes, I saw you: that's all right. He's just projected an image here, and he's saying he passed over into the world of spirit very, very quickly: he was involved in an accident. And he talks very plainly of Paul and Robert,' I relayed.

Suddenly, an attractive young woman right at the front of the fascinated studio audience started waving her hand to get my attention.

'Do you understand this?' I asked, and she nodded enthusiastically as two cameras turned in her direction. 'Just a minute then, I'll get — oh, all right, son,' — the lad was quickly interrupting again with more evidence — 'he was dead on arrival at the hospital,' I repeated.

'Yes.'

'Who were Paul and Robert? These are people you know?'

'Yes, Paul is the chap who went over, and Robert is his brother.'

'OK. If that's the case you've been speaking to his brother about him recently.'

'Yes, I have; yes.'

'And this young man was standing listening to you.'

Obviously thrilled, the young woman was eager to know more; but unknown to her, I could hear

Paul gently sobbing at my right-hand side, for he knew we'd found his special lady and his emotions had overcome him.

'All right... he's crying,' I reported softly, 'because you're the one we want. You love him, and he loves you — and he wants to get through to his loved ones. "I love my brother," he says, "and he's never got over the shock."'

'No, he hasn't,' she replied positively, just as Paul was urging me to state that he was often with his brother Robert, and he wanted him to know that he'd tried to personally contact him.

'All right, Paul, I'll tell her: I heard that so clearly. He said, "Tell my brother his best mate speaks to him." He says, "They placed some flowers for me, but I don't want them to go there; I want them just to think of me and send me their love." Do you understand that?'

'Yes, I do,' she said knowingly, after which the lad went on to mention some earrings and a place called 'Station Road', and that there was another person involved in the accident. His lady then confirmed to the audience that he'd lived just near Station Road and that she understood the mention of the earrings, but she wasn't sure about the third party involved in the tragedy – she would check this out.

'"Tell her I followed her here," Paul said, "and it's time she tidied up her shoes!" He's getting good at this now,' I announced with a smile, asking the young woman, 'What does this mean?'

'Oh yes, I have lots and lots of shoes and they're in a big pile, and I *have* to sort them out!' she grinned, and later informed me she'd made that *very same statement* a few days previously.

Then Paul delivered two accurate facts which, looking back on them, show that he'd cleverly prepared his spirit message, long before it was to be transmitted; and these statements proved all the more evidential because of their intimate nature. In speaking of his roadside death, and of his precise words to his mother on the day that he died, he drew immediate confirmation from his girlfriend:

'He's saying that two people rushed and tried to resuscitate him, but they couldn't resuscitate him.'

'Yes, that's right,' said his startled lady, her eyes glinting.

'And he also tells me, "I used to go out and say to Mum: tarrah, Mum" — but he never said it on that day.'

'No, he didn't,' she agreed.

'Oh, you knew?'

'Yes, I know,' she said.

Then Paul continued, '"I never said it on that day, Stephen, and I've waited now to say: it's not goodbye, Mum – it's not tarrah, Mum; I'm all right, and I'm with Bill and Annie" — these are probably friends or relatives (I interjected) "and I'm safe, so don't cry for me."'

I took an emotional breath for all of us, smiled at his girlfriend, then gently asked, 'Now, will you tell Robert that he's been?'

'I certainly will, *yes!*' she beamed from ear to ear. 'I'm seeing Robert tomorrow and I shall *certainly* tell him.'

It was so lovely to see the young lady's happy smile that I almost forgot to let Paul finish his contact, which he did with a final flourish of, '"God bless you, my darling — and tidy up those shoes!" Thank you very much,' I said, completing my mediumship with a smile as big as Paul's and his lady's.

'Thank you *very* much,' was her warm and bright reply.

Millions of television screens across central Britain, which were flickering like candles in the darkened corners of living-rooms, then suddenly switched pictures as the station ended this video-recording and immediately went live to the studio to reveal Linda Mitchell, one of *Central Weekend Live*'s presenters, who addressed my recipient.

'Can I ask your name, please?'

'Andrea.'

'Andrea, who exactly was contacting you there?'

'My boyfriend.'

'And what was his name?'

'Paul.'

'How close were you?'

'We were engaged. He'd asked me to marry him the night before the accident.'

'When you hear those sorts of things, what's your reaction?'

'I'm happy – *elated,* knowing that he's still carrying on.'

'Don't you feel a bit creepy? I mean, he died — how long ago did he die now?'

'Two years this January.'

'And you've had this message from him...'

'Yes, I'm *happy*! It's not creepy at all, because it's Paul. How can it be creepy? I know him so well, why would he want to frighten me now?'

'Are you a believer in Spiritualism?'

'Yes I am.'

'Do you regularly go to Spiritualist churches and meetings?'

'Yes.'

'Has Paul spoken to you before?'

'He's impressed people and given them similar situations as to how the accident happened, but he's never come through with such positive evidence as he did with Stephen. He's never come through like that before.'

'Really? What was it about what Stephen said that impressed you so specifically tonight?'

'My shoes, my earrings, his brother, his mum — his mum still does get very upset. Just everything really, and I know he'd come through with things like this, you know.'

'OK. Thank you, Andrea. Well,' said Linda, looking directly into the camera, 'the question is simple: can Spiritualists contact people who have died and put them in touch with living relatives? Leading medium Stephen O'Brien regularly fills town halls up and down the country with people who are eager to know if the answer to that question is yes.'

She then turned towards the colourful studio set where I was seated with two others (ready to do battle). 'Stephen, that's quite an amazing thing, isn't it, to talk to somebody who's been dead for two years? I mean, you said you felt emotionally wiped out by this.'

'No, it's not unusual,' I answered brightly, 'it's quite a commonplace occurrence for me as I go around the country – but it didn't emotionally

18

wipe me out,' I gently corrected her. 'The link was much longer than that, Central TV has edited it down; what happened was this: my communicator began to cry, and because he was in attunement with me I sensed this very strongly.' Linda nodded understandingly as I finished with, 'But I tried to sincerely deliver what he had to say to his fiancée.'

'And you've never met Andrea before tonight?'

'No, I've never met the young lady before,' I said. In fact, that was the first time I'd heard her name, and her intimate relationship with Paul had only just been revealed to me.

Linda then brought into the discussion the celebrated illusionist Mr David Berglas, who was then the President of the British Magic Circle, by saying, 'David, isn't this proof that there is something in Spiritualism?'

'I have to say: no,' he replied — which came as no surprise because he'd been engaged to voice a counter-viewpoint to try and systematically destroy the evidence I'd given to the elated young woman, after which he had to confess to viewers that he'd spent the previous forty minutes since the recording of my link in defending me backstage, because, as he admitted about Paul's spirit evidence that I'd just delivered, 'You got an amazing degree of accuracy.'

And then he offered the rather meagre sum of £10,000 to me, or to any other medium, who could prove to his satisfaction the reality of a life after death — I say 'meagre' simply because on previous occasions I'd turned down £250,000 from sceptics on TV!

'I'm not one bit interested in your money,' I

replied instantly — and I wasn't. A great part of my work is to bring comfort and hope to people and also to help them to be more aware of the undying nature of spiritual love and of the continuity of life. I also teach that soul-liberating spirit teachings, guidance and inner strength are available to every one of us; they are often transmitted to me by discarnate loved ones from an eternal world of spirit beyond what many still consider to be 'death'. For decades I've tried to publicly achieve these objectives by consciously joining two worlds together as one, as best as I could, and often in some very difficult psychic conditions.

But I don't think many sceptics want to accept that a medium's purpose is to *serve*: we're not out *to prove* anything.

Sensitives provide a service to people on both sides of the thin veil called 'death', so that they can contact each other.

Common sense tells us that after telephoning friends in a distant land, you don't then demand of the handset, 'What did you set out to prove?' It has simply provided an invaluable service — and even when communication lines have been opened up, there are still a number of electronic and weather conditions which can adversely affect the clarity of the transmissions that they carry and receive.

Similar difficulties can hinder psychic communications, except that the problems in mediumship arise because of the presence of inharmonious minds, and the lack of soul-sensitivity in the medium.

But let's get back to *Central Weekend Live*:

David Berglas was still stating his case against

mediumship and was about to deliver what was intended to be a stunning showstopper but, unknown to him, and to everyone else, my spirit friends had forewarned me of his 'secret' intentions while I'd travelled to the Nottingham studios on the train — so it came as no surprise to me at all. He served his volley by announcing, 'As a magician I can always duplicate what any medium demonstrates, which I've often done.'

To this obviously prearranged statement the presenter replied, 'I'd like to see you do that, David,' — but the whole exercise fell flat on its face because I instantly scotched it with, 'Maybe you *could* get up and mimic a link like that, but yours would be trickery, and mine is Reality — and that's the difference between us.'

There was immediate spontaneous applause from the audience. Mr Berglas stayed firmly in his seat, and my comments were later hailed as making 'good TV'.

Then the presenter threw some red meat to a pack of wolves, so to speak, by opening up the discussion to the ever-eager-to-argue audience — which was one of the show's trademarks. Or, to put it another way — she might as well have said, 'Let the bun-fight begin!'

Suddenly, a whole basketful of bread went flying, and a barrelful of hoary old chestnuts that the sceptics usually throw at sensitives also whizzed past my head, all flung in quick succession.

When a rather pious Christian gentleman said, 'Regarding people on the Other Side, I don't feel we have a *right* to contact them' — I instantly corrected this with, 'But Paul contacted *me,* sir. I didn't contact *him, he* contacted *me,'* which drew more hearty spontaneous applause from the studio audience.

After this, the presenter brought into the discussion a new contributor, Jean Bassett, an official of Britain's Spiritualists' National Union.

'Jean, you're an ordained minister in the Spiritualist Church, people are talking of charlatans and frauds: how do you deal with that big credibility gap which a lot of sceptics in the audience don't seem able to bridge?'

'We can only work through it with sincerity,' replied Jean, warmly. 'Everybody's entitled to disbelief, this is their prerogative — but we can then come in and prove to them that survival is a fact,' she went on, truthfully adding that hundreds of genuine mediums visit small Spiritualist churches up and down Great Britain each week, receiving only their travelling expenses and not personally knowing their audiences, and yet they still offer accurate spirit messages to the public.

The presenter quickly changed tack.

'Stephen, why does it always seem to be pretty minor information? If we're hearing from the spiritual world why do we never hear the answer to the AIDS problem?'

'If anybody would care to look at their life, Linda, it's quite mundane,' I said. 'These messages may sound trivial — but *not* to the one who's sending them, and *not* to the one who's receiving them.'

'So you're saying it's a way of proving the link?'

'Yes. This young lady's man isn't going to come back and speak about Einstein's Theory of Relativity — he's going to talk about her and him.'

It's worth mentioning at this point that spirit messages are often full of personal information which is meant solely for the ears of the two parties involved, which is why other witnesses can never truly judge the meaningfulness of the nuances that may be hidden within them.

And so the studio argument raged on for a good twenty minutes or more, coming to an end with resounding applause as we all trooped off to the green-room for coffee and cakes, where David Berglas made a special effort to congratulate me on my work. Oh well, I thought to myself, *c'est la vie*.

But it was all worthwhile in the end because the programme caused quite a stir in the country and I received much favourable mail from viewers who, after enjoying it, were now interested in investigating the paranormal.

Television, of course, instantly makes one's face a familiar sight, and to my great dismay this means that I'm now often recognised in public, which — quite frankly — has been one of the biggest blights of my private life.

Such embarrassing intrusions, however, can sometimes be made more tolerable when they serve some greater purpose, as one did quite recently when I was coming out of a marketplace.

I'd just gathered the folds of my voluminous mackintosh about me while stepping through a set of those terrifying lightning-fast automatic doors — I'm positive that one day they'll shut too quickly and slice me completely in half! — and as I stepped into the bracing air, a loud male voice suddenly called out behind me, 'Excuse me!'

Startled, I swivelled on my heels.

'Pardon me, but you *are* Mr O'Brien, aren't you? Stephen O'Brien, the medium?'

Standing before me was a tall swarthy-looking man in his mid-twenties, and he seemed rather troubled. Although he was wrapped up warmly against the chilly February winds, his face was reddening in the breeze as I studied his smarting eyes; and even then I didn't know what to expect — strangers can deliver any kind of unwelcome surprise these days.

'*Are* you Stephen O'Brien?'

'Yes, I am.'

'I thought so; I've seen you on television. I hope you don't mind me stopping you like this, but I've been worried sick. Can I ask you a question, Stephen?'

Suddenly, there was a note of genuine anxiety in his voice: this young man needed help, so I nodded and he spilled out his sad story.

'You see, I lost my father this year, and when he died I was completely devastated. He was a great bloke and it's the worst thing that's ever happened to me,' he said, pathos filling every space of the psychic atmosphere around him; and my heart went out to him when I sensed the grief of his great loss.

'What can I do for you?' I asked, pulling my scarf around my neck against the sharp air.

'Well, the problem is I'm a Christian, you see, a Catholic, and my people were very unhappy when I told them I'd been to see a medium. Actually, it was after I'd read your books.'

'Oh,' I said, keeping an even tone when, in fact, I'd already sensed what was coming next. 'Look,

I'm sorry about your father,' I added sympathetically, 'but as you've probably found out by now, there's no such thing as death.'

'Oh yes,' he said enthusiastically, 'your books have been an enormous help to me; and the medium I saw at the Spiritualist Church gave me an excellent message from my Dad, proving his survival. She told me things that only he and I knew. It was a magnificent moment, and I can't tell you what it meant to hear from him again, Stephen.'

'That's great,' I said, 'and you're very fortunate to hear from him so soon.'

'Yes, but my problem is my family. You see, they're good people, but they're born-again Christians and... well, now they won't even speak to me. They've cut me off from the fold, and they told me Dad's message had come from the devil who was impersonating him, and that now I'd be damned in hell-fire for eternity, for trying to contact my father...'

His words trailed away helplessly and he deeply furrowed his brow. I stared into his face and couldn't believe my eyes when I saw the strange psychic shadows falling across this young man's features as he remembered his family's fearful threats, and sensed the pain that he'd felt when they'd withdrawn their love from him.

'Please,' he pleaded, rather like a lost child, 'can you help me, Stephen? What do you think of what they said?'

'It's absolute rubbish,' I replied.

I was amazed that his relatives seemed to care more for their religious dogma than they did for the feelings of one of their own bereaved.

'Look,' I continued, trying to appeal to his reason and to his religious sense, 'In the Bible it says that Jesus told his disciples to seek and they would find. Well, you went out seeking for your father, and you found him. So you've done nothing wrong at all. If God had thought communication was evil, He would never have allowed His chosen prophets to speak to the so-called dead, would He?'

'No. I suppose not,' he agreed, brightening a little.

'And the Bible is a book packed with psychic and spiritual experiences, miracles, and healings. It's full of stories about spirit messengers — angels from the next worlds — sending help to Earth; and it says that Jesus himself spoke to the "dead" prophets Moses and Elias on the mount when they appeared to Him.'

'Yes, He did, didn't He?' he said, his whole face lighting up for the first time.

'That's right; and the Master's message was all about Love, as well as about promising that we would do much greater things than Him, because He ascended to the Father. Do you remember that text?'

'Yes. That's right,' he enthused, 'He did.'

'Well, there's your explanation. And remember this: your dad, just like everyone else who's ever passed on, is still alive in another world. So don't take your family's views too much to heart; I'm sure they don't really mean to hurt you — they're only speaking from their own understanding, you know,' I said honestly, and with as much compassion as I could muster in the circumstances.

'You know, at the end of the day, this is *your* life my friend, not your family's; and it's you who must live it, breathe it, experience it and seek out its meaning for yourself, in your own way.'

There was a thoughtful pause.

As I watched the young man's face registering the new thoughts our conversation had brought him, I lifted my collar against the cold wind.

'Stephen,' he said, at last, 'thank you... But tell me, why on earth would my people claim communication is evil?'

'Probably because of fear,' I replied. 'Fear of what they think is the unknown — when, in fact, the next world has been well charted for anyone who wants to learn about it. And perhaps your relatives have misinterpreted certain of their religious sayings,' I added. 'And It's worth remembering, by the way, that Christianity isn't the only faith in the world. There are other beliefs that are much older. Besides, all roads lead to the Godhead in the end, so no single Church can possibly have all of the truth — but each faith might have a small portion of it.

'And as for the so-called devil — I don't believe in him.'

A smarting gust of February wind caught my ears, so I pulled up my scarf and went on, 'My own spiritual faith is built on direct knowledge and experience of the God-force. It's man who draws upon this Power of Life and then wickedly twists and contorts it, and uses it to say and do ignorant and unkind things. Man is the only devil I know,' I concluded.

The stranger's face now beamed out psychic light,

and for the first time his eyes showed a youthful sparkle.

'Listen: do you love your father?' I asked.

'Oh yes, very much.'

'And do you think he still loves you?'

'Oh yes, with all his heart; he told me so before he died, and again in that medium's message.'

'Then that's all that matters,' I returned. 'Never forget that love is stronger than death.'

'Stephen,' smiled the young man, reaching out and warmly clasping my hand tightly in his, 'I feel so much better about it all now. Thank you very much for talking to me. It's been a great privilege to meet you; and I think your books are marvellous.'

'Listen, don't be too hard on your people,' I advised. 'They're only doing what they think is right. Why don't you pray for them, and do your best to help them to understand, and then to share in what you've found – what, in your soul, you already know.'

'I will,' he replied.

'And the greatest thing of all, of course, would be if you could learn to forgive them; maybe then they'll accept you again — not for what they'd like you to be, but for what you really are and for what you truly believe,' I said; and he shook my hand again.

'I'm really grateful. Thank you.'

'My pleasure,' I said, calling after him as he went on his way through the busy crowd of cold shoppers, 'and if you continue seeking, you'll discover much more!'

As I wended my way home, I couldn't help

thinking just how deeply some careless words can hurt, more than those who speak them may ever know; and I was conscious, too, of the Nazarene's mission, which, after all, seems based on loving others as we ought to love ourselves.

As some readers may be aware, just like this young man, I've suffered from similar narrow-minded bigotry, and not just from born-again Christians, either (who, I regret to report, have been the most forceful and violent of all my critics). Even some sceptical scientists have been willing to have a go at me. So I've now come to the conclusion that some people lead such sad and inadequate lives that I'm obviously their principal amusement.

Poor souls.

Still, I've become quite philosophical about it: they also serve who stand only to be humiliated.

You name it and it's been hurled at me. In fact, I'm now so proficient at ducking, I've got a crick in my neck.

But the public hasn't been one bit deterred by any of these 'professional debunkers', and each year they still attend my meetings in their thousands. Despite the several crippling economic recessions Britain has suffered from – situations so bad that many household-name stars were forced to call off their performances through lack of ticket-sales – my meetings have never been cancelled; and all of them seemed well received, though attendances did fluctuate, of course.

Such public interest in the paranormal under-lines the fact that man is slowly entering a new phase of consciousness, a New Age of Awareness in which materialism is on the down-trend and matters of the body, mind and spirit are rapidly ascending.

Over the years, the people have given to me something more precious than their welcome encouragement: they have given me their love.

And they still send me small gifts through the post: this year someone even had some trees planted in my name on Holy Island.

But most of all, I get sackfuls of letters in which people continue to express their condemnation of the noisy critics and ought-to-know better bigots for exhibiting their bad behaviour in public.

But to me, the people have pledged their undying support. I hope that doesn't sound arrogant; I didn't mean it to, but it's true. I've received letters from nearly every country in the world, encouraging me, thanking me, and asking me to share more of my life-story and the spiritual teachings I've received.

Letters have come from places where my books haven't even been published, so it seems many a battered copy has gone 'on holiday', even if I haven't. Funnily enough, a woman from England wrote recently saying she was reading one of my books, *In Touch with Eternity,* languishing on a sun-drenched Spanish beach, when suddenly she was 'accosted' then avidly chatted to by two sun-burnt *senoritas* who'd recognised my face on the cover, declaring they'd seen me at one of my meetings!

It certainly is a small world.

Most of the thousands of letters I've received have been quite touching and emotional, full of sincerity and sensitivity — and others have positively glowed with such compliments and praise for my work that I'm far too embarrassed to record them here.

I'd like to thank everyone whose kindness, thoughtfulness, and sincere prayers have indeed strengthened, uplifted and encouraged me to continue sharing the spiritual truths I've found with millions of souls who are eager to hear them.

I still answer my mail personally, and my prayers immediately go out for all of my correspondents and their loved ones.

And thank you, too, for being patient in waiting for your replies. My wish for you all is that you may find true peace of mind – and especially for the correspondent who felt inspired to ask, *'What has developing your sensitivity given to you, and of what use is it?'*

Such a questioning spirit will no doubt lead its possessor on to an exciting path of inner soul-discovery; a road I feel privileged to have walked, and which I'm still dutifully treading. Mind you, it's been a tough yet paradoxically marvellous, spiritual journey – but it's been a personal quest well worth the effort.

What has unfolding my soul-awareness given me? Well, so many remarkable and comforting things that I'm delighted to share with you.

It's revealed to me what awaits every sentient creature after death, and how the incredible Universal Laws of Predestination and Freewill fit into, and control, every facet of our lives.

It's brought me a more profound understanding of who man truly is, of where he comes from, and of what will be his ultimate destiny (and what will be the fate of all other souls).

Awareness has created within me great joy and has made me conscious of each being's unbreakable link with the One Living God; and of how, through man's hidden psychic powers and connections with this Supreme Power and Great Light, he can heal not only his own body, mind and spirit, but also the tortured souls and hearts of others.

My increasing depth of awareness has revealed to me the true nature of the Infinite Great Spirit in all Its pristine beauty and Its supernal magnificence and spiritual majesty.

Sensitivity has fanned within my spirit the radiant lights of soul-knowledge and many eternal spiritual truths which I can now, in my own small way, shine into the darkness of other people's lives, into the hearts of souls who are desperately dissatisfied with the greed of acquisition and an all-consuming lust for materialism.

And the great news is that by developing a responsiveness to the inner things of the spirit, all people who are craving knowledge of spiritual realities and seeking the inner peace that passes understanding can experience these indescribable joys for themselves. They can also benefit from the wonderful power of unconditional love, as it enriches their lives.

My personal awareness has helped me to link with developed minds that dwell deep within realms of brilliant light far beyond the Earth, and I've been able to receive, and then to share, some of the wisdom of the ages which has been secretly revealed to me by these souls, whom I consider to be spiritual masters.

My quickened psychic senses have revealed to me angels by my side.

There have been innumerable blessings.

And now, when I stand on a summer riverbank and look into the rushing stream, I can feel its spiritual source and power. In the glinting eyes of an old woman I've seen a shining, bright soul-light; and within the breast of a young man, the true nature of his loving heart has shone forth, openly before my vision.

Nothing can hide from the soul who can truly see.

On many quiet Sunday mornings when drifting breezes carry the resonant peals of church bells across a tranquil valley, their music strikes its psychic harmony deep within my soul.

In so many things, I've intuitively felt and heard the rhythm of life.

At violet twilight when, on the warm breath of night, silent voices come speaking to me from another world, or the radiant forms of people who have long forsaken this cold Earth for a much brighter land appear before my eyes, their vibrating peaceful presences are so very real to me that they may as well not have 'died'.

And when I gaze into the heart of a perfumed flower, I can appreciate its unique beauty in fullness: I don't have to analyse it, or consciously think about it — it isn't a sense experience — it's a spirit-to-spirit link. In the gazing, I seem to become a part of its being, and its energies blend with mine.

The unfolding of soul-sensitivity has opened for me doors to luminous inner worlds, which if they were ever to close again would leave me bereft of any real meaning in my life.

Greater heart-realisations have also shown me that war and hunger, and hatred and tyranny, burn all the love out of the breast of humankind and serve only to increase man's poverty of spirit.

Such inner revelations have urged me to choose the much gentler, more spiritual pathway of trying to practise and to make known the benefits of unconditional love, harmony and brotherhood between all life-forms.

These noble thoughts are so easy to accept, but are sometimes so tremendously difficult to enact in daily life — but they form the core of what I've tried to share with as many millions as I could, in the living hope that one day — even though it may come gradually — peaceful toleration will fully establish itself on the Earth.

I realise that every voice for peace is important; and that each life expressing it must lead the way, one step at a time.

Looking back on my spiritual journey so far, no one on Earth, or in Heaven, could ever persuade me to forsake one jot of the sensitivity I've developed through the many hardships I've experienced during this personal soul-quest.

So, I shall continue to seek out, and do my best to express, the powers of truth and love.

As this inner awareness continues to unfold, it seems to me now — as I look around at what often seems to be a mad and rushing world, still bereft of peace — that through my subtle spirit senses I may have experienced more of actual reality than some people, and perhaps a good deal more of spiritual truth than most.

Passing By

feathered birdwings arc a brilliant sky
  and kiss me quietly
    as they fly,
      stirring my sleeping soul
        like a lover's sigh
          as they pass by

mother earth
  blesses me,
    as I tread her soil she tries
      to energise my thirsty spirit
        passing by

tall trees swaying way up high
  draw their veil across the sky
    and shadow youth with coolness —
      many times they sang their sigh
        but my eyes were deaf
          and I passed on by

summer sun lift up your voice
  so I can lift up mine
    and fly –
      how many years have I rushed along
        without a second glance
          and passed you by?

sparkling eyes of the hungry children
  shining bright and making me cry —
    can you still love me now?
      will you open your hearts
        and try?

that I might easily forget
the burning shame
of ignoring you
when you passed me by

my dearest friend with the golden heart
you loved me once —
I was special, set apart —
but time was nigh:
and now I'm old
and soon must die,
like a loveless child
passing by...

Stephen O'Brien

2

Disembodied Voices

The atmosphere in the theatre auditorium was electric: it had been quite a good public meeting, one in which the audience had radiated their loving thoughts into the atmosphere, providing just the right kind of psychic conditions in which to receive clear spirit communications, and many voices had come in thick and fast.

Grateful husbands had successfully returned to their wives, children had relayed some lovely memories to ease their parents' grief, and lovers had comforted their best friends. They'd all done remarkably well to get me to hear their sometimes faint voices clearly enough to represent them faithfully; and their messages had been sprinkled with special thoughts and evidential, quirky turns of phrase that had sent us into stitches of laughter. There'd also been a few quiet tears when communicators had remembered their most personal and poignant last moments on Earth.

And now time was swiftly passing us by: it was nearing ten o'clock and the end of the meeting, a time that can sometimes be heartbreaking when I'm conscious of many more invisible friends desperately hoping for a chance to speak. But the clock had nearly beaten us and I was just going to finish — when I suddenly heard a woman's urgent disembodied voice calling out from behind me. Terribly anxious and excited, she seemed desperate to make her special connection.

In an instant, I knew she wanted to reach her two daughters seated in the crowd. But where were they? I hadn't the faintest clue. Unless I'm told where people are sitting, I just have to call out the facts and hope the link will be placed. It's almost impossible to pinpoint recipients with phrases like, 'This message is for the lady two rows from the back of the upper circle; she's wearing a green coat.' Sometimes I can't even *see* the audience because of the bright spotlights, and people sitting underneath deep galleries and in mezzanines are often shrouded in darkness.

I quickly sent a thought to the worried spirit mum, 'It's OK,' I reassured her, 'don't worry about the clock: I'll *make* time; I won't turn you away,' I said, after which I located her two girls, who immediately stood up and shouted back their replies in loud, excited voices.

This spirit mum's link seemed quite evidential and comforting, containing the kind of love that any devoted mother might send to her treasured daughters. But afterwards, her girls surprised me when they revealed the hidden significance of their mum's clever final phrase, which had been, 'You see, girls, I came here anyway!' This had thrilled them and had made them 'float on cloud nine' because, as one daughter — Alison — explained:

'It was absolutely *amazing*! Our mother passed

over only last Friday. In fact, we'd bought her a ticket and she was supposed to be here tonight at this meeting! She really believed in you, Stephen, and was so looking forward to meeting you. So when she said, "I came anyway," we were thrilled. We couldn't believe it was happening! To have a message like that from our mum was incredible. Thank you so much.'

Then Alison and Jan threw their arms around me, kissed and cuddled me, and all of us were stunned by their mother's evidential remarks. And later, Alison, who had found her mother's death particularly hard to bear, wrote to me saying, 'You brought me a fabulous message from my mother last year at the Middlesbrough Town Hall, and it's helped to keep me going.'

This kind of spirit message serves to remind all mediums what their calling is about: it's a sharing of mind-liberating knowledge and spiritual truths, as revealed to them by their compassionate inspirers in the Beyond. Communications can bring a wealth of comfort and hope to those who mourn, and to those who feel lost in a seemingly senseless and purposeless existence since 'death' robbed them of their special people.

Mediumship can remove the dreadful fear of annihilation which is inherent in the mind of man by unveiling 'death' as nothing more than a false shadow: in all the universe there is only life. God alone knows, this sad world of ours often needs some greater spiritual revelation, as well as a constant reminder of what the power of unconditional love can achieve when it's allowed to beat within the hearts of men and women everywhere.

Unconditional love is the greatest power in the universe, and this power alone will help man to save himself from his own all-consuming greed and selfishness.

I can't grieve for the 'dead' for they are most certainly alive; my heart is sad for the so-called 'living', those billions of people who are blindly wandering in the deepest darkness of ignorance, when they could be feeling utterly secure, and living as free men, basking in the effulgent light of spiritual truth.

Spirit, which is our true essence, can never die: it's eternal, and some communicators are very good at reinforcing this fact by delivering clever evidence of their survival – a spirit dad did so at one of my London meetings when he addressed his beloved daughter.

'Your father wants me to tell you, "I'm still alive. And I'm going to make an appearance on the next wedding photograph when it's taken,"' I informed her.

'He's done that once before,' was the astonishing reply.

'Well,' I rejoined, 'he's going to do it again — complete with a red carnation in his buttonhole!'

The audience was much amused and intrigued, and so was a London journalist who followed up this message by obtaining the woman's next wedding photo, complete with her spirit dad's 'extra' image on it, just as he'd predicted – and an interesting article then appeared in a popular women's glossy magazine.

But other spirit links, delivered at my live theatre meetings, have frequently drawn quite different and often emotional, or serious responses — such as the message that linked together two British soldiers.

'I have a Tony here,' I solemnly announced, 'speaking of Bill and Brian, and I'm sensing the presence of a soldier whose life was tragically lost in an Irish sectarian killing. He says, "I was blown up — the IRA murdered me," and he's repeating two Irish place-names: Ballymena and Belfast.'

Before I could get any further, a well-built and mature, grey-haired man in the front stalls quickly, and somewhat emotionally, claimed the contact.

'Yes, it's me,' he said, 'I know him.'

And through the glaring lights I could see that his eyes were glinting with emotion, as I went on, 'Well, he tells me, "I was really bitter when I first came over, but I'm learning to understand now, Corp."'

'Yes, I was his corporal. As a punishment I sent him out on jeep duty in place of myself. He was travelling from Belfast to Ballymena, the places you mentioned, and terrorists bombed the vehicle. It —' and here his voice suddenly caught with tears as he placed a trembling hand over his mouth — 'I'm sorry,' he apologised, 'but it should have been me who died, and not him.'

There was a stunned silence in the auditorium. The air became still, and not a soul moved.

'No, please,' I said reassuringly, breaking the tension while mentally re-establishing my contact, 'please don't be upset. He must have been ready to go,' I added, trying to comfort his ex-corporal by stating the spiritual law which decrees that no one crosses over before their time, no matter how they make their transition.

But then I heard the murdered soldier seething at me through his teeth, 'Those IRA bastards killed me; I'll get my revenge on those bastards' — which I didn't transmit, of course. However, I felt a gentle spiritual lesson was in order — so I told the audience, and his friend, 'I'm afraid I can't tell you he's one hundred per cent happy on the Other Side because he's just said something unkind about the people who took his life. He's still very angry with them.'

And then I spoke directly to the spirit soldier standing behind me, gently counselling out loud, 'It's no good feeling such bitterness, you know, son; it can't change what's happened to you and, at the end of the day, you should try to forgive them — that's the only way to progress.'

The spirit lad obviously appreciated my remarks, and privately replied, 'I know you're right, mate; but I think I was too young to go,' after which I continued the rest of his message to the corporal.

'He says, "Don't worry about it too much, Corp — this is a much better world, anyway,"' I reported. 'Oh, and he's sending his regards to "Taff, Smiffey and Smellie."' I laughed.

'Yes — they're some of the boys he knows.'

His corporal was visibly relieved when I ended with some comforting words from the colleague he'd once thought 'dead'.

'"No more guilt, sir,"' I conveyed, then added from myself, 'because your friend is still alive.'

It was plain to see that the ex-corporal had been spiritually moved by the entire experience, and this message, I believe — judging by the way it was received and sent — will undoubtedly have changed both of their lives for the better, which must surely be the true purpose of any spirit contact.

Such a candid link also highlights for us that peace of mind can never be ours unless we personally attain it; the young 'dead' soldier still had much soul-growth to achieve, even though he'd arrived on the Other Side.

But then, *death doesn't change us, and spiritual progress is gained only through self-mastery of the character, mind and emotions.*

However, not every spirit connection I've given has been so gratefully received, or been placed at the time of its transmission. There are dozens of valid reasons for the non-acceptance of messages but the fault lies mostly with recipients who won't, or feel they can't, publicly speak up and claim their links. This was illustrated when I relayed another tragic passing which went unaccepted, at first, but was later fully verified, highlighting one of the many difficulties mediums encounter when working with large audiences.

The rather poignant tale had been unfolded by a young lad called Anthony who had been killed outside a nightclub. The youngster specifically told me, 'I was stabbed through the heart, died at the hospital, and three people attacked me.'

I was unwilling to publicly mention his manner of death because such descriptions can sometimes be traumatically received by sensitive relatives, but I soon had to relent because I was ordered to do so — by Anthony himself. He commanded me to 'Give the message exactly as I said it!' — so I did;

but not a living soul claimed it in the silent theatre.

So I relayed a few more names, which Anthony assured me belonged to his 'workmates', and then went on, 'Look, he's clearly telling me his friend is in the audience,' I repeated again. 'Please speak up! Where are you?'

Utter silence; not a sound from anyone...

'Well, he won't give in and go away, ladies and gentlemen,' I persevered, echoing Anthony's determination, 'and he's adamant that I must state: "The man who killed me only got a manslaughter charge, that's all; and he's just come out of prison after serving only eighteen months of a two-year stretch." Where am I going with this contact?' I spoke through the microphone, peering into the dark theatre, shading my eyes from the glaring spotlights with my free hand.

But still the link was unaccepted; the only thing I could do was to be faithful to the boy and quickly do my job. I gave his link of love and survival, plus his warning that his assailant was 'out and about in town again, so be careful,' and then reluctantly, and rather sadly, moved on to the next message. With such large audiences I can't wait for ever – it simply isn't fair to the rest of the communicators or to other members of the public who'd be more than happy to acknowledge their loved ones.

However, it came as no surprise that after the meeting, during my autograph session, a blonde teenage girl, about seventeen, stepped forward and fully acknowledged every detail of Anthony's message as correct.

'Yes, I know him,' she admitted, her remarks being witnessed by a long queue of people and two stewards. 'Everything you said was right, Stephen: his name, the stabbing, the three attackers — *everything*. But I was too overcome to speak up.'

Such circumstances render me powerless to make communication successful.

Then Anthony's girlfriend wanted to know, 'Did he say anything else to you?'

'I'm afraid his contact was only brief,' I explained again (having already taken great pains to state this to the audience at the beginning of the meeting), 'and I can't just click back into his mental wavelengths. It's very much his personal effort at the time which brings the connection.'

She said she understood, and I followed on with some more helpful advice.

Later, after the public had gone, one of the stewards asked, 'How do you feel in situations like that, Stephen? It must be very hard to stand on stage in front of hundreds of people and look a complete fool because of somebody else's reticence.'

'Well it isn't very pleasant,' I said, 'and I know full well that the press were in tonight and they'll probably report Anthony's message as a load of rubbish because no one claimed it. But did you hear the young girl's acceptance?'

'Yes, I was gobsmacked,' he gushed. 'But the sceptics won't be, will they?'

'Oh, they'll think whatever they like, anyway,' I rejoined.

'But doesn't it annoy you like hell?'

'Let me tell you something,' I said with quiet conviction, 'when I go to bed tonight I can sleep with a clear conscience because I represented that boy faithfully. I listened carefully to everything he said; I gave his message, and provided a service. I know this, God knows it, and he and his friend know it. Two souls were brought together by the power of the spirit, and the truth touched them both — and that's all that matters.'

Realising that I have no control over who'll accept spirit messages has made me philosophical about these seeming failures. Indeed, one never knows who'll communicate successfully next.

One night a famous spirit visitor made a guest appearance at my meeting in the Manchester Free Trade Hall, when I was contacted by the celebrated poetess Sylvia Plath, who had committed suicide years previously. Strangely enough, I wasn't even aware that she had 'died'.

However, I was quite specific when stating her identity, for she surprised us all by giving her full name. 'Oh, I have Sylvia Plath here, trying to reach a young gentleman. She says she's been regularly contacting him with inspiration and poetry.'

From up in the circle, a surprised man in his twenties accepted the link. 'Yes, Stephen, *here*! She contacts me a lot!' he shouted out.

Ms Plath then gave him some personal but very sound advice about his future, which flummoxed us listeners, but he said he'd understood it all 'perfectly'. After showing intimate knowledge of this man's life, Sylvia then promised to give him guidance whenever he might need it.

Such comforting connections reassure us that our spirit friends are often very near to us, each day of our lives, and that they're caring not only for our close family members, but also for our animals and household pets — and even for wild creatures. This has been proved to me many times.

One day, while returning from shopping, I found a wild sick pigeon crouched outside the block of council flats where I lived, and a gentle spirit voice asked me to, 'Please look after her; she's awfully tired and ill.'

The dishevelled bird gave no resistance when I quietly lifted up her thin and bedraggled form: she seemed nothing more than protruding bones and feathers, there was very little healthy flesh on her gaunt frame; it was so sad.

'You must have flown an awfully long way, my lovely,' I whispered to her, gently smoothing her feathers while carrying her home, where I placed her in a warm upstairs room, on some cosy woolly jumpers.

She slowly blinked her deep nut-brown eyes when I caressed her emaciated body. Because she was utterly exhausted, I moved slowly not to frighten her, and tried to make sure that she felt safe with me.

'God bless you,' I said. 'You sit here quietly, and I'll get you some corn from the town.'

After settling her down I walked two miles to get the food, just as the kind man from the RSPCA had instructed me to do on the telephone. But as I walked along, I couldn't help feeling disgusted by the thought that some nasty person must have kicked the poor bird, which probably explained the dents I'd felt in her tiny breast.

How wicked and cruel some people can be.

With my mind full of these thoughts, I made my way home carrying the special corn and vitamins, when — such an odd thing happened. Out of the blue, the wind blew one stray, mud-caked pigeon feather right across my path on the street. I stopped dead in my tracks and felt my heart sink, immediately recognising this as a psychic omen. It was then that a disembodied voice said, 'The bird will pass.'

I was so hurt and concerned by the news that I rushed along the roads, running as fast as I could all the rest of the way home. I dashed upstairs, but was instantly greeted by the smell of death. My new friend's soul had quietly left this world; her little body was already stone-cold, and her silent head was resting way back upon her motionless grey wings. Her half-open eyes were staring up at the blue sky through the open window, as if gazing, almost forlornly, into heaven itself, where she must have longed to have flown.

The poor bird had died like an angel with gracefully folded wings, just as the disembodied voice had told me she would.

My only consolation was that in my heart I'm positive my spirit friends had helped her to cross over with the least amount of pain and with as much spiritual healing and dignity as possible.

'She had called out within her soul for kindness and rest,' revealed the voice again, 'and it was given.'

Although feeling sad, I comforted myself that at least her last memories of man were, I prayed, ones of brotherhood and thoughtfulness.

Over the years of our association, such predictions given to me by the spirit people have usually come true: they've rarely been wrong.

For instance, they'd correctly foretold that

because of my mediumship millions of souls would be touched, through television appearances and public work, the written and spoken word; and, of course, on the radio, my voice being carried on those mysterious airwaves that people from all walks of life tune into avidly each day.

I hope my broadcasts have helped millions of people who are seeking knowledge of an afterlife to realise that there's life awaiting all of us in the Beyond.

But I still find it quite a spooky thought to picture countless surprised men and women sitting in taxis or at home, or working in factories or offices, suddenly stopping what they're doing when my voice comes out of the radio at them, saying things like:

'You will live after you die; and it isn't something I believe in — it's something I *know*.'

And this could still happen to anyone, at any-time — just as it did in early 1990 after the release of my first volume of autobiography, *Visions of Another World,* when I was invited to appear on the following two networked radio shows.

3

Medium Wave

London, 3rd February 1990: edited extracts from the live BBC Radio 2 show hosted by Anne Robinson, who later became the renowned quiz-mistress of television's The Weakest Link.

Anne Robinson: Do you believe there is life after death? Do you, furthermore, believe that when a loved one dies it's possible for them to speak to you from the dead?

Indeed, is it right or proper that we should even attempt to contact those we've laid to rest?

My guest this morning is a psychic and medium, and he claims to regularly make contact with those who've passed on; and he does it, he says, because he's found he has the power.

He does it, he says, not for profit; and he's about to embark on a nationwide tour. Stephen O'Brien, good morning.

Stephen: Good morning, Anne; thanks for inviting me in.

Oh, it's a pleasure – I think most people are

fascinated by clairvoyance, fortune-telling, and mediums. Can you start by explaining how you discovered this power of yours?

I was born with it. I can remember when I was a young boy sitting at the bedroom window just twisting my hair on hot summer nights and watching the strollers go down the road — and some of them, when they approached the brow of the hill, would just vanish or fade away, while others carried on walking.

Of course, being a lad, I didn't question that at all.

But I think the most important event happened when I was ten: it was about two o'clock in the morning when I was woken by hammering on our front door, and I woke up, startled.

At that time I slept with my brother and I tried to wake him but he wouldn't move — he was sound asleep; and so was my uncle who slept in the same room with us, because we were quite a poor family. And my mother and father next-door were sleeping, too: no one woke, bar me.

I even pinched myself at the time to make sure I wasn't dreaming.

That eerie phantom hammering went on for so long that, being young, it did frighten me.

But now I know, after having developed the power of mediumship and now being able to hear the Other Side, the people Over There who work with me have since said, 'Behold, we stood at the door and knocked.'

But it was when your mother died that the power came to the fore, wasn't it?

Yes. I absolutely adored my mother — you couldn't find a nicer woman: she used to help old people in the town; she was a lovely soul.

But she died of cancer when she was forty-nine; and we all felt so desperately helpless, as we had to watch the light of this wonderful soul go out.

But three months after my mother's death I came home one night to an empty house, turned the key in the lock and I heard my name called from above: 'Stephen! Stephen, come up!'

And when I turned around I saw my mother in a brilliant blaze of light, standing at the top of our staircase and beckoning to me. When I went up to meet her, she came across and kissed me on the left-hand side of my face, just as I'd done to her when she was lying ill with cancer — and she laughed; as good as to say, 'Well, what are you all worrying about? I'm OK.'

And from that moment on I remember thinking to myself, if *she* lives, then *everybody* lives – that's something I must tell the world.

And that's what I've been trying to do for many years now.

So *what form does your getting in touch with people's relatives and loved ones take? How does it work, and where is the setting for it?*
Absolutely anywhere.

For example: your listeners today are hearing our voices through a receiver which is tuned to a certain frequency or wavelength – and it's exactly the same idea when we contact the world of the spirit.

The message I've got is that we cannot die: we

take our last breath here, and our next breath in another world which vibrates at a higher frequency than this one.

What they've got to do from the Other Side of Life is 'tune in' to our world, to attune their minds to the wavelengths or frequencies of our minds. Once they do that, contact can come anywhere — either as a sighting through the ability to see clairvoyantly, or perhaps we might hear or sense them.

When I take my public meetings around the country, as I stand on the platform there could be any amount of people present — up to a thousand or more — and I have to listen to the call that's coming in and say to the caller, 'OK, I'll now try and place you with your loved one.'

And once we get the right call with the right recipient, hopefully the messages will start flowing and give that great comfort which says, 'I haven't died; I love you.'

That's spine-tingling, Stephen. I want to ask you a million more questions, and a couple of things occur to me immediately. The first one is my feeling that when we lose a loved one we need to practise some acceptance that they've passed on, and whether what you do is really preventing us from having that experience?

I don't think that's the case. Grief is a perfectly natural process and people will grieve when they miss the physical presence of someone they've lost to the world of the spirit.

I don't think that what I do stops this grieving process, because people *have* to accept their loved ones are no longer with them physically.

But I get sackloads of mail — I received about three hundred letters this week as a result of a tabloid feature — and people write saying, 'I've lost my child; my mother; my father — can you tell me, is there any word from them? Are they OK? Do they miss me? Will you tell them I love them?' And they don't realise that they can send their own thoughts to their loved ones on this wavelength we've been talking about.

What I do doesn't stem or stop grief, it adds knowledge to people's faith.

A lot of religions take one to the graveside and say, 'Here we leave you with love and faith.' But what I do takes people one step further and says, 'If you're willing to search and seek, maybe to that faith you can add some knowledge and comfort.'

My lovely mum died three years ago and I think if you got her on your magic telephone I know what she'd say — she'd say what she told me for forty years: she'd tell me to 'Sit up straight and hold my shoulders back.' She'd tell me to 'Wrap up well' when I'm going out, and to look after myself and, 'For goodness' sake, put some money in the bank for a rainy day!'

Don't we all know what our parents would say? They're like long-playing records we've heard so often.

Yes, but supposing you and I were total strangers and you came to one of my public meetings in response to an advertisement, and I got a contact from your mum, who might be able to give her name and describe the way she died, or she might even call for you, giving some kind of clinching detail that would pinpoint you in the crowd. A radio-mike would go to you and I'd start a three-way connection.

Then, if she *does* say those very things, that's exactly my point: no one else *could* say them, bar your mum; you'd go away saying, 'My God, she's still alive.'

As indeed, your dog will be — I know you're an animal lover.

Well, I'll tell you what, Stephen, when my dog gets up to those Great Kennels in the Sky she's going to be very uncomfortable, because it can't be as good as she's had down here! (both laugh)
Oh, I think it could be better, you know. But animals do survive, and they're loved by friends on the Other Side.

There's a trend at the moment in many religious quarters to say that animals do not have souls: but I can say that they do. This, I know, will comfort a great many of your listeners.

I think it's just because we're often in so much need of comfort, Stephen, that I fear the sort of powers you and others claim would be very attractive to the vulnerable.

As you know, not everybody has really got the powers they claim, and it's an area where I feel the vulnerable could be 'taken' emotionally or financially.
I agree with you, which is why I say to people who are investigating whether or not life continues after death: read and be as educated as possible. And when they attend a Stephen O'Brien meeting

they mustn't come thinking, this is going to be good. People shouldn't pin all their hopes on me, or on anybody else.

They should wait for the message to come.

They must take with them all their reasoning powers; they must sift the evidence – and it needs to be specific.

But my meetings are not held purely to dispense comfort, they also educate people as to what lies beyond death, as well as presenting some specific evidence to show that we survive beyond the physical, which is just a world of illusion.

You know, as broadcasters, journalists and producers we all have good days and bad days; tell me: what if it's one of your not-so-hot days, Stephen, and there you are with a hall booked, there are thousands of people coming to see you, and you're really not terribly switched into your telephone line to Them –

– Oh yes: that happens –

– *do you say, 'Go home and have your money back?'*

No, I explain that the meetings are experiments in communication. In *Visions of Another World* I wrote a chapter called 'Behind the Scenes' which highlights the fluidity of communication, and how sometimes I can mishear something or not quite 'see' it correctly.

Like you and your colleagues I do get off-days, but the people just bear with me and appreciate that at any given time I'm trying my very best to help them.

Though, sometimes, I do feel inadequate when

someone, for example, has lost a child. A man recently wrote to me from Merseyside — his son was killed on a motorway and he was absolutely desperate to know if his boy had survived. Now, when someone pins all that hope on you, I think it can hamper communication because then the investigator is sitting there waiting for what *he* wants to hear — and, of course, I can't command what the spirit people want to say.

If your mother communicated —

— She'd be frightfully bossy, Stephen! (both laugh) *I was reading in your book,* Visions of Another World, *which has just come out and in fact has had to be reprinted, that you mention one incident where you connect somebody here with somebody 'up there' and they were suggesting that this person 'down here' was going to have a baby —*

That's right —

— and it was completely wrong!

Yes, I remember that! Someone from the world of spirit, an aunt who contacted her niece, said to the girl, 'You are with child; we're delighted!' and the girl had only found out about it that morning herself.

Then the aunt predicted that it would be a boy; but nine months later this woman came to me at a public meeting and said, 'I had a girl. What does it mean?'

I said, 'It means your aunt was quite wrong!'

(Anne chortles)

You see, when we die we're not infallible: death doesn't confer upon us any abilities that we don't have now.

When we take our last breath here, we take our next breath There, and we take with us everything that we've earned for ourselves: the growth of our mind, our spirit, our soul, our education, and our morality — or our lack of it.

This Earth, in my view, and in the viewpoint of the spirit people working with me, is a schoolhouse — a grounding-place where we learn about consciousness, self, emotion, feeling, and where our minds can expand through experience.

And then death is nothing at all; it's just a hiccup in the line of life.

So are our loved ones on the Other Side growing still, and becoming more experienced?
Yes, progression is the law, a natural law, not a man-made law but a God-made law, if you like – the Law of the Great Spirit that fashioned this universe. The eternal law states that progression is open to everyone.

We're all progressing, there is no going back.

Wouldn't we be better staying at home and just saying a nice prayer to our loved ones that have gone?
Of course you can do that: love is the link — that's the link that joins the two worlds together.

Stephen, do your powers also extend to meeting someone and being intuitive about what's going to happen to them?
Yes, that's what I call a psychic impression; psychic coming from the Greek (meaning: soul). So psychic

powers are soul-powers. Everyone has a soul, I believe, and therefore we're all psychic and we can meet strangers and think, 'I don't know what it is but I just can't take to you at all.'

But about others you might say, 'What a wonderful soul.'

I believe that this power is a part of the soul — of the auric fields of electromagnetic energy-wavelengths which surround us, and which have been photographed by people — 'picking up' these impressions.

And would you say that quite a lot of us are probably psychic if we ever 'tuned' ourselves nicely?
Oh yes. At my public meetings when I ask the audiences how many of them have had various psychic experiences, usually over seventy per cent of the hands go up, and then I say, 'You see! I'm not the only strange person here!'

Now you say you haven't made any money out of your powers –
– Yes, I've helped charities, over the years –
– *but in fact you're going on a nationwide tour from February to June, and you will be charging for that?*
Yes, today the cost of venues, and advertising which is so desperately expensive, has to be made back, or I can't get to those areas to serve the people.

I did do an extensive nationwide tour last year — after which I thought it was time for my own funeral, I was so physically exhausted! — and I didn't get a penny for that. In fact we helped nineteen children's hospitals across the nation.

It's been a great a pleasure to talk to you this morning, Stephen — thank you very much indeed. Lovely to meet you, Anne: it's been delightful.

*

Extracts from an interview with the usually turbaned author and TV personality Molly Parkin, which was nationally broadcast live to Wales from St David's Hall, Cardiff, on BBC Radio Wales's Level Three Show in March 1990, in the presence of a live audience.

Molly Parkin: It's an absolute pleasure to see you, Stephen.
Stephen: Hello, Molly.

He's young, isn't he? (laughter from audience)
Well, doesn't she look young herself? Doesn't she? (audience agrees vocally) She looks lovely.

Well, I've got no hat on today. I've bared my head in your presence! (more laughter)
  Now, an old lady told you when you were young that you would become a medium. How did you react to that as a young boy of ten?
  Well, I didn't understand what she meant, really.

And yet, in a sense, you kind of did?
Yes: I've always felt ill at ease in this world, as though I was in the world but strangely not of it.

When I was a boy I used to hear voices and see people, and have psychic experiences which my peer group didn't have.

I remember waking up one morning just before dawn and I heard a choir of schoolchildren — I must have been younger than ten — and they were singing 'All Things Bright and Beautiful', and I suddenly realised –'I'm in bed. This is silly.' And it stopped. Then I got up and looked out of the window, but there was no one there.

It's a wonderful enrichment of a childhood, of course.
Yes.
I think more and more people are getting interested in the spirit world. But back to you: you went into rather boring jobs when you left school.
I did, yes — I've never really been happy in this world, Molly.
But you're happy now, this minute.
Yes: I'm happy to be here — but there's an inner longing, a yearning. The real person is within —
Yes –
 — and this physical overcoat is just a shell, a vehicle of expression for the mind and soul, given for an allotted time. And then you drop this body and the true person, within, goes on.

You believe that of everybody?
Oh yes.
And the fact that you're a medium means you're able to express it because your conviction is so strong.
Yes: I've seen, heard and sensed so many people

from the Other World that I've come to realise my true place is not here at all; I belong, I believe, in the eternal world, and I think I'm just here for a time. Just like the rest of our audience today, we're here to achieve something: to grow and to learn –

– And to help each other –

– that's it.

Then at the point of death we'll take all that with us into the next stage of learning — into the junior class; this is the infants' class.

So this life isn't a haphazard occurrence, but the first step in a growth process.

I accept all that; I believe all that.

When you have your very large audiences, of course, you're very eloquent when you talk about these matters and you have a great stage presence: how much do you think going to a drama school — after those other boring jobs — helped you with all that?

A lot. It gave me confidence to face an audience and project whatever little personality I have. It gave me an inner certainty of knowing that although I was standing before anything up to a thousand people — not knowing who was going to communicate, or where the link was going — I could confidently say to myself, 'Stephen, if you don't get anything it doesn't really matter, you can still talk to the people.'

A few years ago I studied to try and develop my own psychic powers because, at one point, I thought I might go in that direction myself: to become a medium and a healer — and I know you're also a healer.

Did you have any training of that sort? You went regularly to a Spiritualist church — and I say that because other people might like to develop their gifts.

Yes, that was where I found people who understood the powers of the soul. The people who understand these are the people who've already developed them, and they are within psychic centres or Spiritualist churches.

What was the reaction of the Spiritualist Church when you became a professional medium and you had your larger audiences, because there is a view that if this is a gift from God then you shouldn't commercialise it.

I agree with that.

So some cynics might say you're in this to make a lot of money for yourself; but this isn't the case, is it?

No... (awkwardly) At the risk of embarrassment I'll announce it on radio: I've recently fought a case for the repossession of my council flat... for non-payment of rent, because the money went into last year's United Kingdom tour.

But I've won it; so I've still got a roof over my head!

Well, we're very glad about that, aren't we? (applause from audience)

What do you say to people who say that visiting a medium, or dabbling in the occult, may be dangerous?

I would say: believe nothing, and test everything. If

you consult a specialist about your health you're not obliged to accept his opinion: you can get a second opinion.

If anybody's going to see a medium, sensitive or psychic then they should accept only that which appeals to their intelligence and makes sense.

May I give an interesting example?
Yes.

One of Britain's well-known mediums, Estelle Roberts, who's now passed over, during a private appointment with a woman who'd lost her husband was able to tell her, 'Your husband is here. But I'm very sorry I can only hear him saying something rather silly, and that's "Rabbits, rabbits, rabbits".'

To this the woman replied, 'Mrs Roberts, when my husband was dying he took my hand and said to me, "Look, love, if there's another life I'll come back and I'll give you a code-word, and the code-word will be *rabbits*."' (Molly gasps)

So you see, it's only the recipient who understands the full import of the message that's being given.

Talking about rabbits, animals do survive in the spirit world, don't they?
Yes, they do. Are you an animal lover?
Oh yes: I'm a lover of everything!
Are you?
Yes!
Oh, *that's* interesting to know, isn't it? (Molly chuckles wickedly, and the audience joins in)

Regarding animals, I remember once giving clairvoyance in the Midlands and there was a blind

man at the back of the hall with his guide dog at
the side of him, and a message went to him from
his people on the Other Side.

But as I was working with him I saw in a silver/
golden light that at the *other* side of him there was
a spirit guide dog, sitting at his feet.

I was told its name was Sandy, and when I gave
that to him he started to weep, because this was his
previous guide dog which had died.

Sandy proved that loyalty persists, and that love
is stronger than death.

Oh yes, and most enduring — that's in your book
Visions of Another World *which was published in
1989 and did very, very well, and continues to do
well.*

*Your audiences are packed, I know, Stephen; is
the tour going well?*
It is.
*And I see you're on in London at the Wembley
Conference Centre; that's a very, very big venue,
and I know you're going to fill it to capacity.*

*I'd like to go on and on, but we'll talk to you
again later on in the programme.*

And we wish him luck, don't we everybody? (the
audience applauds)
(over the clapping) Thank you very much, Molly —
it's been lovely today.

4

Psychic Signs and Portents

Just like the millions of listeners who tuned in their radio sets to pick up my broadcast interviews, in order to contact us the spirit people have to attune their minds to approximate the wavelengths of our thoughts on Earth; and some communicators are expert at doing this, especially when they need to give an urgent psychic warning.

One such memorable spirit sign was given to me on a swelteringly hot summer's day in June 1985. It happened while I was ambling through a musty antique market in Swansea, my hometown in Wales; I was idly gawping at ancient clocks and other Victoriana but not really concentrating on them because I was in a turmoil.

As readers of my other books will know, I'd received a baffling prediction from my spirit guide friend and teacher, a splendid North American Indian, whose tribal name was White Owl, in which he'd foretold that I'd move away from Wales to live in North-east England. In due course, exactly as he predicted, I received an offer of a council flat in Gateshead, a windy town on the banks of the River Tyne, and then I didn't know whether to obey or to ignore White Owl's advice to move. 'Should I, or shouldn't I go to England?' I questioned, over and over to myself. Then I asked my spirit friend to prove that this traumatic wrench would be worthwhile. 'Let's have a bit of indication from Up There!' I quipped. 'Do you think I should I go to Gateshead, or not?'

Several days had passed by in Other-Worldly silence, and now here I was browsing amongst the Victoriana and antiques when suddenly I stopped near a box of battered sepia photographs, pictures that had been taken in the early 1900s. 'These look interesting,' I thought, noticing that there were about a hundred postcards, all bunched together like a dog-eared pack of cards. Quite at random I idly divided the deck once, and there in front of my eyes was something which made me gasp: it was a snapshot of the main thoroughfare of a North-east town, with rusty tramcars trundling along beside busy shoppers who were to-ing and fro-ing, many of whom were women wearing long black dresses that trailed in the muddy road. And underneath there was a printed caption:

Gateshead High Street, circa 1901.

I was amazed! But being a shrewd person I spent the next five minutes sorting through the box of cards and scrutinising every single picture, and — as you've probably guessed — the postcard of Gateshead was the *only* one in the box.

This was undoubtedly the psychic sign I'd asked for.

'Well, it seems I'll be moving,' I acknowledged out loud, much to the amazement of a wide-eyed toddler passing by, who nearly dropped his sticky lollipop as he craned his neck to find my invisible companions.

And that's how I ended up living in England for two years, during which time the spirit people planned that I should meet several new mediums and help them to firmly establish their psychic talents. These new friends and I still keep in touch today, and it was that clever spirit sign which brought us all together — it reunited a spiritual family of long-separated spirits who belong to a soul-group. Over the years I've received several strange psychic warnings worth recalling; you might experience some similar happenings yourself. (Who knows?)

One of the more unusual ones occurred when my grandmother, Polly, lay dying in the hospital. Her doctors kept insisting, 'We don't know how long she'll be in a coma like this. We're not God.' But through the power of their special vision, my friends on the Other Side delivered their own peculiar prediction one cold December evening, just as the sun was sinking in the frosty sky.

At the time, I was alone, taking off my slippers and putting on my shoes, when suddenly I caught sight of something odd: on the beige-coloured wall right beside my head, five black houseflies had appeared from nowhere, had settled themselves down, and were merrily fanning their wings, as if it were a bright summer's day instead of an icy December evening.

I did a classic double-take, baffled as to what these flies were up to: they shouldn't have been alive at that time, let alone sunning themselves on our cold wall. I blinked, but they were still there; so

I glanced away and tied my shoelaces; and when I looked up again — they'd vanished.

At the time I didn't make the connection between these five phantom insects and the fact that I was getting ready to visit my grandma at the hospital; but much later, it dawned on me that *five* flies had appeared on the wall, and *five days later* Polly's coma suddenly ended, and she passed away peacefully in her sleep...

Of course, it wasn't easy to tell if my father, who was her eldest son, was upset by her death, because it was often troublesome to gauge what he was thinking. My mother, however, had no bother at all in clearly reading my father's mind, though not while she was alive on Earth: she developed this telepathic skill only after she'd 'died' and had passed into the spirit world; and one day she used this ability to deliver a pointed psychic warning to me.

I recall it was the mid 1970s and Dad and I were living under the same explosive roof that was daily raised by our personality clashes. Mam had been 'gone', as they say here in Wales, for about two years before she displayed her uncannily accurate mind-reading. By then, of course, temper-flares between my father and me were so bad that we couldn't be in the same room without the wall-paper catching fire. Our personal relationship had always been stormy and lamentably predictable.

'Oh, why won't you leave me alone?' I'd pitifully moan.

'Because you're a lazy good-for-nothing swine, that's why!' Dad would shout back, furious because I was then unemployed, and he wasn't. But try as I might he wouldn't listen, and I didn't care, which is why my mother had felt it necessary — as she had lain near to death months previously in a semi-conscious state – to clasp him tight and plead with him, 'Ron, promise me you'll take care of Stephen... Promise me...' Dad said he would, but after her death, matters just got worse and worse...

Then one day I came up with an ingenious but rather naive plan. 'I know: I'll kill him with love,' I reasoned.

Anyway, I gave this youthful idea my best shot for months. Whenever he bawled his lungs out at me, I refused to retaliate and just sat very quietly, perfectly relaxed, and ignored his angry and rude remarks, and kept absolutely still and thought, 'No comment' – and it worked!

It was a truly brilliant plan. 'He'll soon be quiet,' I thought, 'because after a while all he'll hear is his own loud voice, and that'll shut him up.'

Incredibly, I was right. My young logic proved more than effective and an unearthly silence, like that of the grave, fell eerily about our house.

The blissful peace was heavenly and golden, and I gratefully drank it in like a thirsty cactus that had been deprived of water for months on end. My silence worked like pure magic, and I felt quite proud of myself, until the night when I received a spirit sign from a medium at a public meeting:

'I've got your mother with me, Stephen.'

'Oh?' I said, rather surprised.

'Yes, and she says, "Don't think the current trend will continue."'

'Thank you,' I replied, not knowing what my mother's words might have meant.

Her psychic warning was given on a Saturday night, but its importance became clear early on Monday morning when the balloon went well and truly up at home!

Quick as a flash, Dad suddenly bounced back to being his old self with a vengeance, and started his usual shenanigans. True to my plan, I sat silently on the settee and maintained a deathly hush, but in the twinkling of an eye my mother was proved correct: *father went berserk.*

His loud voice just kept on booming and rising higher and higher in pitch, until it reached its maximum decibel effect, a frightening squeal beyond which it was fatal for the victim to move a muscle without getting clocked by two shovel-like hands — and I was trapped helplessly on the settee, with a madman in front of me and a wall at my back. I couldn't move.

'My God, he'll explode in a minute,' I thought; and I wasn't disappointed.

Suddenly he yelled, 'You're no bloody good! You sit about all day without a job! What the *hell* are you doing with your life? You... *you...* you lazy–' and in the next instant he shot out of his chair, pounced over to the sofa, yanked me to my feet by the scruff of my neck and then, his face white with rage, pulled me to the floor by my hair and delivered a few deft kicks into my ribs...

So much for my 'killing him with love'.

I made no effort to retaliate — he was far too strong and frenzied; besides, he was my father. He had also been a powerful amateur boxer in his younger days and had broken all his knuckles in fights.

After venting his spleen, he stormed angrily upstairs, huffing and puffing, and I was left huddled
on the floor, unable to understand how someone
could feel he possessed the unchallengeable right
to inflict such pain upon another being.

Some people may be shocked to learn that I was
twenty-two when this happened. My mother's
psychic warning had materialised. 'The current
trend' (of peace and quiet) had most certainly 'not
continued'; and her spirit message also strengthened my conviction that our Reality is Thought —
she had clearly seen what was in Dad's mind, as
naturally as we'd watch a brightly lit movie on a
screen.

The accuracy of this type of telepathic reading of
our thoughts by the spirit people had also been
confirmed to me by my first mediumship tutor,
Mrs Palmer.

One day her spirit guide (who, in life, was an
Arab horseman called Ahmed) shocked her to the
core of her being when he told her, 'Your mind, to
me, is as open as the Sahara Desert.'

'Good Lord, just imagine that, Stephen,' she'd
gulped, awestruck by the embarrassing implications. 'There'd be nowhere to hide in the Sahara,
would there?'

'No,' I replied timorously, remembering some of
my own dubious thoughts, and thinking of the
Bible being right when it states 'nothing is hidden,
all is known.'

Such startling psychic signs and portents are
quite common occurrences throughout the world,
as many people know. A mother once told me that
on one night during the Second World War, while

she was washing the dishes, quite out of the blue she suddenly reeled backwards, clutching her stomach as if she'd just been kicked in it, and announcing, 'Arthur's been killed.' This was her beloved son who was on active service at the time — and the War Office later confirmed that he had indeed 'died' at the very moment when she'd received her psychic shock.

I believe that Arthur, himself, had transmitted this paranormal signal: the dearest object of his thoughts had instantly received his traumatic and powerful emotions because he'd sent them to her through the mighty power of his love — just moments before he'd died.

Many thousands of people have experienced similar 'hunches' and have felt similar sensations in the solar plexus area (just above the navel) because this is one of the main psychic registration points in man. It's often been medically referred to as 'the second brain of the body'.

Animals also possess this type of acute psychic instinct, much more so than modern-day man does.

Although our psychic senses are still operating, they don't function as strongly as they must have done in ancient times when prehistoric hunters needed to 'know' when life-threatening danger was approaching, especially when they couldn't see on dark moonless nights: this vital sixth sense would have been essential to protect each precious family unit.

My grey-and-white (with black stripes) female cat, Sooty, exhibits these psychic instincts in abundance, and when she was recently ill and had to be spoon-fed a course of chalky tablets, it became remarkably evident!

Medicine is anathema to Sooty, and the moment I nonchalantly saunter off to get it, her psychic senses are immediately activated! She whizzes past me through the hall at top speed to hide herself in some inaccessible corner, all hunched up and clamped to the ground, immovable and ready to do battle – or to wait until the danger passes. (Only it never did because I'd usually winkle her out with a strategically placed broom-handle.)

Her psychic awareness also operates in response to music, it seems: on some days when I play the piano she miraculously appears from nowhere and drapes her luxurious warm fur coat around my neck and purrs away merrily for all she's worth. 'Oh, I'll play well today,' I muse to myself — and invariably I do.

But on other days, when stress makes me hit more cracks than notes, suddenly she vanishes! I'll just catch a quick glimpse of her fluffy backside scooting up the stairs to bury herself under a soundproof duvet. She seems to 'know' when there's a monstrous cacophony of music coming – and she's particularly 'aware' in the evenings, when she squints her yellow peepers into slits and shiftily 'eyes up' the invisible spirit friends whose presence I haven't sensed.

'Do let me know if it's anyone important, madam,' I often say.

'*Miss*,' she seems to reply haughtily. 'Do you mind?' (I don't think she's ever forgiven me for that operation, but her unearthly caterwauling knew no mercy, so neither did the vet's scissors.)

Soul-sensitivity seems to be on the increase these days. In fact, since the 1950s there have been countless strange psychic signs reported by people claiming to have sighted UFOs – Unidentified Flying Objects – in the skies. Worldwide, ordinary folk say they've seen them, and I'm no exception.

One evening, after Dad had expertly waltzed me around the room, I hurriedly left and took refuge on a bitterly cold park bench. Miserably numb, sitting on an inch-thick frost and forlornly gazing heavenwards, I was trying to lose my anger in the incredible beauty of the dark night sky. It was then that I spotted the pulsing silver light. I'd seen satellites like this one many times before: they look just like fast-moving stars as they arc the black sky in a perfect curve. But this one was different: it was a particularly bright object – an entrancing sight, until it unexpectedly changed direction.

Only then did I realise it was a UFO.

Dumbfounded, I tracked the distant shining ship, and I watched it swivelling in the high atmosphere before it quickly shot out into space, away from the Earth, in completely the opposite direction to its previous path; and then it vanished.

Friends were suitably amused when I quipped, 'Mind you, if the saucer had landed I'd have been up inside it like shot — no messing about. Well, there's got to be something better than this, hasn't there?'

And more laughter followed when I added, 'But with *my* luck, as soon as they realised who they'd picked up they'd probably open the rubbish chute and drop me into the sea!'

Even though there are many theories about

where these reported space visitors originate from, I believe a great majority of them are human and that they could come from our own future, where time-travel has been perfected to such a degree that they can visit the Earth's past – us.

But I also think that strict regulations may have been fixed, instructing them not to land or to associate with us, for fear of causing a tremor in the time-stream.

However, many reports of such important face-to-face meetings (close encounters of the third kind) are firmly on record throughout the world.

It's easy to dismiss other people's stories as fabrication, fantasy or nonsense, but not when you personally know these folk and can vouch for their honesty and integrity. One sensible colleague of mine, Lin Martin, encountered a spacecraft close up; and her experience proved to be a remarkable psychic sign, for, after it had occurred, much wider psychic powers unfolded within her — and today she's a public medium. She says she's been sensitive since childhood and that this awareness seemed to burgeon following her sighting.

Strangely enough, serious investigators have now collated much similar evidence which points to the theory that after a close contact with a UFO many percipients often develop a heightened telepathic power, or somehow have their psychic faculties boosted. After her experience, Lin Martin extended her talents to encompass the rare skill of psychic portraiture: she sketches the faces of invisible spirit communicators. Here's Lin's description of that fascinating encounter which boosted her psychic powers:

On the day it happened the sky didn't have a cloud in it, but a certain coolness had descended over Corby, in Northamptonshire, early on that June evening; not enough to give a chill, but just enough to be comfortably pleasant after a hot summer's day.

I was eighteen at the time, in the early 1970s, when this sighting took place on the common, which my then boyfriend and I had chosen for our walk.

The grass was dotted here and there with other couples also enjoying the pleasant evening.

Visibility was very good – it was a clear summer's night, with just a few trees around, as we walked.

Then, for some inexplicable reason both my friend and I were oddly compelled to simultaneously look upwards, and there — about 50 feet directly above us — was a strange object hovering in the sky.

We were both taken completely by surprise.

To this day, I couldn't be sure of its exact size but it seemed a little bit bigger than a helicopter; though, of course, it wasn't one.

Our first reaction was one of utter fright — and to run away as fast as we could, but we seemed to be transfixed to the spot: neither of us could move. We were just motionless, staring open-eyed at the spacecraft up above us.

We also lost all sense of the passing of time — for all we knew we could have been standing there for hours, yet it may have been just a few seconds. Unfortunately, we didn't think of checking the clock afterwards.

The hovering craft was saucer-like with a dome-shape on its top, and large windows extended all around this dome — and an orange luminescent light seemed to be vibrating or pulsating from within them, rotating and circling at high speed inside the ship.

I didn't register the colour of the craft itself, because the bright orange light commanded all of my attention.

It was as though I was mesmerised by it.

And another odd thing was — there was *no sound* coming from the object. I couldn't hear any motors or engines.

The silent spaceship was tilted towards us at an angle, so we couldn't see its underside. And even though the windows were quite large neither could we discern anything inside them — yet we both *sensed* that we were being watched, somehow observed.

After what seemed like an eternity, the spacecraft quickly moved vertically upwards — shooting off on a zigzag course at high speed, right across the evening sky — and then it disappeared from sight.

No words were spoken between my boyfriend and me, we simply exchanged disbelieving looks in silence, as we made our way back to the house where we were staying.

We were only young, and discussed nothing whatsoever, not until we felt completely safe behind locked doors — and then it emerged that we'd both seen exactly the same thing.

Just like this lady, all mediumistic people radiate an abundance of psychic light and energy into the atmosphere around them, and spirit intelligences can often use this to send us signs and warnings.

This frequently happens to another acquaintance of mine who's both a healer and a clairvoyant, and who has remarkably vivid dreams which often contain psychic predictions — a phenomenon that I'm sure many of us have experienced.

One of his more notable warnings involved the deceased filmstar Marlene Dietrich, who, in her latter years, had confined herself to a Paris apartment where she died peacefully, aged ninety-one.

He was an avid fan of hers, having written to the screen legend for over twenty years.

He'd regularly received personal notes and photographs from her, and he'd also telephoned Marlene, but she became a trifle eccentric towards the end, not allowing herself to be seen, interviewed, spoken to, or photographed by anyone.

Living as a recluse, she discouraged visitors and all personal publicity, and made the telephone her single lifeline to the outside world.

Sometimes when he rang she'd be quite lucid and able to hold short conversations, but at other times — probably because of her great age — she'd behave in a most peculiar way. Once, she answered in a mock-French accent, 'Zees eez Madame de Pompadour. You 'ave ze wrong nomberre. Please 'ang up and do not call zees nomberre again!' — and then she clomped the receiver down.

On another occasion, because her initials were MD (medical doctor), she rattled out in gutsy German tones, *Der Doktor ist aus*. The doctor *ist* busy: go away!' And click went the line again.

Poor Marlene.

However, about a week before she died in her Paris flat, my acquaintance says he heard an almighty thud from one of his upstairs rooms.

'I ran up and discovered Marlene's latest signed photograph, which she'd just sent me and which I'd framed, had crashed to the floor. The frame was all smashed but the glass was still intact, and I immediately felt something was wrong, taking this as a serious psychic warning.'

Straightaway he telephoned Paris to check on the actress, but I'm afraid she gave another of her amusing performances. There was loud Italian music playing in the background, which he commented on. 'There is no music!' blurted back Marlene. 'Music is not playing. This is the maid, and the doctor *ist* out!'

Then click — and she was back in blissful seclusion again. But, within the week, the psychic sign proved to be quite correct and the screen legend passed away peacefully.

Marlene was sometimes a highly controversial celebrity whose openly bisexual lifestyle had gained her much unwanted publicity, as had the fiercely guarded privacy she had imposed upon herself when she locked the doors of her life, and rejected the attention of the world's media for most of her latter years.

Readers may remember that Marlene Dietrich and I met in Cardiff in the 1970s, after one of her world-famous and impressive cabaret shows, when she kissed me on either side of my face. I never dreamed we'd speak again — but we did; only this time it was after her death, while I was undergoing one of my out-of-the-body experiences.

I was doubly pleased to see her, of course, especially as Miss Dietrich had firmly stated in public that she didn't accept or believe in an afterlife.

Marlene and I met again in the astral world — those planes of thought nearest the Earth — in a large and airy, peach-and-beige-coloured apartment with huge picture windows overlooking deep green fields and extensive parkland. There were bright flowers everywhere in the grounds outside, and inside, too, in large pots, tubs and vases. It was a stylish, lovely place.

In the spirit world she could now walk properly; in her new body all signs of her difficult leg problems, caused by a nasty fall off a stage in Washington, had vanished. She was a radiantly beautiful woman in her prime, at the height of all her personal charm. Her skin was exceptionally clear and she looked about thirty years old, possibly a little younger. She was wearing a black backless dress on her small frame, and there was a delicate gold bracelet on her wrist and some kind of gold locket adorning her slender neck.

She was a glowing picture of loveliness.

Her features were nicely rounded and not sharp or angular, and she radiated, as all true celebrities seem to do, a remarkable sense of her own presence.

Seated with her legs folded underneath her, she was reclining on a hugely padded sofa. And when she spoke in those famous husky tones, her voice and mind generated great magnetism.

'My dear, I didn't give a damn about what people thought about me: I did what I wanted to do,' she said, 'because I wanted to do it.'

I nodded and sunk down into a nearby plush armchair, asking whether she remembered our brief meeting all those years ago. She said she did, but when I tried to make some small talk about life, she rapidly interrupted with:

'Life!' she huffed, stretching her famous legs from underneath her and crossing them – a little provocatively I thought – 'I lived my life to please myself, not others. Life is for living, and I lived it to the full, and I won't stop now.

'If I felt attracted to someone, gender didn't matter at all, you see. I made love to them, and loved them completely, because I followed my true self, not convention. But,' and here she waved a cautionary be-ringed finger in my direction, 'although I was highly sexually driven, love mattered the most, my dear.'

I smiled, agreeing with her sentiments.

'Gender doesn't count: love the person; celebrate the body and the mind. What are the alternatives?' she asked. But I didn't have a chance to answer because she carried straight on with, 'Indifference, or hate; and who needs those?'

'No one,' I said, at last. 'If more people loved each other the world would be a much better place to live in, that's for sure.'

She looked across at me, as if recognising my intelligence for the first time. Then she half-whispered, quietly, 'That's right; that's right, my dear...' and I sensed her thoughts were becoming more contemplative during the short pause which she gently ended with:

'But my social conscience has been pricking me lately just a little. If I can think of anything to help the idea of love on Earth — lovingness — I'll do it.'

She then rose gracefully out of the massively

padded sofa and moved (almost regally glided as if in a costume drama) towards the picture windows where she thoughtfully looked out at the magnificent grounds, before continuing:

'But first I have to learn how to throw my thoughts into another person's mind, people down there on Earth. I've tried a few times with my family, but I haven't had much success.'

'Have you been back to see them?' I asked brightly.

There was a sudden flash of anger across her eyes as she swivelled to face me again.

'They photographed all my private things, my stuff! I was annoyed. It made me really angry, at first...

'But then, what the hell? I can't hide for ever — no one can.'

'No,' I agreed, knowing that the inquisitiveness of the voracious press makes them ever-eager to buy exclusive stories about the rich and famous.

'My dear, the public wanted glamour,' she emphasised, with both arms opening wide — as if to silently indicate that this quality was now filling every available space in the room — 'and I gave it to them. They wanted to laugh and cry, to feel emotions intensely, and I gave these gifts; and that's why they'll remember me.

'But in the end my own image trapped me, my dear. My people were the most important, but the legend had to be kept alive, even if I was dying a little bit more each day.'

Then she slowly dropped her arms to her sides, turned away, and began staring rather vacantly through the windows at the distant trees, a woman deep in thought.

'I never believed in surviving death, you know,' she said, casting me a half-glance over her bare shoulder, then resuming her passive coolness and gazing once more at God's country; 'but we live and learn. Now... only now I think... there is a growing belief in a God within me; an overseer...'

She gently inclined her shoulder-length golden hair outwards towards the fields and the pageant of nature, then sighed to herself and folded her slender arms; her back was towards me.

'Of course, I realise now — now that I've had a lot of time to think — that real beauty, true beauty, is something within a person, and not on the skin's surface,' she said giving me another momentary glance, before turning back toward the window.

'But when I got older, everything sagged, my dear; so I had to hide myself away...'

She wasn't looking at me now, and perhaps not even speaking to me any more, and a marked tenderness crept quietly into her thoughtful voice.

'The picture of my face will remain, I think, but I'll be doing some hard work here, groundwork, to promote the idea of love... true love in all its forms, just as soon as I settle in...'

5

The Silver Cord

Some people may not believe in an afterlife, but innumerable others have been forced to accept the reality of the hereafter, particularly when they've undergone a sudden out-of-the-body-experience (an OOBE).

It stands to reason that if we can obtain proof to indicate that we can exist outside of our physical bodies, complete with our established memories and personalities, then our survival after death is assured. But is there any evidence available?

Yes, there is – and let's take a look at some of it.

The following emotional and quite touching account of a typical OOBE is given by a young man in his twenties.

But is it a genuine spirit-excursion or simply a dream; or perhaps it's wishful thinking, rather than a real journey into the next world?

What do you think?

As a child I spent a considerable time with my grandparents, especially 'Bamp', my grandfather, whom I'd see twice a day on my way to and from school.

Years later, when both of them had gone, I was especially devastated by Bamp's death, for we'd always been close. I was heartbroken.

But about a month or so after he'd died, one night I was asleep and dreaming that I was returning home from one of my regular jogging runs on the street, when on the way back I thought, 'I know, I'll go and visit Bamp.' So I ran faster and faster, gaining great momentum as I reached the door of his house, and I burst through it — then suddenly, from out of the kitchen, came my grandfather.

I can't describe the emotion I felt when I saw him, and we hugged and hugged each other for an age. I was so happy and overjoyed to be with him again.

'There's a letter from Australia in the front room,' he said. (We have relatives there.) 'Go and sit down and I'll make a pot of tea,' and then he went back into the kitchen.

I was incredibly happy, but at the same time I couldn't understand why I hadn't seen him for so long.

I went across to the table, and as I picked up the letter I instantly 'remembered' that Bamp had *died* a couple of months back, and an icy feeling suddenly gripped me when I realised I must be standing inside his home in another world.

I immediately panicked and in sudden fright I fled from the house — but all the time that I was trying to get away I could feel his strong hand gripping my arm and could hear him saying, 'It's OK to stay awhile.' But my fear got the better of me and I belted through the door as fast as I could go, and I ran and ran and ran.

Then I woke up in bed with a start, feeling completely drained, as well as being drenched in a bath of sweat; and for a short while I was sure I could still hear Bamp calling to me.

But after a while, I settled down a bit and realised how silly I'd been, because Bamp would never in the world harm me, and so I chided myself for being so stupid in running away from him.

But then I was upset, and I cried to myself.

Looking back now though, it was a remarkable experience — so clear in my mind — and I truly really know my grandfather has survived death, and this visit to him showed me where he is. I've been there for myself, and I've met him in the next world.

At first glance this seems like a touching reunion between a grieving grandson and a much-loved relative, but whereas many could accept this young man's experience as a genuine OOBE, others might seriously question it; and some psychologists would have a field-day explaining it all away.

As for myself, I accept it as authentic, for the percipient is well known to me, as indeed are all the other excursionists we'll soon meet (and whose identities I've withheld in order to protect their privacy). I can personally vouch for each contributor's mental stability and sincerity; and I also possess signed affidavits of their 'journeys'.

But what of the experience just related? Does it offer any conclusive evidence that an inner spirit body, and therefore a consciousness, existed 'somewhere' in 'some place' outside of, and apart from, the percipient's physical body? What do you think?

Before passing judgement or taking a critical look at these phenomena, here's another interesting case, but this time it comes from a man in his thirties and he shares with us an unusual journey which he undertook, he claims, while lying fully awake in bed, and in which he experiences a deep sense of soul-peacefulness — a feeling that has been reported by countless percipients. But is the following experience a real occurrence, or is it just fantasy?

When I was about ten, and even when I was younger than that, I used to leave my body at night; on many memorable occasions, I knew I was slipping out of it, at will.

While still fully awake, but with my eyes closed, I learnt a clever trick of sinking down through the mattress — in my other body — and then going further down again, right through into the small confined space between my bedroom floor and our kitchen ceiling beneath.

While there, I could clearly see all the thick, grey, plastic-covered electrical cables, and plenty of fluff and dust running along the wooden support beams.

Then I'd make myself fall further down again — right down through the floor and into the kitchen — until I could see the kitchen ceiling directly above me.

But I was always horizontal and looking upwards, never looking down.

Then, whenever I decided I wanted to get back to my bed (and this was also a conscious decision), I'd simply reverse the falling process — and I'd suddenly be back inside my physical body. However, it was always so much easier to float down than to go back up; funny that.

Much later, as an adult in my twenties, I can also recall finding myself travelling upwards through space, very quickly, right up into the night sky. This happened quite often, and when I realised where I was I'd think, 'I've got to get back,' at which point I'd return with such incredibly fast speed that I'd actually bounce on the bed when I woke up, as if I'd hit it with great force — and my heart would be thudding away.

But on every occasion when I existed outside of myself like this, whether as a boy or a man, I was always struck by the tremendous sense of peacefulness within me, and I was really happy to be light and floating.

The problem raised by these two gentlemen's accounts is that because they were the only people to report their experiences, they're purely subjective experiences: no other objective witnesses can confirm them.

OOBEs, if verified as genuine, would undoubtedly prove that because each excursionist is existing outside of the body, the seat of consciousness cannot possibly be the brain.

To discover whether or not such astonishing journeys can really be made by astral projectionists, we must first ask ourselves if anyone has ever 'brought back' some objective evidence or any previously unknown facts that were gleaned by them while out of the body, and which they later discovered to be correct.

With these criteria in mind, does this next

account of an OOBE help us? It's reported by an intelligent self-employed businesswoman who is approaching her late thirties.

When I was nearly fourteen I fell in love and was totally besotted with my first real boyfriend, and I expected to meet him every day.

Unfortunately, one week he had influenza and I didn't see him for three days, by which time I was convinced he'd decided to drop me for someone else. In this state of anguish, I found it difficult to sleep at night, so I tried a relaxation technique I'd seen on TV, where you concentrate on your feet, imagining them getting heavier and heavier until totally relaxed, and then you move on to the next bit, etc.

By the time I got to my shoulders I was wallowing in a state of deep calmness, but my mind was still very alert. (I now call this state 'twilighting', where I'm fully able to hear a telephone ring but simply can't be bothered to make an effort to do anything about it.)

Lying in bed, naturally I was thinking of my boyfriend and wondering if he really did have a bad cold, or whether he was just making excuses not to see me, when I suddenly found myself standing in the hallway of my home and I was dressed only in my nightwear. The walls around me seemed sort of indistinct, shadowy even.

I walked downstairs to the back door and went through into the yard, pausing at the gate because I knew it was old and rusty and would probably make a tremendous noise if I opened it. I was in a dilemma because just standing there in my nightie and bare feet there was no way, I thought, that I could climb over it. But while looking up at the big gate I instantly found myself on the other side of it, out on the roadway.

(At the time, and even now, nothing seemed extraordinary to me; I just accepted it.)

My boyfriend lived about half a mile away so I began to walk towards his house and, as I did, I took more notice of my surroundings. It had been raining and the tops of the nearby hedges were being bent by a strong wind, but I felt nothing of it at all, not even the cold October night air all about me. Although I knew it was late at night, there was enough light for me to see every twig and berry in the hedgerow, so I gazed upwards to see if there was a full moon, but there wasn't, because the sky was deeply overcast. And yet there was this mysterious, hazy grey-blue light all around me which didn't seem to have any source at all.

When I eventually arrived at my boyfriend's place, walking towards the back door I wondered how I was going to get inside, and then how I'd be able to find his bedroom. I'd never been there before.

So I closed my eyes to think more clearly, and when I opened them again, I discovered myself sitting on a windowsill on the inside of his room! The place was strangely lit by this same blue-greyish light and I could clearly see my boyfriend moving fitfully in his bed, coughing and sneezing as he tried to sleep. I was looking at a room I'd never seen previously, and as I gazed around me I took particular note of the wallpaper pattern, the dressing-table and his wardrobe. I also noticed there was an unfinished letter resting on his bedside table.

Then I became scared of waking him, so I didn't try to read the letter but instead admired the deep blue colour of the curtains and carpet, and then realised it was the first *real* colour I'd properly noticed. (In hindsight, I suspect that this colour's intensity prevented the grey light from diffusing it.)

I don't remember returning back into my body, in my own house, but the following day my boyfriend turned up, still sneezing, to say how much he'd been missing me. And when I told him what had happened the previous night and fully described his room exactly as I remembered seeing it, *my description turned out to be perfect in every detail*. But instead of beaming with the delight I'd hoped for, he looked very dismayed and seriously asked me if I was a witch.

(I was only fourteen!)

The accuracy of my description, even down to the unfinished private letter on his night-stand, had given him, he said, 'the shivers', just to think that I'd 'wandered in a dream' inside his own house and 'right into' his bedroom.

And being young he quickly made me promise never to tell anyone else, or I might get 'locked up, or something'.

Does this incredibly detailed excursion provide us with sound evidence for the separate existence of our projectionist's mind from her sleeping body, thereby indicating that her soul would survive the death of her physical self?

Many would think it does, but the ladies and gentlemen of the famed Society for Psychical Research (SPR) would strongly disagree, and would declare that a portion of the 'traveller's' mind may have engaged itself in 'distant telepathic contact': that the girl had 'seen' the appearance of her boy-friend's bedroom by somehow distantly linking her mind with his.

The SPR would then produce volumes of similar cases from their extensive files to support this theory.

But does this explanation ring true?

(By the way, let's keep in our minds that odd 'grey-blue' light which our last projectionist mentioned, because we'll meet it again shortly.)

So where do we go from here?

Well, if we could find only *one* occurrence of a physical object being moved or dislocated by a projectionist's spirit hand, while at the same time this event was being witnessed by people who were physically awake, we'd be on much firmer ground.

And here's exactly such a remarkable case, given by a man in his mid-forties:

One bright summer's evening I went to bed for a rest. The bedroom was quite light, and I must have fallen asleep quickly.

All at once I was aware of rising up off the bed, fully conscious, then I realised I was standing at the bedside looking down at my physical body which was fast asleep next to me. For all the world, even though I looked as if I were dead, I wasn't frightened.

I felt great: at peace with myself, and as light as a feather. But my bedroom was now much darker, sort of shadowy and a kind of misty grey-blue to my sight.

I left the room and went downstairs in the usual

way, where I knew I'd left my mother and father watching television. At the bottom of the stairs I naturally opened the living-room door with my left hand — to about two feet wide — and both my parents were startled. They turned around to see what was going on, but the look on their faces told me they couldn't see *me* at all. Even our old black dog lifted his head and crooked his neck to look in my direction.

I can't remember if anyone spoke, because it's a long time ago now. But what did strike me as odd was that when I'd gone to bed, the living-room had been quite bright (the electric light was also still on), but now, during this experience, it seemed to be dimly lit; shadowy again.

Both my parents, who were staring at the empty doorway, had their mouths wide open and looked dumbfounded; so I shut the door, turned, walked back upstairs and went over to my body in the bed, and simply got back into bed.

I think I must have just slipped back inside my body, and then I must have fallen fast asleep again.

But the next day, my mother told me about the door opening on its own, and there being no one in the hall outside.

This man's amazing experience certainly indicates that the seat of consciousness cannot be the brain, for his brain was 'fast asleep' upstairs while his personal awareness still functioned in another dislocated vehicle of expression — another body just like his physical one — called by many paranormalists *the astral body*.

The fact that physically 'awake' or conscious witnesses reported exactly the same physical event that the 'sleeper' experienced (the door opening of its own accord) rules out hallucination, and considerably strengthens the case for the survival of the soul outside of the body.

The above case defies any reasonable scientific explanation other than the percipient had undergone a genuine out-of-the-body experience.

It's also interesting to note that a high number of percipients all report the same unusual sense of lightness and peacefulness while conscious in their soul-bodies. And when our last excursionist speaks of the rooms being 'light' upon retiring, and then much 'darker' when seen by his spirit vision, his observations tie in with the previous account of this same 'grey-blue' light – a phenomenon which has been consistently reported by countless astral travellers worldwide.

Here's my spirit guide's explanation of this blue-grey light:

The atoms of physical matter which make up the physical body are vibrating at much slower and lower frequencies than the atoms constituting the spirit body, which are vibrating quite fast.

Therefore, when a person is conscious in the spirit body, the physical world, to their perception, will be a very slow-moving place.

To an astral traveller, the Earth environment appears grey-blue, dull, shadowy and sometimes lightless, because the slow-moving particles of physical matter create a 'denser', 'thicker' or 'foggier' atmosphere to his spirit vision, which is fast moving and is 'finer' and 'lighter'.

When uncountable projectionists experience broadly the same sights and sounds (as they do when vast numbers of cases are studied), they provide us with a body of impressive evidence for the separate existence of the mind outside the physical frame.

Several noted clairvoyants have claimed that the astral body is connected to the physical by an ethereal silver cord or lifeline, which joins the two vehicles of expression to each other. Just as a baby is linked to its mother by the umbilical cord, so it's claimed the astral and physical bodies are similarly joined by an energy power-link.

When this 'cord' dematerialises, death occurs and the physical body starts breaking down into the elements from which it came.

However, in my experience the silver cord isn't a cord at all, it's a fine magnetic energy-link which sometimes manifests itself as light; and there are many of these links constantly moving between the two separated bodies during an OOBE. When your astral body returns to its physical shell after travelling, just like lightning that jumps from one heavily-charged raincloud to another of lower potential during a thunderstorm, so the astral body's cosmic energies 'jump' to the physical, and it is these fine power-lines which are often seen by clairvoyants as silvery threads.

But these energies can also appear in other colours. Some people claim that the silver cord emerges from the solar plexus of the astral body (just above the navel) and enters the physical through the base of the brain — but it must be remembered that energy can cross at any number of points. I've often clairvoyantly seen the 'cord' linking the two brains.

Incidentally, I've also seen the spirit bodies of people I knew, while their OOBEs were taking place – but these people were still physically alive but were sleeping, and no cord or threads of light were visible to me at all.

We're all linked to one another by numerous psychic connections no matter what world we live in, and it's along these power-lines that telepathic messages can be instantly transferred.

Take the case of my Aunt Charlotte, for example. Her elderly mother lived in Germany, and she and her family lived in Wales, hundreds of miles away, but one night while my aunt was out socialising, she suddenly clutched at her blouse in irrational panic.

'What's wrong?' asked my uncle.

'It's my mother,' she said, 'I've just heard her calling to me, "Charlotte! Charlotte!" twice.'

My aunt became so agitated that no one could placate her and she had to be taken home. Later, she received a telegram informing her that her mother had died at the very time when she'd heard her supernormal voice calling to her.

Just by thinking about someone we will immediately produce fine psychic energy-links, and then project them towards the object of our thoughts; and distance is no obstacle.

Now here's another interesting account, this time involving strange telepathic powers operating between individuals. It's not an OOBE, but our percipient, a sensitive businesswoman in her sixties, raises intriguing and unusual implications in the light of her experience.

I was a newly appointed lieutenant of a Sea Ranger Crew and we were at summer camp just outside the old town of Brecon in South Wales, years ago now. I'd never been to Brecon before and, as far as I knew, neither had most of the girls in my crew.

It was a lovely sunny morning and, after inspection was over, the captain called us together and said, 'I have business in town today so I've arranged transport to take you all to the river where you can hire boats and canoes.

'I'm putting the lieutenant in charge and I want you all to assemble at the photographer's in the town at 5 p.m. on the dot for a group photograph.'

We were thrilled, and all piled into the back of a lorry, and were soon paddling our way down the river and having a marvellous time.

At 4.15 p.m. I blew my whistle and we went back on to dry land. Then I thought, 'Where do we go from here?' because not one of us could remember the name of the photographer's we were supposed to meet at.

'Skipper didn't tell us the name, or the street,' said the girls. Youthful panic started to set in, so I asked a passer-by about photo shops in the town and was told there were four, but some only worked part time.

Then suddenly I felt very calm and immediately and confidently took charge saying, 'Follow me, girls!' And I led them through the town, winding my way past shops and houses — purposefully — and trooping them in and out of small, quaint old streets. Then I turned a corner and there it was!

Skipper was waiting outside at exactly 5 p.m.

'Thank goodness!' she said. 'Do you know, I couldn't remember if I'd told you the photographer's name and address.'

'You didn't!' chorused the excited girls.

Now, years later, as I look back on that odd event, I'm puzzled by three things:

1. How could I possibly have known exactly where to go in that unfamiliar town, getting there so purposefully and calmly, without the slightest hesitation?

2. Could it be, I wonder, that I knew the old streets because I may have lived in Brecon before, in some 'previous life'?

3. Or is it possible that my mind, or some part of it, somehow travelled ahead of me and the girls, and then 'guided' us all to the meeting place?

Each of this lieutenant's explanations is a valid possibility, but I've included her account because it may also indicate some others:

It's possible that she may have been astral travelling on the previous evening, while her physical body was sleeping, and that in the astral world she may have planned the following day's events with 'Skipper'.

Or perhaps both 'Skipper' (who fully knew what she intended for the girls) and her lieutenant's minds had been in some kind of telepathic contact during the previous night's sleeping hours.

Or perhaps their thoughts may have linked up imperceptibly on the very day of the trip?

But, whatever the explanation, it certainly seems that some sort of psychic sense had been active; some kind of power had been operating outside of the lieutenant's head.

If only *one* of the above cases defies rational explanation — and I think the witnessed account from the man who opened the door with his spirit hand *does* — then the massive edifice of survival evidence, so painstakingly built up over the years by millions of dedicated spirit people, may stand intact, and hence merit our serious consideration.

Looking at our projectionists' stories, and recognising that they were fully able to exist in another plane of being as complete individuals 'outside of' and 'at a distance from' their physical bodies, I'm happy to accept that *the seat of consciousness is not the brain.*

And because of my many thousands of encounters with the so-called 'dead' – during which I've been privileged to relay their messages to their loved ones still on Earth – I can state that when the brain (with the body) dies, we will stand unscathed, and will survive the transition known as death, as complete and conscious, thinking individuals.

But where exactly *is* this Other Side of Life, this Other Dimension which our astral projectionists have briefly visited?

And why is it that this ethereal realm, which contains the so-called 'dead', frequently eludes the physical senses of millions of people?

Furthermore, is it possible for us to locate this spiritual world?

I believe it is...

6

Beyond the Veil

I was alone in a deserted lecture hall, in which I'd earlier been teaching mediumship, and now I had an hour free. Upstairs, directly above me, sixty-odd students from around Britain were listening to the continuing seminar.

More than grateful for my break, I wandered on to the empty platform and lowered my weary body into a big armchair: it felt as comfortable as a favourite old coat, and so welcoming that I quickly relaxed. Gently closing my eyes to regain some of the vast amounts of nervous energy that teaching burns up, I revelled in an inner silence, wonderfully liquid and golden, which was punctuated only by the muffled sounds of a distant tutor's voice coming from the room above.

Entranced by the shining darkness behind my eyes, I began to wonder what occupied the immediate space directly around my chair in the spirit realms. Although I was seated in a deserted small hall, about 30 feet wide by 100 feet long, I knew that within this area many invisible dimensions might exist. And then it happened – all at once.

Without warning my psychic vision opened up

and before me was revealed an utterly different world. I found myself somewhere near a very real and dusty street, full of old-fashioned wooden buildings, and the scene resembled that of a country settlement in 1930s America. My spirit sight took in every detail of the stained slatted buildings with their hand-painted signs swaying gently and creaking in the breeze; and all around me was the bustling sound of hurried activity.

It was high noon: the sun's shimmering heat was being reflected everywhere, and the humidity was palpable. Although I didn't see many people, I somehow knew that most of them were sheltering from the heat inside the various quaint shops.

Suddenly my attention was caught by a rickety old Ford car: shiny black with large wheels, it came chugging along the street right in front of me, spluttering and shaking, and leaving little dust clouds hanging in the air as it passed by. It was perfect in every detail, not a shabby replica but the genuine car itself.

I was fascinated; and I remember thinking, 'This world I'm seeing must be far removed from the hall I'm sitting in on Earth.'

And this Earthly thought, of course, brought about an immediate change of scene; and in the twinkling of an eye the dusty road and the car vanished.

And next I found myself seated in a similar high-backed leather armchair — in exactly the same spot — but this time there was no sign of the empty lecture hall back on Earth. Instead, I was now sitting inside a vast amphitheatre, which had quite a high ceiling. There were brown oak-panelled galleries all around me, as well as a dress-circle of seats, whereas the hall on Earth had seating only on the ground level and it had a much lower ceiling.

I noticed that some of the upper-gallery chairs were occupied: several people of various ages were grouped here and there, all watching me on the platform, almost as though they were waiting for me to start speaking or to take some kind of service.

It then occurred to me that they were witnessing a live event: they were watching my experiment.

But I made the foolish mistake of quickly opening my eyes to compare the two different places, and this action instantly brought my awareness back to grey Mother Earth — and I was once more seated in the quiet lecture hall, entirely alone again, and right back where I'd started.

But I knew exactly what had happened: I'd experienced two very brief existences in the astral worlds, in those shining spirit-planes that vibrate very close to the Earth.

I was then struck by the incredible realisation that in just one small space there are probably millions of different worlds, all existing simultaneously, each plane of thought separated from its neighbour simply by the rate at which it exists or vibrates.

But for the most part, the inhabitants of each sphere are blissfully unaware of their neighbours, unless someone breaks into their consciousness as I had just done.

There are countless worlds within worlds, within worlds, which all coexist together; and each world *interpenetrates* the others.

The experience I've just described might set us on the path to locating these worlds of spirit, which we can visit when we're out of the body. But before we can get a firmer grasp of their reality we need to consider the simple explanation of why 'ghosts' can walk through walls, and we can't.

Science tells us that physical matter is nothing more than an open network of atoms all vibrating and circling one another at such a fast rate that they give 'the appearance' of being solid, whereas, in fact, what seems to be 'solid' is actually an open structure. It's the incredibly fast speed of an object's atomic particles that makes it seem 'solid'.

Everything is constantly moving, and is in a state of continuous vibration.

The spaces between vibrating atoms are relatively vast: if we try to visualise the distance between our own sun and the Earth, this gives us a rough idea of the immense gaps between each of the vibrating atoms that are making up and 'materialising' this book you're reading, which may seem 'solid' enough to you — but it isn't 'solid' at all.

To help us locate the worlds of spirit we need to understand this: atoms which vibrate at slower 'physical' speeds make up the physical objects that we can see and sense in 'the physical world'; and these atoms cannot pass through any other physical objects because the speeds of the two sets of atoms are fixed at roughly the same rates of vibration.

For example, if you were to throw this book at the nearest wall it wouldn't go *through* the bricks but would bounce off them, because the atoms of the book are vibrating at roughly the same rate as the atoms of the wall, within a small waveband known as 'the physical world'.

Furthermore, physical matter, so the spirit people tell us, is simply spiritual matter (or high-frequency spirit energies) which are manifesting at lower 'physical' wavelengths.

Here's a helpful example: imagine that Spirit, or Life-essence, is like a fine morning mist. Soon it condenses into heavier rain, and afterwards it freezes to become ice: this ice-state might represent for us the physical world. The basic life-stuff or essence of all three states is the same (it's water) but it materialises itself in different densities, according to its rate of vibration.

This is why 'ghosts' can walk through our walls. The bodies of the ghosts are vibrating at higher frequencies than the particles of the walls are, which therefore can't prevent their passage.

'Life is Spirit, and Spirit is Life,' says my Other World teacher, White Owl, 'but Spirit functions, or manifests itself, in different worlds or planes of thought — plus in multifarious life-forms, and also in other universes.

'Man foolishly assumes he is a body with a mind, whereas his essence is pure Spirit, registering through a temporary vehicle known as the physical body; but even this is Spirit, existing at a much lower frequency than his mind.'

Here's another allusion to help us grasp why we can't see the spirit world with the naked eye:

If we boil a kettleful of water, it becomes steam that we can see and feel. Simply by quickening the vibration of the water molecules we've changed its state from a liquid into a gas. But if we then heat up the water much more (and hence, further increase its vibratory rate), it becomes supersteam which we *can't* see, but it still exists and will certainly burn off our flesh if we put a bare limb through it.

The spirit worlds are similar to this: they can't normally be seen by our Earthly senses because they're existing, or vibrating, at faster frequencies than the atoms of our physical eyes.

The Spirit Spheres formed in early times as a result of evolution. When the newly-born hot planet Earth started to cool down, it became denser and smaller, and the heavier, slower matter gravitated to its centre, while the finer, quicker and lighter matter cooled off around the central mass in successive layers upwards and outwards into space, creating several spirit spheres, or circular planes of life all around the Earth, which resemble the many skins of an onion.

So the Earth's core and crust are vibrating at a slower rate than each of the successive spirit spheres around them. Because the atoms of each spirit layer are moving faster than the layer beneath it, the natural divisions created between these layers are similar in appearance to fogbanks. Fog is made up of two streams of identical air, but one stream is cooler than the other – or one is vibrating slower than the other — and where they meet, they manifest in our atmosphere as fog.

Interestingly enough, the spirit spheres contain similar fogbanks where each fast-vibrating etheric atmosphere meets the slower vibrations of the layer beneath it; and the spirit people often refer to these clouds or borderlands as 'the mists'.

The spirit planes of thought aren't easy to locate geographically because the more evolved realms — and therefore these are the 'older' spheres — extend outwards to beyond all known time and space, and they aren't simply circling around our small planet.

The spirit worlds are thought-worlds, and, as such, they occupy all space and time at once; and there are many realms of existence in the Spiritual World:

'In my Father's house (kingdom) there are many mansions (planes of life),' says ancient scripture.

The spheres nearest to us are called the astral worlds — 'astral' is derived from the Greek word *astron,* meaning 'a star (or starry)', and they're aptly named because they exist in a shining light (fast-moving particles emit greater light and heat).

Because of their nearness to the Earth, these astral planes of thought are inhabited by recently 'deceased' persons; and recent can mean a few centuries in spirit.

However, the people of the astral worlds have frequently proved their awareness of what makes up our own lives here on Earth.

I've received proof of this on countless occasions.

One such spirit newcomer made a surprising appearance in the cemetery while I was conducting her funeral service!

Hannah, and her daughter, Jenny, had followed my calling right from its beginning and were often seen in the crowds at my public meetings, lending their emotional support. Hannah, who was very petite and in her seventies, positively adored me ('I

think the world of that little boy,' she used to say),
and she wouldn't have a thing said against me.
Despite the fact that she was small-boned and
under five feet tall, she'd been known to stand her
ground against a number of six-footer brutes and
vigorously defend my reputation.

'They're only jealous people, out to belittle you,'
she'd say, poking a lethal finger in what I assumed
to be their imaginary eyes.

When Hannah passed over, Jenny asked me if I'd
conduct the interment of her ashes at the family
grave, and I agreed without hesitation. One freezing cold November morning about fifteen people
assembled in a grassy cemetery; the wind was
bitter and cutting, and during the personal service
(for I never follow books or manuals) suddenly the
heavens opened and we mourners were pelted with
icy sleet.

Apart from the atrocious weather, everything else
had gone fine: I'd read a poem and had spoken
some comforting words to everyone gathered
around the graveside, had offered up a prayer of
thankfulness for the gift of Hannah's life, and then
we'd all paid our respects by dropping small white
flowers into the grave, to symbolise 'that another
soul has risen into freedom,' as I remember saying.
After that, we sent out silent thoughts to our de-
parted friend – and this was the moment when
Hannah chose to make a surprising appearance to
my psychic vision. I saw her standing opposite her
burial place, as large as life; she was leaning on the
gravestone as if nothing at all had happened to her.
With pitiful eyes, she looked across at me and then
around at the blue faces of the elderly mourners —

it was such a cold day — and then spoke to me with typical concern. 'Oh, God help them,' she said. 'God love him, too. Thank you all very much,' she added, in obvious gratitude for our presence and for the kind words I'd spoken.

Such a natural occurrence as this, highlights the nearness of the next planes to Earth, those astral thought-worlds in which our thinking has a more direct effect upon the ether around us than it does upon the materials around us here on the Earth.

Our thoughts create every circumstance and condition that touches and affects our lives.

It was this wonderful thought-power that drew Hannah to her graveside service, and it was lovely to see her again.

I believe we should monitor, and be very wary of, our thought-patterns, for my spirit work, and the assistance and counselling I've given to the patients of psychotherapists in the past, has taught me that old habits die hard, and that they can effectively trap us in thought-cages of our own making if we're not careful.

If a man lives in a certain kind of house all his life and then he 'dies', his thought patterns will propel him to a plane of thought (or to a world of spirit) in which similar houses exist, and he'll probably continue living in one of these until he thinks he no longer needs such a lifestyle.

Your thoughts will 'control' and 'condition' your existence, both in this world and in the next.

We need to be careful about what we think because the immense power of negative thought can cripple a soul's psychological progress, and its penetrating effects should not be underestimated.

My own father was a man who, I believe, was trapped in a self-created thought-prison. He was a person by whom you could set your clock: in his later years he went to exactly the same places every day, at exactly the same time, met his usual friends for a drink, ate at the same café (placing a regular order), and then he came home.

With no offence to Dad, such a daily routine could hardly be described as exciting or as living life to the full; in my opinion, his habit-patterns and mind-tracks created a listless and unprogressive lifestyle. Yet untold millions exist like this each and every day of what I consider must be their potentially half-lived lives.

The trouble with Thought is that it's capable of easily creating illusions: it can fool us into feeling psychologically secure by shackling us into regular but stifling mind habits, and unless we make conscious efforts to break these chains and alter these crippling, negative thought-patterns, we'll suffer the unfortunate consequences.

How many lives, I wonder, are only partly lived because of the illusions of Thought? How many unfortunate souls are daily existing in a strange kind of 'waking sleep', barely conscious of the great pulse of life?

I think they would number more than the grains of sand on a beach.

But change we must — it's absolutely inevitable. So why waste any more time?

Let's all start now.

It's from the astral thought-worlds that a great majority of spirit people relay their messages in my public meetings, of course, and because these communicators are relatively new arrivals in the spirit world, they will not have had the time to acquire more wisdom — and this should be remembered when considering any advice these personalities might offer.

The astral levels of consciousness are the easiest for mediums to contact, but communicating with more advanced and progressed souls is a much more complicated process because they exist deep within the inner spirit realms, and they're infinitely more difficult to reach.

To communicate with such enlightened beings, mediums require a refined sensitivity and a highly developed psychic awareness; physical sensory equipment is quite unsatisfactory for registering subtle vibrations.

Slow-vibrating physical eyes can only perceive light existing within very limited wavelengths.

We can see the brilliance of a golden sunrise, but its 'secret' vibrations of ultraviolet light remain hidden to the naked eye.

We can watch the lightning as it flashes through the heavens on a dark and stormy night, or be entranced by the crackling flames of a forest fire; and yet we're unable to see the X-rays that penetrate our bodies whenever we're examined for illness.

As mere physical computers, our fleshly brains are limited to perceiving a minuscule range of sensory data; yet some animals can hear the ear-piercing sounds of dog-whistles that thankfully escape our notice, and they can see the hidden wavelengths of infrared light.

I often have a quiet chuckle when sceptical academics reject the mind as being a separate vibrating entity from the brain, and when they say there can't possibly be a sphere in which it functions after the body is 'dead'.

We can't see the air we breathe, but it certainly exists.

Just because something is 'invisible' to physical sight, doesn't mean that it has no reality. Just think about the ordinary sound waves from next-door's television coming right through the wall when you don't want to hear them: they penetrate the bricks and mortar and travel in the atmosphere; they undoubtedly exist, but we can't see them with our naked eyes.

And what about the powerful forces of love and anger? We'd be hard-pressed to slap hatred on an operating table for scientists to dissect it.

On radio I once flummoxed a rather confused sceptic of the paranormal with, 'If one of your ardent admirers declared, "I love you", how could you see it, believe it, or even prove its existence, I wonder?'

He was cornered into silence.

So much of what makes up our lives is taken on trust and is experienced subjectively, by us alone.

I also find it illogical to believe that 'invisible' sound and light vibrations can pass through an empty nothingness; all energies must surely be carried by a medium of some sort. The spirit people tell us this universe is filled with an 'invisible' substance called ether — which is yet another vibrational aspect of an Infinite Spirit — and that this ether is the vehicle or medium through which all energy vibrations are conveyed.

By lowering their mind-vibrations, the people on

the Other Side can contact us by sending their thoughts through the ether into our own minds.

Some spirit people are also quite clever at manipulating the ether and drawing power from it, and us, to accomplish seemingly impossible feats. Theories behind the reproduction of matter into clone-like versions of original substances are now being taught to most schoolchildren, but I can cite an impressive spirit-world example.

Someone from eternity must have been very close to me one morning when I grumbled about the talcum powder in the bathroom. 'The silly thing,' I said, vigorously shaking the sealed can to get the last dregs out of it, 'it doesn't last five minutes. Why don't they make it everlasting?'

Little did I know that someone on the Other Side had overheard me, and they then set about doing just that.

I continued to use the talc in its lightproof tin every day, but after a few months I began to suspect something...

'This must surely be coming to the end by now?' I mused; yet the supply just kept on sprinkling out each day.

Eventually, the penny dropped when I heard a young spirit child saying, 'I've been practising my skills in matter-reproduction' — the talent of multiplying physical atoms by manipulating their spirit vibrations through the ether.

'I *wondered* what was going on!' I replied to the moist bathroom air.

The darkness inside the tin must have provided the perfect conditions for such physical manifestations to occur, for the talcum powder carried on pouring for an incredible *eight consecutive months,* after which it suddenly dried up and I had to buy some more. (Now that's what I call value for money!)

The ether and the spirit worlds are all around us. 'Nothing exists without the Power of the Infinite Spirit,' states my spirit guide. 'With Spirit there is consciousness and life; without it there is nothing.

'We are all constantly bathed in a vibratory sea of Spirit Power, an indefinable life-energy that permeates every aspect of being: physical, mental, emotional and spiritual. The Power of the Spirit is everywhere, within you and "outside" of you.'

Though in reality, of course, as I'm sure many would agree, absolutely nothing can ever reside 'outside' of ourselves, for whatever we are conscious of appears to us as a subjective thought or as a mental experience.

My spirit friend has often taught that we exist within the Infinite Spirit's Essence: everything in this universe can be likened to a great sea of spiritual energy viewed as an endless vast ocean, and we are like small jellyfish floating in it, and being supported by its power.

Therefore, we're made up of the power: it feeds us, it is within us and without of us; *we* are *it*, and *it* is *us*. And all manifestations are linked to this Infinite Spirit, and therefore we cannot be where It is not. But I'll have more to say on this later, when discussing the nature of the One Living God.

I believe everything exists because of the Power of Consciousness, even the spirit worlds; and other philosophers have stated something similar by declaring they don't think that Earth-life is a reality, it's a mere dream.

In many ways, I wouldn't disagree.

Life — both here and in the realms of spirit — is a certainly a thought-experience: a dream, but a very real one to the dreamer, nevertheless.

Just imagine that one night you experience a vivid dream and then, in this deep sleep, your physical body suddenly 'dies' and never wakes up — for you, that continuing lucid dream would now be your reality, wouldn't it?

Life's like that, no matter where we exist.

The next worlds of vibration contain countless billions of such 'dreamers', including my spirit guide, known as White Owl; but, dreamer or not, he's a 'dead' man who continues to receive hundreds of personal letters from people in different parts of this world each year.

As a frequent spirit communicator and teacher of natural law and spiritual realities, he seems to have made a considerable impact on many Earth lives. His teachings are the result of what he claims to be the benefit of a much wider spiritual vision, gained through his great age and his vantage-point in the spirit world.

Perhaps we should question this?

Maybe it's time to place him under the critical eye of a glaring public spotlight.

Let's peer now through the divisions between heaven and Earth, through those cloudy fogbanks and vibrating spirit mists, and lift the veil on one of these interpenetrating spirit realms so that we can take a glimpse into its vast store of wisdom as revealed by my spirit guide in his own world of Thought.

Perhaps then we may discover exactly who — or what — White Owl truly is...

'Our message is one of toleration and peace, and our task is to touch and awaken sleeping materialistic souls to the eternal power of the spirit within them, and to reveal the wonderful opportunities for growth and service that this affords.'

White Owl:
the Native American Indian
Spirit Guide of Stephen O'Brien

7

White Owl Speaks
A Guide in the Spotlight

White Owl, who are you?
I am a soul who has undertaken a mission, in co-operation with many other minds more advanced and progressed than my own, to help enlighten mankind and bring his thinking back onto paths of peacefulness and to a deeper understanding of spiritual realities. We are endeavouring to spread knowledge of who and what man is, where he came from, where he is going, and why he has incarnated on Earth.

I am a very close friend of the medium.

How old are you?
I am ancient.

Physical age and your timescale mean nothing to us here. If I told you I was a hundred years old, seventeen hundred, or even a million years old, would these figures matter? Can wisdom come from the unwise? Can the darkness of ignorance spring from the mind of a knowledgeable being?

If your world judges me by my teachings, by what I say, then I think it will be apparent that I have tried to achieve my goals through the power of love. I have never dominated or suppressed my medium's freewill (limited though it is).

I have consistently advocated that man should use his faculties of intelligent questioning and reason, and that he should accept only that which is in accordance with the highest principles of wisdom, and of love, one toward another.

Were you an American Indian only in your last incarnation?

'I' am not a Red Indian at all. The astral body of this balanced personality known as 'White Owl' is just a vehicle for my thoughts and teachings. I am a much older soul who uses the instrumentality of the gentle Indian, just as the Indian uses the mentality of Stephen O'Brien.

It is like a stepping-down process, a transmission of higher knowledge and vibrations down through various 'transformers' or 'mediums' until it reaches your present understanding.

Neither is my teaching entirely my own. I receive guidance and instruction as to what shall be transmitted at any given time. I, too, am a medium.

Where did your soul originate, White Owl?

Souls do not originate, they are part of the out-breathing of a Universal Spirit; they have always been.

There is no beginning and no end to existence; it is eternal.

Here, we cannot say that we had a starting-point, or indeed that our lives will eventually finish.

God is an Infinite Being, and such boundaries

would demean this almighty power and make of It a mere finite entity, and that is against all that we have found. An end to existence, to God, would be illogical.

Where do you live?
Close by, geographically speaking, and yet, to your slow physical senses, I am sometimes very far away, it seems. I occupy space and move through time in dimensions beyond the narrow confines of Earth, existing in planes of thought which are interpenetrating your world at this very moment.

Can you describe for us the sphere in which you normally exist?
I have no adequate words with which to convey to you an exact description of my world. You could not compare it with anything in your physical plane, which is but a very pale shadow, not even a flickering candlelight flame, when set against the radiance and wonder of the realms I inhabit when in my natural state.

Having now been many years in this world — which you are forever trying to locate beyond death but which, in reality, resides within you — I have earned for myself the right to exist in planes of thought far in advance of this astral world, which is full of mental illusions, and from which I am now communicating.

My true place is in a world of indescribable light and incredible beauty.

It is a realm where the power of thought instantaneously brings its beneficent effect.

Here, all the finer aspects of the soul are perfectly

free to express themselves, within the limitations of the Great Spirit's Laws.

The living and vibrant colours of our vegetation cannot be fully appreciated or captured by you, imagined by you, or reproduced by any means currently at your disposal, for our manifestations are self-luminous and have an iridescent brilliance which lights them from within.

We have animals here, too, but in a progressed state of evolution, and their companionship is wondrous in its innocence and purity.

But this plane from which I am now addressing you is a dark and grey sphere (to my vision), and one that is very slow in vibration because of the often selfish thoughts and intentions radiated into it by the people of Earth.

Such is the state of the lower astral worlds.

However, the realms I *could* exist in, but have relinquished for the time being to undertake this two worlds' mission with my medium, are filled with unutterable beauty and fineness of spirit.

Because the majority of our loved ones live in those astral worlds: when you said those places are 'full of mental illusions', what did you mean?
Simply that the mind is not the man, it is merely an instrument which creates a self-awareness of its own reality; it thinks, it pictures, and it gives life to its own mental images — but it is not the man. The real man is the essence, the soul.

Mental illusions operate as follows:

When you inherit my world, having left the slow vibrations of the Earth behind you, your thoughts will have a more immediate and direct effect upon your surroundings here.

If a man 'dies' but still feels he is a very important person, he will perpetuate an over-inflated opinion of himself, needing — he thinks — to be regularly told how wonderful he is. He will then draw around him others who will fulfil these wishes and convince him of his false 'kindness'.

But this is not Truth. It is an illusion that is far from the real state of this man's soul. He will be living within the illusions of his own making.

Your Earth-plane is full of people like this.

Earth is, in many respects, a dream-world full of beings who are building up false impressions of themselves, and of others, within their own minds; but to them these thoughts become very real.

The true inner reality of their soul-state is usually quite different. Yet man's mind — the deceiver and the master illusionist — continues to create these supposed 'realities' and stops at nothing to try to sustain them.

But the only Reality is the Spirit, Consciousness, and this can only be experienced when the mental dross and shadows of illusion have been gradually dissipated and discarded, which often takes a very long time.

But if we are not our minds, then what are we?
You belong to the Essence of the Great Spirit; you are Consciousness, which is the vibrant life-power that your clever mind uses to generate and main-tain its reality, as well as its many falsehoods and delusions.

So when we discard the mind, or as you call it 'the

127

deceiver', what will be left?
God-consciousness; a greater awareness of union with your Originator.

Are you a part of the medium's 'deceiver'? Are you a secondary personality of the medium, another part of his mind impersonating a guide?
No, I am not 'a secondary personality', though I am a part of my medium's individuality.

What do you mean when you say you are a part of his individuality?
For people who are still registering through the flesh, concepts of the spirit are frequently difficult to grasp. Because my vantage-point is significantly different from yours, language often obstructs my meaning.

There is a tremendous difference between 'the individual' and 'the personality'. The personality is that to which you have given a name because it seems to manifest in the physical body you are currently using. But your individuality is much greater than this.

I am a part of my medium's individuality.

There are a number of personalities currently incarnated on Earth – and who now have contact with Stephen to support him and his mission – and there are a few more to be introduced to him as yet. There are also other people here in my world who are all fragments of the one individual, which 'incorporates' us. We are parts of one whole.

We are all seemingly separate persons, but in fact we share the same common nexus, link, or essence, and this is our individuality.

What happens to our individuality after death?
Do we live for ever, or are we to be eventually
merged back into God, into the whole?
I have been on this side of life for many, many
years, as you would gauge time, and I have heard
of no one who has 'lost' or 'diffused' their individuality back into the Godhead from whence it came.
Once individuality has been characterised, it seems
for ever established.

Often I am privileged to take counsel with many
great teachers – the Ancient Shining Ones – who
are aware of all our thoughts and of the work we
are undertaking through mediums on Earth. They
come to instruct and guide us, and they teach that
a greater awareness of individuality will be
afforded to each soul as it progresses towards the
Light.

They do not speak of annihilation, back into a
primordial source.

But that is not to say we will always have an outward tangible vehicle of expression, for eventually
we will have no need of this. I have communed
with some greatly advanced souls who have
remained perfectly individual in their essence but
who have no outward form of any kind. They are
points of consciousness, pure thought and feeling:
time and space is open to them.

But I am speaking now of souls who have existed
here for aeons, and not newcomers who have been
here for a mere few thousand years.

We are told that individuals from the Spirit are
frequently close by us: does the next world guide

us daily?
Most assuredly, and often imperceptibly.

We are near your minds, and not only when you are awake: when you are asleep at night, we are also present as you cross over into our realms. Our guidance and inspiration reaches you through the power of thought.

We can throw images into another's mentality, for his or her consideration. It is quite easy to do; you yourselves are transmitting these thought-forces every second that you exist; but we are specialists at it.

Why is it that so many guides, as given by some mediums, are supposedly Red Indians, or Zulu warriors, or even ancient chieftains or Chinese mandarins, and suchlike?
You have answered your own question: they are not. Much is relayed through certain unreliable mediums which does not emanate from us.

Mediums are all at different levels of soul and psychic development. Some are more sensitive to our influence than others, but we cannot make our thoughts clearly felt or perceived if the abilities of the mediums we must work with are under-developed.

A great musician can play beautiful music on a finely tuned instrument, but the same performer can hardly be blamed for the sub-standard sound at the concert if the tools you provide him with fall short of high quality.

You have to learn to distinguish between what is coming from us, what is coming through the medium from his or her own subconscious mind, and what is pure delusion.

Are you implying that we should never trust mediums?
I always advise caution in accepting utterances from any source, in whatever world, without first pitting them against your keenest intelligence.

Surely you would not expect me to say otherwise?

But now let me ask you a question: do you think it important to know who guides you?

Yes. I do.
So you will want to have a recognisable identity, a guide-personality either given or revealed to you by another sensitive?

Yes. I would like to know who guides me.
I must tell you: it is very easy for me to clearly read that thought from your mental aura. Let me now explain what could happen if you keep this idea in your mind.

Through the Laws of Attraction, you will draw to you someone from my world who would like to work with you, but they may well be hindered by this dominant guide-thought in your mentality.

Your spirit friend will want to get on with the important work, while your dominating desire will be to know your guide's identity. Furthermore, if you wish for a certain type of guide, a colourful personality — such one of those you have already mentioned — then the intelligence working with you will be obliged to meet that powerful desire-force, in order for the lines of communication to be opened up, so that the work may progress.

You mean they would lie to me?

No, they would meet your need: it is you who would lie to yourself.

We are not interested in names, positions and high-sounding titles, we are concerned with helping the Great Spirit's Truths to liberate man's mind from ignorance and fear.

But your remarks indicate that mediums may mislead people.

Mediums are only human beings, my friend, and quite fallible ones at that. They, like we who are in Spirit, will doubtless make many silly mistakes.

As far as Our Side is concerned, communication is not as easy as it might sometimes appear. We try to blend our minds and personalities with those of our mediums and we are not always as successful as we would like to be, owing to mental, spiritual, emotional and physical conditions obstructing our efforts at the time of contact.

So, are some guides purely thought-forms, or thought-images that have been created by the minds of their mediums?

Yes, some are just that.

Thought-forms of (let us say) an elderly Chinese mandarin would appear just like pictures hovering within the mind of the sensitive who has formed them, created by his desire-force because he wants this kind of person to make contact with him.

These 'images' have no real life of their own, but they can be seen by us, and sometimes psychically aware people on Earth are talented enough to attune their perceptive powers into the mental frequencies of the medium and clearly register

these very thought-forms—
– Through telepathy?
– yes; and then the psychic describes this thought-image to its own creator, to the sensitive.

The medium then goes home believing he has an old Chinaman as his guide, which is exactly what he thought he had, and what he wanted to hear, is it not?

Yes. But genuine guides do exist?
Oh yes; I am one of them.

Can you tell us something about your own guides, your superiors: who are they?
What do you mean by the term 'superiors'?

Those who are much higher than yourself, those for whom you work.
I am guided by the Mind and Will of the Great Spirit, who is the epitome of all perfection and all wisdom.

Perhaps you are referring to the individuals through whom this inspiration reaches me?

Yes, the hierarchies in the world of the spirit that we've heard about.
There are many wise souls, yes, but even they are ruled by the limitless Natural Laws. We have no governments here, not as you understand them.

Here there is service and a constant search for truth and wisdom, with a gradual unfolding of greater understanding. But most of all, we know the blessings of true friendship, love and service.

It is love and friendship which motivates us, and

it also binds souls together.

So how do you reach the Earth, to guide, exercise 'control' over, or to inspire your medium friend?
First, I must think myself close to the Earth by remembering what the conditions of its slow and ponderously heavy atmosphere felt like to me when I lived there, many centuries ago now. I then move through the surface of the astral world and descend to the Earth.

Upon arrival I am able to move within what is known as the aura of the medium: his electromagnetic fields of vibration, which are an out-picturing of his soul.

By an intricate process of mental attunement I can then gain access to the frequencies of his subconscious mind, and it is from here that I can inspire him with my thoughts.

It is always a willing co-operation undertaken to forward the Divine Plan.

What is the nature of this plan you've so often spoken about through Stephen?
The plan is now in full operation, and will not fail. It is organised by a vast conglomerate or group of minds who have taken upon themselves the mammoth task of liberating the mind, heart and soul of man, and delivering spiritual light to the human race.

We shall uncover to his gaze his true spiritual nature and his real state of soul-evolution. Man has scientifically evolved in a technological way, but his spiritual evolution has certainly not gone hand in hand with this advancement.

Man on Earth remains, in the majority of cases, a self-centred, selfish creature who expresses little concern for the development of his self, the stewardship of the world in which he lives, or the respect that he should have for the other life-forms existing around him.

It is this blinkered vision and ignorance which we seek to dispel with our teachings, by always appealing to common sense.

But surely organised religion has undertaken this task for many centuries?
I would disagree with you.

You are gravely mistaken.

Many organised religions, to use your phrase, have — by setting up their narrow mental and spiritual boundaries, sects, divisions and 'isms' — caused immeasurable strife, hardship, darkness of the soul, and hindrance to the light of true spiritual knowledge spreading throughout your world.

Hypocrisy has always dwelt within the Earthly mind of man: what he preaches is seldom what he practises.

So we have decided to go outside these organisations, creeds and theologies, and to reach the masses with our spirit teachings through the loving hearts of all those who are specially incarnating now, and whose work will eventually lead the human race forward, out of spiritual darkness and into the liberating light of truth.

Will you deliver your teachings through sensitives other than Stephen? We've received reports about you speaking in various psychic circles.

My influence is brought to bear where I believe it is needed, but my channel for the spiritual truths that I have promised to deliver is through Stephen O'Brien.

People on Earth, through no real fault of their own (it is just their somewhat restricted viewpoint), do not fully appreciate the many and complex intricacies involved in the processes of spirit communication.

I was diligently trained for this task over a long period of time. I then chose my medium, and he, me. I then had to guide him and gather together the others of our band of spirits.

But now we are an established team, a bridgehead, a partnership: and we two, in a wider sense, are one. After all this time and effort it would be foolish to seek out others through whom to deliver my message.

We understand, but Stephen won't be here for ever.
What I am charged to deliver will be given during his allotted time of service. When the work is finished, the mission will cease: though I am not permitted to state when that will be. After it expires, my Earth-voice will know silence again, as it did before our work began.

But if I decide to go forward and inspire other channels, they would not necessarily know, would they?

Some are already claiming you're working with them while your medium is still alive.
'Test ye the Spirit'; I think you have heard this

before. Anyone can call himself a medium.

Are mediums born, or made?
Where any form of mediumship is evident, you can be sure that its possessor has earned every jot of that facility through hard work in prior incarnations. Mediumship functions more favourably through certain physical bodies because of their chemical make-up, which is why the incarnating servant selects a suitable family group and personally decides on its own destiny and broad future upbringing, before its life materialises on Earth.

Mediums are born with a mission, to play their part in the Divine Scheme of things.

Then what, in your view, is the true job of a sensitive, or of anyone who claims a conscious connection with intelligences residing in the next world?
Mediums have a sacred calling — but, if you are a public medium, I have a question for you: what exactly are you doing? You are most certainly *not* proving survival of the human soul after death; some of the best scientific minds in your world, and in mine, would find it extremely difficult to prove you are now existing in *your* world, not to mention in mine.

Ultimate proof of survival comes when you pass from the Earth and arrive in my world. Then there is no doubt about your eternal nature.

Then what are all the sensitives in the world doing?
They are providing *evidence* of survival, but not

proof *per se*. They are offering a priceless service to those who feel spiritually lost: to the lonely and the ignorant, and to those who mourn and need knowledge of spiritual realities.

They are comforters and educators.

Are there any other hidden purposes behind mediumship?
Those who are serving in this way chose this time to undertake their current responsibilities — it is all impressed within your spiritual nature, in your pathway, and there are far deeper implications to being a living entity who claims conscious links to us than at first might be imagined.

Mediums should not deceive themselves as to their true role in the Divine Plan.

Do mediums require dedication and commitment in order to succeed?
Yes, for you cannot be a medium once a week on a Sunday, or only when you perform public service.

As an aware soul you are continuously representing God, the Great Spirit, on Earth — in your own unique way, every second that you breathe.

This is an awesome personal responsibility.

So in what way would a medium's prayers affect a guide like you?
Your life is your prayer. You are a flowering tree, and by your fruit shall you be known: for a man cannot lie to himself or to the God within him, or to us, his ever-watchful friends in spirit.

In my world all is known — for here Thought is King — Consciousness is the great Reality, and all else is illusion. We are totally aware of your inner-most motivation for wishing to act as bridges between us and man incarnate.

Do you have access to our intimate thoughts?
If we desire to know something, nothing escapes us; we are alive and monitoring all that touches your lives. We know intimately all those who are co-operating with us.

We know who is with us, and who is against us.

Ours is a very organised world.

Sometimes instruments for the spirit need a gentle reminder about this law.

Service is a sacred calling and the voice of the spirit has summoned you to go amongst your brothers and sisters and render service to them in whatever way you can.

So what would you say to a person engaged on any pathway of delivering spiritual aid to his fellows?
Keep on serving in whatever way you can. Your life is important and your talents are important, so use them, whatever they may be.

Never for one moment forget that you are touching souls, awakening minds and hearts to the Living Power of the Great Spirit and to the fact that It resides in, behind, and through all manifestations, seen and unseen.

You are a spiritual catalyst, a divine channel for the power of God to effect changes for the better in the lives of His children, many of whom are helplessly lost in the darkness of spiritual ignorance and despair.

But you are an ever-burning lighthouse of the spirit, a bright beacon of truth shining out across the storm-tossed seas of life. God, through His Messengers of Light, has called you to uphold this sacred office of mediumship.

Therefore, do not forsake us, for we are doing all that we can to uplift mankind from being a beast into being a saint, from creating vile thoughts into creating purity of mind.

How can we gain a closer awareness of your presence?

Through silent meditation, and a heart filled with love. With all of your love and your willing co-operation we can help the human race to lift itself up from the quagmire of its animal nature and into the light of its Divine Aspect.

Each one of you is playing his part in this cosmic jigsaw puzzle of certain evolution.

Seek within.

Speak with us, and become conscious of the greatest power in the Universe — God, the Infinite Spirit.

But remember that by every thought you think and every act you perform you either degrade and darken your own soul, or else transform and clothe it with raiments of radiant light and love.

Can we earn a place in the state known as heaven by following your advice?

You are building your own heaven right now on Earth, fitting yourself for a sphere of existence in my world, which you earn by the daily purification of your mind and character. Heaven is a state of inner being, of mental perception — it is not a location, but a mental appreciation. In rendering service to your fellow creatures, in whatever form, you are adding merit to your own evolutionary state. Always it is the motive of each action which is the most important factor.

Do your best to help; you can do no more.

The seeds you sow today, will be the plants you will reap tomorrow. Some leaves, however, cannot be picked until you join us here in the light.

Whatever soul-abilities you are endeavouring to express, remember that as true mediums for the Spirit you are engaged in a wonderful work indeed.

You are helping the human race to advance, onwards through the sea of life, helping it to sail towards the light of knowledge and into a tranquil harbour of peace.

We need you to help us in our task of raising a struggling humanity out of the abyss of cruelty and into the effulgent light of spiritual love.

So must we have faith and keep on working to comfort and uplift humankind?
Yes: keep faith, but base your faith on the spiritual knowledge which has been revealed to you.

Blind faith is a barrier to the open-mindedness required by servants of the spirit. You must remove such psychological barriers in order to receive your guidance and inner revelations.

Blind faith obstructs; open-mindedness reveals a pathway.

Fear must also be completely eradicated from your thinking, for it prevents contact with us because our mental and soul-radiations are so fine and subtle that such gross emotions can easily sweep away our subtle influences.

Go forward and serve.

Try to be kind, and keep cheerful, for we are just a hair's breadth away, guiding as much as we can.

Just call on us, and we will respond.

We are standing ever beside you.

I am your Guardian Angel

Weep no more for me,
  for though it seemed to you that I died,
  in truth, I've never left your side.
    I've stood beside you
    through all your grief, your pain and tears;
    I am your Guardian Angel now
    and I'll guide you down the years...

I was there on those quiet evenings
  when you knelt and prayed;
and when you kissed my photograph
  I felt your doubt and fear,
and heard you wondering if I was safe and well
and whether I was far away or near –
     but I was there;
      and remember this:
        the Great God heard your prayer.

For the Cosmic Mind
  that formed this wondrous Earth –
  vast mountain ranges, oceans, life and trees –
  whose Spirit shines in the morning sky
  and whose voice is carried on the breeze,
  the Power of this Almighty God
  beats within each loving sigh:
    The Great Spirit is Eternal;
    and so are you;
      and so am I...

And at some future time,
  in a spiritual world that lies ahead,
  I promise you this: we'll be reunited.

I'll hold you in my arms again
and I'll kiss away your tears;
but for now, I will watch over you
throughout the lonely years.

So weep no more for me,
for you see, love never dies –
I am your Guardian Angel now,
and I'm standing by your side.

Stephen O'Brien

8

'O, Great White Spirit...'

(An invocation delivered by White Owl.)

O, Great White Spirit,
from hidden worlds within, we have come
to bring our truths and wisdom
to all who will listen.

We consider it a privilege
to forsake our right to exist
within shining realms of light,
earned for ourselves
through spiritual progression,
and to return to this dark and often grey Earthworld.
In a spirit of friendship we make contact
as elder brothers and sisters
seeking to aid a human family
which stands in great need of
Thy Divine Light
and
Thy Divine Love.

Soul-sensitivity and awareness
are the fields within which we stand,
waiting for man to lift the veil of ignorance
and to discover our presence...

Within the flowering of spiritual unfoldment
our silent voices will be heard.
Residing in the secret kingdoms of the soul
our tones will resound within
the minds of men and women everywhere —
in anyone who seeks
to know us
and
to love us.

We need only to hear the cry of the spirit
to respond as quickly as we can.
We need only to sense the loving heart
of one who serves,
and we are near.

Where two or three be gathered
in the name of Love,
we will also be there, in the midst.

We are ever surrounding the faithful
as
Angels of Light,
ever ready to comfort and guide;
so that all men may know
that no child of Earth is unworthy of
our co-operation:
and when only one step forward is taken in love
a thousand souls from my world
will step behind to serve.

In the heart which cares,
in the soul which acutely feels empathy,
sympathy,
and compassion

for its fellows and lesser life-forms —
in such a mind our inspiration
is as a Living Spring of Clear Waters
flowing
through the mists of
Earthly consciousness
and out
into the darkness of the Earthworld
as a Guiding Light.

For these, our true servants,
there is no night,
no despair,
no loneliness,
and no sense of irreplaceable loss:
they know not grief,
or sorrow
or any lasting pain
which breathes within emotion.
They see only
the Light of Knowledge
and
a bright Torch of Hope
burning in the centre of
a Universal Heart.

In the silence of the hushed soul
we are waiting;
in the purest breast we reside;
in the quietness of a sensitive mind
the link with us is made —
for we cannot function successfully
where there is doubt,
uncertainty,
fear,

avarice,
self-centredness,
or a grievous lack of compassion.
But we are ever near
the faithful
and
the kind.

May it please the Will of the Great Spirit
to bless our work
with the fruitfulness and inspiration
of The Shining Ones above.

Thy Will be done:
Surely, so let it be...

*

A Visionary's Prayer

(Composed and given by Stephen O'Brien.)

May those who feel lonely and unloved
   meet the arms of another
   and be embraced...

May those who feel lost in the darkness
   seek the light of truth
   and find it...

May those who have plenty
   give to those
   who have nothing at all...

May those who are intolerant of others
   learn patience
   and practise it...

And may those who cannot see
the beauty of the stars
   open their eyes wide
   and be thankful;

   for then their fear may become certainty
   and their vision, clearer –
   revealing each challenge as a friend.

And may peace live in their hearts,
      Great Spirit –
if only for the sake of the children
      as yet unborn,
        who are waiting to come...

9

Farewell to a Chocolate Soldier

I'd been earnestly praying for spiritual healing to help my elderly father, whose ill-health had been getting increasingly worse for some time, when one day my only brother, John, telephoned with some bad news.

'Stephen, Dad's very poorly. You'd better go and see him.'

It transpired that my father, who was seventy-one and morbidly obese at 22 stone (140 kg), and who lived alone, had fallen down at home and had remained helpless on the floor for over an hour and a half, unable to stand up on his own.

'Oh, I didn't know what to do,' he said, fearfully. 'I was so weak; I couldn't sit up, boy. I lay there for ages before managing to drag myself to the telephone cable, pulling it down and phoning an ambulance. They busted the door in, and put me right. But I don't mind telling you, boy, I was frightened. It shook me up good and proper.'

After this, Dad made a slow recovery, but then just before Christmas 1991 another urgent call came from John.

'Dad's in hospital, Stephen: he nearly died.'

So I jumped into the car again and sped straight to Swansea's Morriston Hospital where my father was recuperating.

'I've had a terrible chest infection, boy. It nearly killed me, but they treated it just in time: another hour and I'd have been a goner. I was shivering and shaking from head to foot and burning up like I was in a furnace. They've taken lots of X-rays and blood tests and I've got to stay here for a week or two, they think.'

'Oh well,' I said, 'as long as you're comfortable, that's the main thing, Dad. Do you need anything?'

'No, I'm OK. All I want is to get out of this place, boy. I can't bloody stand hospitals, they're for pregnant women or people who are gonna die.'

'Now come on,' I said, 'cheer up. They'll soon put you right.'

'Aye, I expect they will,' he replied, but I could see he didn't believe it; so my brother and I visited him every day: John went in the afternoon and I went in the evening.

Despite my father's weight, the doctors said he was malnourished and was suffering from a protein deficiency. This didn't surprise us because every day he'd eat at a café where the food was nothing but stodge made up of mashed potatoes and vegetables which had been boiled for so long that, quite honestly, he'd have been better off drinking the vegetable-water.

Hospital dieticians immediately placed him on a high-protein diet, consisting mainly of meat and fish, but mostly fish.

'And how are we today then?' I'd ask chirpily.

'Oh that bloody food's getting me down!' he'd

complain. 'Fish, fish, fish – all the bloody time! Fish every bloody day. I'll grow a set of fins in a minute and bloody swim out of here in the end.'

Poor old Dad always was a bit of a moaner: he'd grump over the slightest thing and it was never a pleasure to be around him. If my father had a pain in his little finger or a cut on his toe he'd swear he was in dire agony, ready to be carried off to the crematorium. And he was always moaning about the arthritic stiffness in his neck and the fact that he couldn't walk properly — but when the doctor told him to go on a strict diet, he paid no attention whatsoever. He would much rather eat and drink as much as he liked, and then sit down and grizzle about it.

But soon another complication set in – Dad contracted a blood disorder: his doctors found salmonella in his blood cultures. They ordered him to keep scrupulously clean and to wash his hands every time after using the bathroom, which was something he'd rarely done, in or out of health. And indeed he continued not to do it despite being given strong warnings of re-infecting himself and of making the nurses ill; but all to no avail.

There wasn't a man in the world more stubborn than my father: he only did what *he* wanted to do, when *he* wanted to do it. He was a remarkably strong-willed man, except when it came to pain — that was another kettle of fish. I vividly recall the time when my mother lay dying of cancer back in the 1970s: after Dad had broken the news of her imminent death to me, which I took reasonably calmly, he said, seriously, 'I don't know how I'm going to get through this, boy. Perhaps you'll be the strongest of the lot of us. I might turn out to be a chocolate soldier.'

'A what, Dad?'

'A chocolate soldier. You know: someone who puts on a brave face, but who melts at the first sign of battle... We'll see,' he added solemnly.

And, as readers might already know, my father did turn out to be a chocolate soldier when my mother passed over: the realisation of her death was too much for him to bear and during her last moments he couldn't face it, so he went to a neighbour's house and my brother plied him with drink and he fell fast asleep. So when my mother died, her husband wasn't in the same house: he was next-door, out like a light.

Anyway, while Dad underwent further hospital tests, in response to our request for more explicit information about his complaint, his female doctor approached my brother and me, and asked, 'Could I see you privately?'

We knew what was coming. We'd already been told he had a cancerous growth in the left lung, and it was I who had explained this to him weeks previously. He knew what he was being treated for — he'd been a heavy smoker in his younger years — but now his consultant had more news for us.

'Your father's tumour is in a very progressed state. I'm afraid the course of Radiotherapy and the chemotherapy injections haven't stunted its acceleration.'

Then she paused before adding, 'I'm very sorry, but all we can do now is help to control the pain.'

We, his two sons, were silent for a moment.

'My brother John and I have already discussed this,' I replied calmly, and with measured consideration, 'and we want to know, will you help our father to die peacefully?'

John nodded solemnly in agreement, saying, 'We know him so well. He's not the kind of man who'd want to suffer.'

The doctor's eyes gently scanned the floor and then looked into my relaxed face, and she said, 'No, I'm sorry. You see, that is something we don't do. We don't practise euthanasia – it's not our policy.'

'But we're requesting it,' I added quietly, 'and I know my father would, too. Why don't you ask him, doctor?'

I noticed that she particularly registered this last pointed remark of mine.

'While I fully understand your feelings,' she continued, 'I'm afraid there's no way we could agree to euthanasia.'

There was another silence while I gathered my thoughts, and presumably everyone else did too. 'Doctor,' I said, 'both my brother and I, and our family, are extremely grateful to you for looking after Dad and for promising him such wonderful care, as he's nursed towards the end of his days on Earth.'

At this point my brother's eyes filled up and he covered them with his hand. His head lowered a little and the doctor looked at him compassionately, then she turned to me and said, 'You've obviously come to terms with losing him?'

'Yes. I believe in a life after death, so the quicker my father passes, with as little pain as possible, the happier I'll be — especially because I know he'll be reunited with my mother,' I replied.

'So for you this is just a pause in the journey, and not the end of it?'

'That's right.'

'And what about you, John?' she said, turning to my brother, whose eyes were still full.

'I don't think like my brother,' he said quietly.

'So how do you feel about your father's passing?' counselled the gentle consultant.

'Well, it's inevitable, and I can face that, but I'd like to be able to talk with him, you know.'

'What about?'

'Well,' he answered softly, 'I'd like to tell him that I love him, I suppose.'

'Then why don't you do just that?'

There was a respectful lull in the conversation.

'Who's going to tell my father?' I asked. 'He has a right to know his true condition. I think it's wicked that people are allowed to die without even knowing the crossing is near.'

'Well, if you like,' she said, 'I'll come up to the ward with you today and the four of us will all have a chat together, and that'll give you the opportunity to speak to your father about the things you want to discuss before his last days.'

'That's a good idea,' I concurred, and we agreed to meet the doctor in Dad's little side-room in fifteen minutes' time...

John and I revived ourselves with hot drinks from the hospital canteen, and in silence we drank them. I was waiting for him to start speaking, as I sensed he wanted to; and when he did I felt we were then much closer than the days when, as small boys, we used to whisper secrets together in the old tiny bedroom we shared way back in the 1950s.

'He won't talk to me,' he said sadly.

'What do you mean, John?'

'Well he just sits there and stares into space whenever I visit him. He won't speak, and I've tried to make conversation, but I just can't break through.'

'What would you like him to say?'

'Well, I don't know... I suppose I want him to tell me that he loves me...'

I gauged this was not the right time for my personal thoughts on this controversial issue, so I withheld my opinions and instead said, 'Listen, the doctor's told us we shouldn't expect Dad to change just because he'll know he's dying. She's watched thousands of people die, and they don't just suddenly drop the habits of a lifetime: they usually die with exactly the same character as they had when they lived.'

Inwardly, I wanted to tell John, who had then just turned forty, what I truly felt about whether Dad really did love us boys; but I let the moment pass.

We finished our drinks and walked silently up to the ward.

Dad was propped up in his bed, coughing, and as we came through the doors he was violently sick. A nurse and I stood on either side of him and John stood by his neck, and I held kidney-shaped, papier-mâché bowls underneath his chin while he filled them four times over with a green-and-brown viscous fluid, the like of which I'd never smelt in my life – it was horribly pungent and acrid.

When the human body is healthy it's a wonderful work of art, but when it's ill, it's such a painful burden.

I glanced across at my brother, as good as to say I didn't think an animal, let alone a person, should have to suffer these indignities, as our father was obviously doing.

But he never made a sound did Dad, not a moan or a grumble. He just persevered with having his mouth wiped several times, then afterwards when everything had settled down he said, just like a child would, 'I don't know where it's all coming from; I haven't been eating.'

'It's probably a reaction to the chemotherapy,' I counselled, honestly. And we both sat down as I added, 'We'd like to have a bit of a chat with you today, Dad, and the doctor's coming along in a minute.'

And in that moment, I think he realised his true condition.

Then the sympathetic consultant arrived and after some very gentle conversation she sat on the bed and took Dad's hand.

'Now, Ronnie, how do you feel? Tell me.'

'Oh, you know — good days and bad days,' he said, rather hesitantly.

'Yes. But how do you really feel?' she asked again, softly.

'To tell you the truth — awful.'

'Well, you know we've given you some special nursing, and I did tell you last week that you've now had the maximum amount of treatments. Do you remember?'

'Yes,' he said — and there was, for him, an awkward pause.

'Do you remember, Ronnie... when you were first admitted you said to me, "There's no point in going on living like this." '

Dad nodded slowly, and there was another pause.

'And do you still feel like that?' she asked.

'Yes, I do,' he replied without hesitation and with deep conviction. Then Dad looked her in the eyes and said, 'You've come to tell me I'm gonna die.'

There was a long silence.

I noticed everyone's eyes glancing downwards, except my own, which fully registered Dad's moment of realisation.

Then the doctor smoothed the aged yellow hand that couldn't now sign its owner's signature legibly in his pension book. John and I looked at him and it was just one of those moments when words were inadequate, and a raft of momentous feelings were conveyed in stillness.

But the wonderful doctor gazed at Dad with such tender compassion, squeezed his hand again and said, so quietly, 'And how do you feel about that, Ron?'

And Dad said something that surprised her, but not us because we'd heard it so many times over the years. He said, 'Everybody wants to get to heaven, but nobody wants to die.'

And the four of us smiled.

And that was it.

The moment passed, and there were no violent hysterics from anyone; my father was remarkably brave about the whole thing.

The doctor added, 'Well, Ronnie, you know I have very strong links with the hospice just along the road, and there's a private room there for you. If you'd like to come, we'd be so pleased to have you with us.'

'Oh no,' he said quickly, 'I don't want to go there.'

'But it's a lovely place, Dad,' interjected John, 'Stephen and I have been there — it's a beautiful place and the staff are marvellous.'

'No,' he said, very uneasily, 'I don't want to go there.' And he really meant it. 'Everyone's got to die,' he continued, 'We've all got to go sometime... I'll just have to face it.'

My brother comforted him with, 'Everything that can be done, will be done for you, and you'll get the best treatment possible,'

'Aye... ' Dad said, 'Aye, I know that, boy...'

So the kind consultant promised him that he could stay a few more days in his little side-room, and that she'd ask him again about a move later on; but we all knew that now he understood his true condition, he'd simply give up the fight and slowly slip away from us — which was to prove correct...

On the way to our separate cars, walking down the steep hospital steps and out into the bitingly cold and frosty January air, I took what I thought was the right moment to broach with my brother the subject of our father's love.

'You know, John — don't be shocked — but it may very well be that Dad doesn't love us,' I ventured.

'What are you talking about? Why do you say a thing like that?'

'I suppose it all depends on what love means to

each of us. But, to me, he's always seemed such an insular, self-centred man. He had a house, he had a wife, he had friends, he had his club, he had his drink, he had his possessions, he had his money and he had his two sons. I'm not at all sure we weren't just another part of his life, rather than a part of an intimate relationship within it, as two sons who were loved.'

'You're talking rubbish, Stephen.'

'But that's how I feel, you know,' I said honestly.

My brother fell silent for a while, then broke the pause with, 'So what happens now? How do you think we should treat him?'

'Like the nurses do: to us he's a man with a history — we've shared time and memories with him — but to the staff he's a seventy-one-year-old sick man who's going to die and who needs as much tender loving care as we can give him, no matter what the past has been like.'

John listened quietly, as I went on, 'Even though Dad and I have never really got on together, we've made our peace, you know. These will be his last days on Earth and, come what may, we've got to be kind to him.'

Then we parted company, both deep in thought...

Immediately after this, the doctors attached a battery-powered injection pack to Dad's chest, filled with a painkiller and medication to ease his sickness. In the quiet early hours of the morning, between midnight and 2 a.m., when I'd often sit with him while he slept, the technology would gently whirr as quite frequent doses of medication were automatically delivered.

Sitting quietly next to the sleeping man, I sent

out my prayers to the Great Spirit, then drew upon the Great Healing Light and passed these energies on to my father as he lay still in the bed. This I did on many nights, praying that it might help him to have a dignified passing. And at such tranquil, early morning moments I was very aware of my mother's spirit presence close by.

'Look after him, Mam,' I said, 'for he'll soon be with you.'

There was no reply, but my soul sensed her acknowledgement: the only sound disturbing the quietness of the night ward was the intermittent ticking and whirring of his injection pack as more medication passed into his body.

On several visits during the next few days, John and I would sit at the bedside while our father, now only semi-conscious, struggled for air.

'He won't be long,' I said.

'No: he could go on for weeks.'

'I don't think so, John. He'll be just a few days more,' I said.

Then one morning at about 1 a.m., while I sat alone at my father's bedside on one of my healing-visits, he suddenly half awoke.

'Hello, Dad. It's me, Stephen. How are you feeling today?'

He groaned something inaudibly.

'You know, I'm glad we made our peace over the last few years, and especially in these last few weeks, Dad. There's no point in bearing any grudges, is there?'

He shook his head very slowly.

'Since you've been in hospital we've had lots of conversations about the soul, Dad, and about the afterlife; and the fact that we don't go into nothingness when we die; remember?'

He nodded again, tired, and then smacked his dry lips together.

'Well, I spoke to help you with the crossing you've got to make. I hope you knew that,' I whispered, as another injection was automatically delivered into his body. There was silence between us, and my father now closed his eyes while his chest heaved for air, spasmodically, every six to eight seconds — interspersed with six or eight seconds of silence and no movement.

'If you like, Dad... I can explain what'll happen to you when you pass through death and move over to the Other Side.' My voice was calm. 'Would you like me to do that?'

And immediately my father's head laid further back to rest on the pillow and he nodded once or twice. 'OK,' I said, 'I'll tell you all about it,' — and I did. I explained how death itself was painless, and how his spirit would be released from the temple of his body, and how he'd then be free — and still conscious in the vehicle of his spirit body. But most of all I stressed that after his passing he'd be standing beside my mother, whom I'd often sensed at his bedside, and who was waiting for him nearby. This news, especially, seemed to bring him a great deal of comfort as he drifted into sleep again; and I went home more at peace with myself.

The following night, which — as it turned out — was to be my father's last on Earth, John and I concluded our lengthy visit at about nine o'clock in the evening.

By then, Dad had fallen much deeper into

unconsciousness and John had expressed a fore-boding that we should stay because he felt the end was near.

However, we didn't. But at the end of the visit I stood up, smoothed my father's brow, leaned over the bed and kissed his forehead, saying: 'Good night, God bless, Dad,' exactly as I'd done to my mother nearly twenty years previously when she was dying from the same horrendous disease. Then strangely I added, 'Say hello to Mam for us.'

John and I walked silently to the doors, stopped, looked back over our shoulders at the old man lying in the bed, and we both knew that his hour was near.

In the corridor, we two brothers started up a much freer conversation, beginning with my saying, 'Just now, in the room, I had a spirit vision of Dad.' My brother seemed intrigued, so I went on, 'There was a field of bright flowers where the hospital wall should have been, and on a small pathway I watched a young couple walking away from me; I could only see their backs. The woman had dark springy hair and was wearing a 1950s flowery-print dress, and he was a stocky man in a sailor's uniform from the Second World War — complete with a hat.

'Then they stopped, and the young man turned and looked back, right at me, and it was Dad – but he was in his late twenties and walking hand-in-hand with Mam, as a young woman. They were together,' I said, 'so he's slowly withdrawing his consciousness, and what we've just seen of our father back there in the bed is only the last throes of the body's nervous system fighting to hold on to life in this world.'

John had listened silently as we walked, but now we stopped and he asked me, 'How long will he be, Stephen? Have you heard anything?'

'Do you mean from the Other Side?' I asked, inwardly quite surprised by my brother's keen interest in my mediumship.

'Well?'

'Yes,' I answered truthfully. 'As a matter of fact, a spirit voice clearly told me, just as we were leaving, "He'll remain unconscious now for several hours." They didn't make it clear whether he'll ever regain awareness in this world; but I feel he won't. We shall see...'

Well, my father's eyes did remain closed and he slipped deeper and deeper into his comatose sleep induced by illness, disease, age, and the effects of the pain-killing drugs, and he never spoke to us again on Earth.

Just over four hours later, that very same night, I was visiting a friend when, at around 1 a.m., I suddenly dropped everything and declared hurriedly, 'I've got to go!' I felt impelled to get to the hospital and I belted out of the house and shot into the car and drove like the wind. As I dashed through the ward doors I saw Dad's side-room curtains had been drawn and a nurse came rushing to meet me.

'He's gone,' I said.

'I'm sorry,' she replied. 'It was very peaceful. We've been trying to reach you at home but there was no answer.'

'I felt compelled to come,' I said, 'I knew he'd gone.'

A sad John came out to greet me, and I asked the

nurse, 'Could we sit with Dad, please?'

'Of course, please go in and stay as long as you like.'

My brother had already been with him for an hour and had recited from the bedside Bible 'The Lord is my Shepherd', as words of comfort.

We entered in silence and closed the door.

The room was all spick and span. In the peaceful light I could see that all of Dad's personal effects had been removed. A small bowl of fresh flowers and a Bible had been placed on his bedside table — and nothing personal belonging to him was anywhere in sight. And there he lay, motionless in death; but, thankfully, at peace.

As soon as I saw the body, I walked over to him, smoothed back the silvery hair on his forehead and said kindly, 'Now you know the truth, old man. God bless you.'

My brother and I then took seats at either side of him and sat and reminisced for an hour about the life we'd all shared.

'It's the end of an era tonight, Stephen. Both our parents have gone now.'

And together we gathered our many thoughts and memories in moments of passing stillness.

'Poor old man,' I said finally. 'I always felt so sorry for him, you know... He always seemed to me to be a sad and lonely person.'

My brother sighed, looking at the body of our father. 'I did love him, you know,' John said.

'I know you did,' I added. 'And in a strange way, in my own way... I suppose I did too...'

It was a bitterly cold and crisp January day when

my father's body was cremated at Swansea's Morriston Crematorium.

Everyone was well wrapped up against the sharp wind as they gathered to pay their last respects. And, just as in the case of my mother nearly twenty years before, I'd offered to take the service but the family had again declined, feeling that my place should be seated beside them in the front pews.

I agreed, but, as a personal tribute to my father, halfway through the service I walked to the front of the altar, near the coffin, to read a poem for Dad; and, as I turned round, I was more than surprised to see the crematorium was three-quarters full. All my father's workmates and friends from his club had turned up in a minibus.

I gently spoke to the gathering.

'I'm sure my father would wish me to thank you for your presence here today,' I said.

'My Dad believed in the Kingdom of the Soul; we spoke about it many times in the hospital, and now I want to give you my one hundred per cent assurance that I know beyond a shadow of a doubt that he and my mother have been reunited in the world beyond this one.

'My father told me he'd thought of my mother, his wife, every single day, and that he'd spent a very long and lonely seventeen years without her since her death. But now they're together again.'

Solemn heads nodded in agreement.

'And in tribute to my father's life, I'd like to read a poem,' I said; and this I did.

Afterwards, in complete silence, I resumed my seat next to Dad's only surviving brother, Billy, who'd lived with us many years ago when John and

I were children. Uncle Billy, moved by the verses, patted my knee in gratitude.

No words needed to be said.

The service concluded, and we all went home...

A few days later I unhappily learned that when I'd announced my personal tribute, some people in the congregation had tut-tutted.

I was disillusioned and, for me, this highlighted once again just how hard-hearted the majority of people can be.

Glad that my father was now out of pain and discomfort, I wondered for how long he'd remain silent after death. But before two days had passed, I received an accurate spirit message from a young medium who conveyed a clear description of him, and then delivered three pieces of evidence which unquestionably proved his survival to me.

The meaningfulness of my father's message was concealed from the medium; but from the world Beyond, Dad felt able to transmit the three things he could never have brought himself to say while he was here on Earth, even though I sensed he might have wanted to speak them on many occasions. These were:

'Tell Stephen: thank you. Tell Stephen: he was right. Tell Stephen: I love him.'

The first was his gratitude for my fully explaining to him his journey through death. The second was something he couldn't ever confess to on Earth, even though he knew I was often right about many things. And the third was the greatest of all, for it was something I'd never heard my father say to any living being.

These three statements addressed the three areas

I'd often considered to be Dad's weakest character points, and this was highly evidential in itself.

And now, I'm extremely happy to report that since his passing Dad has also communicated his love for his eldest and closest son, my only brother John.

In fact, since his transition he's returned several times to give interesting and accurate spirit messages, saying that even though my mother has progressed much further into the world of spirit than himself, they're often together and that, 'I'm not the same man you remember, boy. I've changed my viewpoints a lot and I'm learning all the time, quite fast.'

The light of progression bestows its blessing upon us all, thank God; and I've often sent Dad good thoughts and wished him well in his new life on the Other Side.

And now, whenever I think of my father, of all the memories that could spring to mind, the most poignant is the one concerning the incredible courage with which he bore his illness.

Nearly two decades previously, when my mother lay dying of the same disease — cancer — my father had said of himself, 'Perhaps I'll be a chocolate soldier, boy.'

Well, Dad, in your own time of dire crisis, when you stood uncertainly before your mortality and feared its possible extinction, you faced it squarely, without one grumble of complaint.

You were a remarkably brave man.

You were courageous, and strong, Dad — and you were most certainly not a chocolate soldier.

10

Chuckle-Muscles

These days, whenever I remember my father, many odd memories float into mind, especially those of my teenage years when I was such a home-loving and quiet child — a characteristic that seemed to bother him no end, and which made him issue loud commands like, 'Now, get out *there*! *That's* where life is — outside that window, not in here, boy! Get out there and *live* it. *Shake yourself*!'

So one day, when I was about fourteen, I did just that: I went out and joined the local YMCA theatre group where I spent some wonderful adolescent years, which I still fondly treasure as happy memories. Not only did I 'star' in many of their Christmas pantomimes but I also wrote some of them, and frequently took roles in my own plays, too — many of which were well received.

Our pantomimes were very frivolous and most amusing, and one of the funniest laughs an audience got was caused by the front curtain being sabotaged by a jealous cast member. The heavy drapes rose up by means of a manually operated pulley-system — they were yanked up by pulling on a piece of knotted rope! (None of your modern technology in Swansea's YMCA in the early 1970s.) But our crafty saboteur had nailed one end of the drapes to the foot of the proscenium arch, and when the overture struck up and the curtain was also supposed to go up to reveal a tap-dance routine — only one end of the drapes rose off the stage! The opposite side didn't budge an inch, and the audience was treated to the unforgettable sight of twelve pairs of shapely chorus girls' legs, tap-dancing away for all they were worth, but the troupe was bodiless and faceless! There were hoots of laughter from everybody in the hall until some bright spark unhooked the curtain and the show got under way properly.

Incidentally, one set of those legs belonged to the beautiful Welsh actress, Catherine Zeta Jones. She and I trod the boards together on a number of occasions, but she was just a wee slip of a girl in those days.

After many such jolly times, readers may remember I then attended college, from eighteen to twenty years of age, during which time my mother died, and after this I discovered the Spiritualist Church where she returned to me from beyond death and proved her survival in a remarkable way, as recorded in my first book, *Visions of Another World*.

The psychic impact of my mother's spirit return quickened my powers of mediumship and finally made sense of the many disembodied voices I'd often heard, and the silent guidance and spirit presences and clairvoyant impressions I'd intermittently received throughout my young life.

Suddenly everything fell into place and I perceived the visible threads of a spiritual pattern having woven itself through my days.

Tightly embracing my mediumship with characteristic vigour, I then whizzed off all around South Wales taking public meetings, not only in churches but also in small halls as my work got better known. I soon became 'a special ticketed event'.

I was then instantly and, I thought, rather miraculously accepted by an often staid, older Spiritualist generation: certain people who at first had so bitterly criticised my youth and inexperience, suddenly couldn't do enough to impress me.

A modicum of success meant that previously officious personalities now wanted to hitch their wagon to my guidestar, so to speak — which at first confused me, and then amused me.

But then, I love to laugh – it's a great gift!

And thankfully, the Spiritualists, God bless them, also have the remarkable gift of being able to hoot with merriment at themselves (as well as at everyone else) which is just as well, considering some of the antics and performances that went on in some of their regional churches.

Although hundreds of dedicated and sincerely talented mediums present their services with dignity and intelligence, it must also be admitted that there are plenty of eccentrics in their midst. Some of these are a constant source of laughter, and they often say the most amusing things in public without even knowing it. One such Welsh sensitive is Gladys.

To say that she's the middle-aged Spiritualists' equivalent of Mrs Malaprop (the literary character who always chose the wrong words to mean the wrong things) would be a gross understatement.

Glad frequently got herself into a verbal twist, and one night, during one of her public meetings, she made a most unfortunate remark to a very plain woman indeed. After selecting the lady for a message, Glad had *meant* to say, 'Do you recognise a horse in the next world?' But instead, what she actually asked the poor soul was, 'Do you *resemble* a horse in the next world?'

After an awkward moment's pause, the woman said rather timidly, 'Yes, I do.'

Everyone had an instant fit of muffled giggles; all except Glad, of course, who didn't have a clue what was going on.

Other witty mistakes made by mediums also tickle me when I recall them, and one of these occurred when a rather bumptious London medium pointed to a big woman in her audience and asked, quite imperiously, 'Madam, do you know a person named Constance on the Other Side?'

'Yes,' said the enthusiastic recipient.

'And can you tell me: was she a cook?'

'Why yes, she was,' replied the woman.

'Ah! I *thought* so!' said the triumphant medium with a flourish of her hand, 'because as she made her contact with me I felt a very strong apple-dumpling vibration.'

I still chortle over that silly phrase whenever I think of it.

And then there was the northern medium who copied Mrs Malaprop (and Gladys) when he got his descriptions mixed up. What he'd actually seen from the spirit world was a small, frumpy woman wearing a pillbox hat, but when conveying this to his recipient he made an amusing mistake by asking, 'Do you know this woman who always wore a *pillarbox* hat?'

The ridiculous thought of that frumpy spirit lady tromping around the astral worlds, proudly patting the tufts of hair sticking out from underneath a big red pillarbox stuck on top of her head, keeps me cheerful twenty-four hours a day. Indeed, it's such merriment as this that makes life tolerable and well worth the living!

Speaking of frumps, by the way, reminds me of another occasion when such a person came to a sticky end. It happened when a friend of mine drove me to one of my early small ticketed events at a church right up in the Welsh valleys. The snow was thick on the ground and we didn't think we were going to reach the meeting-place because the road was frozen with ice, and his car kept slipping and sliding all the way.

Then, about a hundred yards from the small church, it suddenly conked out. 'Oh, bloody hell!' he exclaimed. 'Trust the bloody contraption to clap out here. I hope the bloody thing'll start and we'll bloody well be able to get going again afterwards!' (He was very fond of his 'bloody', and still is.)

'Calm down,' I said, 'a spirit man's voice has just told me there's a wire loose in the front of the engine.'

'Don't be so bloody soft,' he returned, 'it's only just been bloody serviced!'

My driver moaned his way out of the car, lifted the bonnet, and the next thing I saw was his astounded face, eyes wide open and peering at me over his large spectacles, and in his hand he was waving the loose wire.

'Well, I'll go to bloody hell, O'Brien!' he shouted. 'You and your bloody voices!'

It was just then that the 'star' of this memory, a now-deceased but extremely frumpy and officious Spiritualist church secretary, suddenly bustled into view outside the nearby church door. The nosey old dear tottered forward on bandy legs, which were swathed in thick black support stockings, and came fussing through the porch into the freezing drizzle. Precariously balanced over her head she clutched a battered copy of an old *Psychic News*, which looked like a soggy pyramid, and it barely covered her permed hair, which itself resembled a tight, shiny golf ball of blue-rinsed curls.

For someone well known for being so bumptious and 'important' she didn't half look a comical sight as she slid dangerously across the icy road towards the car with her newspaper quivering in the sleet. When she reached the windows she glowered at the drenched driver then peered at me through the glass — much as people stare at monkeys in the zoo. (The poor soul was no raving beauty, either: as a matter of fact I'd often heard her quite unkindly described as having the features of a pit-bull terrier.)

Anyway, when she saw me she gasped, dropped her jaw to her chest, straightened her back, shot over to the church and screamed at the top of her voice as she reached its portals, 'Doris! It's *him*! He's come! The medium's *arrived*!' — immediately after which she tripped over the front step, fell flat on her face onto the polished floor, spread-eagled with spectacles all awry, and then performed the singularly remarkable feat of hurtling forwards like an aeroplane, right down through the outer hall — whereupon she amazed the congregation by gate-crashing through the inner doors!

The poor soul.

Oh, I know I shouldn't have laughed, but what with the car breaking down and all those 'bloodys', and then this bumptious woman's fall from grace, I was at bursting-point. (But then I'll laugh at anything, as everyone knows. I even guffawed when the taxes went up.)

It's no great secret to mediums, of course, that members of the public can often *lack* a good sense of humour, and they can also seem quite dense and lifeless when viewed from the platform, particularly when they're confused.

I had to smile when a rather famous medium visited Wales and couldn't get such an audience member to claim her message.

The bemused recipient was wondering why this frowning but silent medium kept repeatedly stabbing the air in her direction, with a maliciously pointed digit; so she kept looking backwards over her shoulder, scratching her head, and thinking that the irate medium obviously wanted someone else to respond in the row seated behind her.

At the end of her tether, the famed sensitive loudly declared, 'No. *You*! Yes, *you* there, turning round! You with the silly blue thing on — *the hat*! *You* with the vacant look on your face!'

(Oh dear.)

But smiles broke out all around the room, and my

overworked chuckle-muscle (my wobbling diaphragm) was certainly quivering away for a good half an hour after that.

Of course, when the messages themselves go wrong it can also be very funny. I remember once linking up a father with his elderly daughter who was sitting right in the front row of an audience.

She must have been in her late nineties, and, although she wasn't wearing any spectacles, I announced confidently, 'Your father tells me, my dear, that your eyesight is rather bad,' to which the dear soul loudly squawked back:

'*Pardon*?'

'Oh, it doesn't matter,' I said, 'I obviously got it quite wrong!' and everyone had a good laugh at my expense.

And now I can't resist quoting the rather funny story of a stonemason's silly blunder. It's said that a man who loved his wife dearly wanted to make her a special tribute after she'd died. Having been such a God-fearing woman, her husband asked the mason to provide a tombstone and inscribe on it the inspiring words: *She was Thine,* which they duly agreed to do. But the following week the man was horrified when he visited her grave because the mason had made a silly mistake on the stone and had left out an 'e'. The unfortunate inscription now said: *She was Thin.*

The furious husband went straight to the mason's and complained, but the manager had gone on holiday and only the young Yorkshire apprentice was on duty. Nevertheless the young apprentice agreed to visit the grave straightaway and to chisel the missing 'e' on to the stone. But the next day the husband was absolutely livid when he discovered the apprentice's further mistake. On the tombstone it now said: *E, She was Thin!*

Humour, of course, also has its pathos, its sadder side, which was once proved to me by one of the most farcical and ridiculous displays of so-called public mediumship I've ever witnessed.

It occurred at a transfiguration service: this is a special séance in which a rare form of physical mediumship takes place in a darkened room while the medium's face is lit only by a small ruby lamp. In these controlled circumstances, spirit people are able to get so close to the medium that they can withdraw an energy from him, called ectoplasm, with which they then try to reproduce their features over the bone structure of the medium's head. The features of spirit faces materialise as a kind of misty, semi-material skin, like a visible 'mask'.

I've been privileged to witness this genuine phenomenon. However, the public meeting I'm about to describe was no such thing.

It was more of a cheap vaudeville variety act, or perhaps it would have been better advertised as a *dis*figuration service, for that's exactly what it was. No one with any intelligence saw any supernormal changes on the face of the plump, deluded male 'medium'.

After suffering through his many gruntings and groanings and his pulling of comical grimaces, which alone could have earned him the title of 'Buster Bloodvessel', to go out with a bang, he then proudly proclaimed, 'My dear friends, there's been so much love in here tonight that I'm going to allow the spirit people to conduct a Cavalcade of Faces.'

'Oh, my God,' I thought, 'spare us that.'

But he didn't.

'Now, friends, as the faces come rolling through I want you to shout out their names and give them recognition. Welcome them into this wonderful séance tonight. And here we go!'

And suddenly — quick as a flash — nothing whatsoever happened to the medium's features.

But to my utter amazement, the gullible in the crowd started seeing things that weren't there at all – and in a trice I wondered where on Earth I was. A sensible woman next to me whispered, 'It's like the Nutters' Night Out.'

And she was quite right. People started shouting out things like, 'Oh look! It's Marilyn Monroe!' 'No, it's Winston Churchill *and* Queen Victoria!' — though how those two beauties managed to get onto the same face together, frankly escapes me. Then someone else yelled out:

'I can see Elvis Presley!'

'No, it's an Indian!' bellowed a woman from the back.

Then to top it all off nicely, the last person shouted, 'My word, it's Bing Crosby! My God, I can see Bing Crosby! That's *amazing*!'

Amazing indeed, for Bing Crosby was *still alive* at the time. Every *true* Spiritualist in that hall was thoroughly disgusted by this man's ridiculous performance, and he didn't receive a return booking.

There's a teaching in the Bible that says, 'By their fruits ye shall know them', and I couldn't agree more.

By the way, while we're on the subject of gurning, over the years a number of my public appearances have been photographed for posterity, and Voices Management had the films processed by a cheeky young chap who's developed hundreds of shots of me, but only a handful have proved worthy of public release. After handing back the last batch, he wittily suggested to my manager, 'You know, Jeff, you could save yourself a fortune on these photos. Why don't you pocket the money and send Stephen for some plastic surgery instead?'

Thankfully another friend tried to redress the balance when she declared, 'But Stephen looked *gorgeous* on the television last night. He must have been down in make-up for four hours.'

'Listen,' I said, smoothing my features, 'I'll have you know I have skin like a peach.'

'Yes, a thirty-year-old peach!'

Honestly, sometimes you just can't win.

I actually learnt the delicate art of 'papering-over-the-cracks make-up' at drama school in my late teens, and also during the long runs of those hilarious Christmas pantomimes I spoke of earlier.

Thoughts of these earlier days trigger off many other poignant Christmas memories, especially the times I spent at the Swansea Psychic Centre, a society I'd helped to found in 1983, and of which I was a vice-president for nearly three years.

Each Christmas, I felt the organisation ought to help some physically and mentally handicapped children. 'Let's get a big fir tree, decorate it on the public platform, and collect presents for under-privileged children,' I'd suggested, and this idea was enthusiastically accepted — and each year we did just that.

Every December the Social Services Department sent us a list of over fifty mentally or physically handicapped children, orphans, or others who were sadly lacking in parental love and care.

Members of the public 'adopted' each child, whose age and background were roughly stated, and then bought them presents which were wrapped up beautifully in coloured papers and foil and displayed under the fairy-light tree.

One snowy Christmas, after we'd had a soul-stirring carol concert, a merry Santa collected all the marvellous gifts: dolls, space games, a huge tricycle for some lucky boy, and my own name-sake's present — a woolly hat and scarf specially knitted and embroidered with a capital 'S' for the five-year-old handicapped youngster called Steven, plus an educational game and some colourful books to help him with his reading.

That night at the Psychic Centre, dozens upon dozens of people had turned up and gathered around a special altar where they'd placed lit candles, to symbolise the illumination of the world's darkness. Then each one had said a silent prayer for their special loved ones who were held in their thoughts at Christmastime.

It was an enchanting evening.

In flickering yellow candlelight and with a huge wave of love washing over the people, warm Welsh voices sang stirring and uplifting hymns of praise.

Later, when the last of the public had filed out after being wished 'A merry Christmas' and 'May peace be with you', Dorothy, one of the committee, said to me as we both gazed out through the big windows at the gently falling snow, 'Stephen, those children will be very happy. It was a grand idea.'

I smiled, nodded, and then lost myself in deep, contemplative thought, remembering the many happy Christmases I'd shared with my mother, when I was young.

'Mind you, Dorothy, I do feel sad,' I said, at length.

'Why?'

'Well... I wish I had the chance to tell those handicapped children that one day, when they inherit the world of the spirit, they'll exist in perfectly formed energy-bodies; bodies free of pain; bodies that are fit and healthy.

'Wouldn't it be wonderful to tell them: one day a balance will be struck?'

'Yes,' she said, 'it would.'

We both stared through the misted glass and watched the snow-crystals falling on the YMCA opposite, where many such children had attended those Christmas pantomimes I'd performed in as a lively teenager.

Then Dorothy broke our reverie by suggesting something which, several years later, turned out to be quite prophetic.

'You should record a cassette, Stephen,' she said. 'An educational tape, to help all kinds of people, not just the handicapped. It'd be an excellent way of sharing your knowledge, you know. And I'm sure there's a real need.'

For several moments I didn't speak; I remained silent, entranced by the swirling snowflakes outside, and watching the scurrying shoppers bustling to and fro, dashing across the busy twilight roads with their heads down against the cold breeze, and their shoes clicking on the hard frosty pavements, all hurrying home with their arms full of brightly wrapped gifts.

A car horn loudly split the atmosphere and, as the vehicle sped past, a tipsy passenger leaned out of its window and called out at the shoppers, 'A Merry Christmas! And goodwill to all men! *And to all the women*!'

Smiling, I gathered my thoughts, turned to Dorothy and very quietly, and rather thoughtfully said, 'Record a cassette? Perhaps, one day, I will...'

And we both gazed out at the falling snow again.

11

What Awaits Us Beyond Death

To meet an ever-increasing public demand for spiritual knowledge, I recorded a series of audio-cassettes, which gave many people a better understanding of many paranormal subjects, plus some interesting and helpful information on what awaits us all after we 'die'.

My first recording, *Life After Death*, was an instant success and it became a bestseller by mail order through Voices Management, the company that arranges all my tours. It was particularly appreciated by people who were partially sighted or who found reading difficult, and others who gave it to friends who were seeking helpful information or a sensible introduction to the paranormal. (My recordings are still available, and details can be found at the back of this book.)

What follows is an edited version of the text from which the *Life After Death* recording was made; many correspondents said they found it enlightening, healing in essence, and that it imparted to them many fascinating insights into life in the Beyond...

Stephen O'Brien's voice:

Before a child is born into this world, its coming is already known.

As a conscious mind you have always existed; there has never been a time when you were not in existence; so, your soul's journey through its many and varied experiences started long before it was born of woman into this world.

We are far greater than at first we might think.

We're not physical bodies with minds attached, but we are minds first and foremost, registering now through bodies of flesh.

You are consciousness itself, which has been individualised and characterised into your present personality.

The soul's journey towards perfection is a long and arduous one. No soul, no matter how great or insignificant the world supposes it to be, has an easy road to travel.

When we come into this life a great many of the challenges, trials and tribulations that we will encounter are already known to our Higher Selves; but through the process of birth there comes a cloaking-down effect, which naturally keeps from our conscious awareness who and what we truly are or were before this life.

We did not 'begin' with our first breath on Mother Earth: we go back much further than that.

Some say that the soul chooses its Earth family, environment and physical circumstances before its incarnation, because these factors will provide the necessary conditions for its spiritual progression. Many people find this concept difficult to accept, but it's certainly worthy of careful consideration.

If we're honest with ourselves, we will recognise that even though the pathway has often seemed difficult and rough, and we've frequently failed to see the lessons in soul-growth that were lying behind all the obstacles, we have emerged from our trials as much stronger people, having gained greater experience and more developed personalities.

And so we come to the point of our birth into the Earthworld.

When it happens, it's just the start of another phase of spiritual growth for us. Sometimes it seems that some individuals are born into highly favoured circumstances, while others inherit abject poverty and cutting hardships. But as passive observers of other people's lives, it's impossible for us to know the full extent of stress, challenge and difficulty encountered by any other soul on any pathway.

And so: birth conveys to the Earth a soul with a mission. No one is born without a spiritual blueprint, which will broadly direct that individual's life in all the facets of its being: in its physical, mental, emotional and spiritual life. This blueprint is constructed by us alone, and it is made up of all our experiences.

The inner self knows that life on Earth is a training-ground for souls: it is a place of learning, of growing; it is somewhere to expand the mind and to become increasingly aware of the developing consciousness.

Poets have often referred to Earthlife as a 'vale of tears', but there is also great joy here — and each life-plan decrees that its creator will taste a wide range of human experiences and lessons of comparison. People cannot appreciate the brilliance and warmth of a summer's day unless they've also known the night. And we cannot truly wonder at the glorious view of the world from a mountain peak, unless we've first dwelt for a time in the shadows of the valley.

Similarly, how can we treasure the gift of peace unless we've first known pain and disharmony?

At some time or other, into every life there comes the dark night of the soul, a time when it struggles to find stability, love and contentment, as well as the vibrant joy which consciousness should bring. These inner battles with ourselves are inevitable — no one escapes them: not the rich man, the poor man, the beggar man or the thief.

Whether we are kings or paupers, each of us is a soul on the road of progression, and in order that we may grow, hardships will be met.

Major soul-growth comes from the interaction of our thoughts and feelings within personal relationships, and within our environment. But there is no force in our lives, no matter how great, which we cannot overcome.

As a wise man once said, 'We are never given a cross to bear, without the strength to bear it.'

Through it all, your human spirit can triumph supreme because your mind is the master, and your body is the servant.

Each soul governs its own journey and moves it forward by positive wilful thought.

Therefore, you should welcome your challenges as friends and not as enemies, for without them there would be no spiritual evolution for you.

Meanwhile, as you struggle on, by simply changing your thought-patterns you can gain a different outlook, which would make living your life much easier.

If a man holds dark, negative thoughts and pessimistic attitudes, then his soul looks out into its world through deeply stained glass, and through its own mind it sees nothing but despair and gloom.

But thankfully, the reverse is also true.

Bright and cheerful positivity always draws to itself a much happier quality of life, and the darkened glass is then cleared.

If we visualise the soul as a shaded lamp, brightly lit from within by a spark of the Great Spirit's Lifeforce, it becomes clear to us that from within the lampshade we are personally colouring our vision and understanding of the Earthworld.

We are continually creating our own heaven or hell, for they are states of mind and are not geographical locations. And we can blame no one for these visions but ourselves. Many souls cause themselves untold misery through holding selfish thoughts: these are the people who always want their own way and create havoc when they don't get it; these are the people who are unaware of others' needs, feelings and desires. The undeveloped soul has thoughts only for itself.

Let's look for a moment at one of the universal laws by which we are all governed: *Like Attracts Like*. 'Birds of a feather, flock together'.

Our general thoughts and feelings are constantly drawing around us, from both sides of life, people of like mind, and it is we ourselves who create a great deal of our personal harmony, or self-harm.

In passing, I'd like to mention that if at present you feel unloved and uncared for, then go out into the world and love and care for others.

And if you feel lonely or uncomforted, then be a true friend to others and comfort *them.*

I think this is what St Francis of Assisi meant in his prayer when he said, 'It is in the giving that we receive' – and he was also right when he said, 'It is in the dying that we are born to eternal life.'

And now we move on to that time which awaits us all — the moment of death, which is a part of the soul's journey that often strikes fear into the hearts of those who don't know what to expect.

When your physical body takes its last breath and gives up your spirit, life is not ended for you, the traveller. My conscious links with the Beyond have consistently proved over the years that death from this world means birth into the next.

And absolutely everyone survives death, no matter how the passing is made.

Whether the passing is made through tragic circumstances, or through natural means, survival is one of the laws that govern this universe, and survival is the birthright of all. And we don't have to hold any particular religious faith in order to enter the next world. In fact, we don't have to hold any faith at all to inherit eternal life: it will happen quite naturally.

Having communicated with the spirit people for decades, I've also come to believe that no one can cross into eternity *before* his time. No matter how near a person may be to death, the time has to be right or the crossing isn't made. For example, I have a dear friend who was once seriously ill; in fact, she was placed in a hospital side-room to die, after having had an exceptionally large cancerous growth removed from her abdomen.

In great sadness all her family gathered around her deathbed, waiting for the end, because the medical profession held no hope of recovery for her.

But while she was in her coma, she underwent a remarkable out-of-the-body experience.

Unknown to anyone on Earth, she floated out of her tired body and found herself on a marble pathway walking towards an archway, under which she met her mother and father, who had both passed over decades ago. Suddenly her mother stopped her and said, 'You've got to go back — you haven't finished your contract yet' — and she immediately awoke in the hospital bed. She was back in her physical body, and slowly regaining her health — much to the amazement of her specialists, all of whom had been completely wrong in their medical prognosis.

After this event, she lived for over eighteen years; so you see, her time to die had not arrived.

This true story also highlights for us that her spirit family knew more of her true condition than her doctors did.

It's because we're part of the Great Cosmic Mind, that vast Breath of Consciousness known as God, or the Great Spirit, that we survive.

God is an Eternal Spirit, and so are you.

The Universal Mind which placed the stars in the heavens, and which makes the seasons follow one another in unbroken constancy, is Immortal; and we are for ever linked to this unlimited power source, which is everywhere.

The Great Spirit is the macrocosm and we are the microcosm.

Let's take a look now at what actually happens when we 'die'.

Sudden or 'accidental' deaths sometimes knock the spirit body unconscious, but this type of concussion is short-lived, and consciousness is soon regained in the world of spirit.

When someone's been suffering from a very long illness, relatives and friends from the spirit world are aware of the imminent passing. Then, as the traveller crosses the threshold of death to life, he or she is met. Sometimes, ill people see those who've come to greet them, and they call out their names: the reason their spirit relatives are present is because they've picked up our thoughts — not only the thoughts from the sick person, but also those from the anxious relatives.

When a thought is born, it radiates outwards. Just as a pebble creates a rippling effect when it's dropped into a pool of still water, our thoughts travel outwards in a similar fashion, and our loved ones in the next world home-in on these energy wavelengths.

If an ailing person's been placed on a life-support system, it's possible that his spirit may have already passed into the next world. If it has, then, technically, the machinery alone is keeping his body alive. But, of course, this is not so in all cases, for some patients make a recovery and are able to breathe for themselves again.

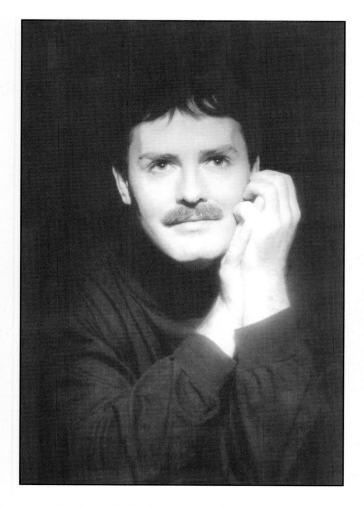

'Soul sensitivity has opened for me doors to
luminous inner worlds,
which if ever they were to close again
would leave me bereft of any real meaning
in my life.'

Stephen O'Brien delivers a spirit message to
a recipient in the theatre circle.

Inset: Stephen's North American Spirit Guide,
who is known as White Owl.

During his British tours Stephen brings messages of love and hope from the Next World to countless people.

'The public have given me something more precious than their encouragement: they have given me their love.'

Psychic Art and Mediumship

Two famous mediums work in unison before a London audience of over 2,000 people.

Renowned psychic artist, Coral Polge, draws the spirit communicator while Stephen provides the survival evidence.

Queues waiting for an autograph, a handshake and a chat
with Stephen after one of his public meetings.

Two days after his death, Stephen's father, Ronnie,
returned to his son with impressive survival evidence.

British TV
Broadcaster,
Gloria Hunniford

Singer,
Michael Ball

Broadcaster and quiz-mistress of
The Weakest Link, Anne Robinson

Healing by sunlight:
a rare moment of relaxation for Stephen.

'A man has time to think in the country;
its sights and sounds refresh his spirit.'

'Thank you'

Loved ones who are in comas, and who may occasionally regain consciousness, are similarly passing in and out of their physical frames.

At this point I'd like to say a few words about people who have taken their own lives:

Suicide solves no problems, because we cannot die.

Suicide victims find themselves still existing, but in another world. So I must stress that I am most certainly not advising anyone to take his own life; for life is about growth which comes from facing our challenges and working through them, and not from running away from them. Conquering our challenges provides us with essential opportunities for soul development and character-building.

If we can't cope with our lives here in this world, then we shall not be able to cope with them in the next life, for we'll take this 'inability to cope' with us into eternity.

So, suicide doesn't solve any problems.

I'd like to say, however, that suicide victims are not in an outer darkness or in some place of punishment, as so often taught by some. They are alive, but they will still have to resolve their mental attitudes and their problems in the next world.

Death itself is painless — in fact, we all die every night when we go to sleep. As soon as the physical body relaxes, the spirit body loosens and departs, and travels out into the next world.

But on some evenings we might not visit the Other Side, but remain close to the Earthly body in a state of semi-sleep. Our spirit counterparts then absorb cosmic energies from all around themselves and then channel them to our sleeping forms; and we awake refreshed the next day.

At the point of death, the spirit body, which is more or less a replica of the physical but without any of its deformities, slowly exteriorises and moves away from the Earthly body.

At these times, some clairvoyantly gifted people have seen the two bodies separating and have noted that the spirit form is linked to the physical by a powerful magnetic connection, which has often been seen as a fine silver thread of light.

When the physical body ceases to function, the consciousness then expresses itself through the vehicle of the spirit body. The link between the two forms breaks, or dematerialises, and the spirit is then free.

Death can best be described as the releasing of a trapped bird from its cage: the bird is your soul, which will fly out into freedom and into a world of light where it can express itself more fully.

In your new energy-body you will have perfect health, and you'll experience a vibrant feeling of youthful strength.

And there are many places (or spheres) in which you may exist Over There, but it is those worlds of spirit nearest the Earth — called by some the astral worlds — which contain the counterparts of everything that we know here in our daily lives; this is because those spheres have been created by the thoughts of their inhabitants. The people who have passed over have built the kind of world they're accustomed to seeing and experiencing.

'Thought is King.'

'Thought rules Supreme.'

In the kingdom of eternity, there are cities and

towns, rolling countryside, magnificent flowers and birds, sunshine, water and trees: it's a very real world to those who inhabit it.

The spirit world functions or vibrates at a much higher frequency than the world of physical matter does, which is why it often remains unregistered by many people on the Earth. Yet, in its own world, the spirit body has dimension, shape and form, and it is as real to its possessor as our physical bodies are to us.

On arrival in the next life the soul will eventually take stock of its completed mission on the Earth, and it will ask itself questions like, 'Did I achieve what I intended to do?' Or, 'Is the Earth a better place for my presence having been there?'

We will review our lifetime's experiences and, of course, we will be reunited with our loved ones.

The following words were the conclusion to my book *Visions of Another World:*

And
when we stand
on the shores of eternity
and look back
upon our experiences
in Earthlife,
we will notice
how all the things we did,
happened
in just the right places,
at just the right times;
and
we shall say to ourselves:
it is good.

195

After a period of settling down, nearly all spirit people make the journey back to Earth to visit the loved ones they've left behind. Many of them even attend their own funeral services. I've officiated at several of these and have often seen the spirit forms of loved ones listening to their own funeral tributes, or standing close by their relatives with their arms around them, comforting them as best they can.

I've also seen the spirit bodies of people *before* their physical bodies were buried.

One difficult old lady visited me the night before her committal, and with her walking-stick she poked me in the ribs and ordered me to, 'Get it right, and do it properly!'

We certainly don't change when we die — at least, not immediately.

People who think the act of death bestows upon us untold wisdom couldn't be more wrong. We won't suddenly become the possessors of all the secrets of the universe when we 'die'. Nothing could be further from the truth.

We take with us only what we are: our minds and our characters, and everything we've developed during our growth here on the Earth.

If we couldn't see the future when we were here — then we won't have that ability Over There, because death doesn't confer upon us any skills we haven't already mastered or earned.

So: looking to the spirit people to solve our problems is of little value.

Our difficulties are our own and therefore we must solve them; besides which, the spirit people most certainly don't have all the answers: they are progressing, just as we are.

Regarding their work in the Beyond: the spirit people are very busy indeed. If they choose to do so, they can follow the arts or sciences, or pursue further education, or perhaps learn about spiritual healing. In fact, they can study or practise anything their hearts desire.

There's no need for them to work for money, though, for in the spirit world it's largely unknown. Over There, work is undertaken because to serve others is the best way to make personal progress and to gain a deep and lasting sense of self-worth.

In fact, many opportunities that may have been denied us in our world, perhaps because we didn't have the necessary qualifications, may then be available to us in the Beyond, because Over There the most important criterion of all is *the inner motive*.

Some spirit people who have passed over tragically young — let's say, in a motorbike accident — often decide to help other youngsters who are crossing in similar circumstances, because they're well equipped to help them to understand what is happening.

Progress is open to every soul, and this includes the souls of all the creatures in the animal kingdom.

So, if you've lost a loved one, remember there is no such thing as death — it's just an illusion.

What seems like the end, is just the beginning of a new adventure for the soul who is making the crossing.

And when your own time comes to make the

transition, have no fear in your heart.

I wrote the following comforting words in *Visions of Another World:*

> I have stood on the mountaintops
> of the shining lands
> and experienced countless visions
> of other worlds beyond death,
> and I am not afraid to die;
> for death is the Great Liberator,
> the Bright Angel
> who leads all living things
> into an eternal life,
> which is their natural birthright.

Here is one of my poems, taken from my second book, *Voices From Heaven,* which I think sums up the message of comfort and hope I've tried to give to so many people during the course of my calling.

It's just a few short lines but, as I read it, perhaps you'd like to replace my voice with that of someone you dearly love, who's passed into the higher life.

If they could speak to you now, maybe your loved one would say:

Do Not Forget Me

Do not forget me when I go,
For go I must, I cannot stay;
But do not forget my face, my love,
Nor my life, I pray.

Yet, if you should forget awhile
When I am gone — do not despair,

But keep your tears at bay,
For the silver love we shared
Will never fade away.

And one dawn soon,
Together we will stand
Upon some silent mountain, in some silent land,
And gaze into each other's eyes once more;
Then, hand in hand
Along some distant shore,
We'll remember all the times that slipped our minds:

    Our fond goodbyes;
    The times we loved;
    The time we met;

My love, we'll not forget.

12

Questions and Answers

The text of the second side of my educational cassette, Life After Death, *is based upon the following interview, which was originally conducted in a question-and-answer format:*

Stephen, I'd like to start by asking you if everybody survives death?
Yes, of course they do: there is no such thing as death. Every soul survives; even animals have souls, and they survive too.

And do the spirit people eat and sleep?
Yes, if they want to. The spirit body is the energy body; only the physical Earthly body needs food. The spirit body draws its energy from God, the Great Spirit, so people don't need to eat when they're in the next world — but of course if they want to, they can, because all manner of fruits and foods are duplicated Over There.

They can also sleep, if they wish, but mostly when they want to rest they just lie down on a grassy bank or on a couch, or they take up another mental pursuit – because a change of scenery is very often as good as a rest.

And what about clothes, Stephen; do they wear any?
Oh yes, of course — well, nearly all of them do! The spirit people clothe themselves by thought, in the same way as we do in this world. When you get up in the morning you have to take thought before you can don your clothes for the day, and it's the same Over There.

If a woman who has passed over had a favourite outfit, by exercising her power of thought she can 'clothe' herself in that same costume; she can visualise it into existence. But mostly the spirit people wear robes that are — how can I describe them? — they're a kind of loose-fitting robe or universal garment, made up of self-luminous light and energy, and they can be of any colour.

And what language do the denizens of the Next World speak?
Any language they choose; but mostly they would speak in their mother tongue. If a person were French or German, then his mind is ingrained into the habit of speaking that particular language, so when he passes over he'll continue to use it.

But what we have to remember when thinking of the spirit world is that behind everything is the power of Thought. Thought is the reality; and thought can be conveyed from one soul to another without the need to speak any language.

If a mother loves her son and wishes to convey that love to him, she doesn't have to express it in speech, she can send it to him telepathically, through a mind-to-mind contact, and he will receive it.

Can you tell us something about day and night in the spirit world?
Yes. There is no night Over There; the spirit people exist in everlasting daylight.

Because Mind conditions its surroundings, there is eternal daylight in the Beyond.

There's no night Over There because the spirit light — the glowing sun that lights up their world — is set very, very high in their sky: there's such a high atmosphere in the Beyond that they experience a kind of everlasting day. Their sun never sets, so to speak; however, areas of shady twilight do exist in the Hereafter because they've been created by the minds of people who desire them.

What about the concept of Time in the Next World. Does time exist?
The spirit people don't follow the clock Over There because they have no day and night, and they don't mark out the days, weeks, seasons, months or years as we do: there's no chronological or clock-time in the spirit world.

However, they do experience the passing of Time, but not as we know it.

Time, as we know it, is an illusion. We're trying to classify it and mark it out chronologically, and that's the illusion.

What the spirit people are aware of is the true sense of the passing of time, and this is known as 'living in the Eternal Now'.

We also have this on Earth: we're also living in the Eternal Now; and even as we think about this, that particular 'Now' has gone and its place is immediately taken by another 'Now'.

The spirit people experience a succession of Eternal 'Nows' – there are no clocks there.

You mentioned briefly how important Thought is. Do the spirit people use this power to travel from one place to another?
Yes, they do. In a way, we all travel by thought.

If we want to make a journey on Earth, first and foremost we must think about where we want to go, and then we must use the power of our minds to take our physical bodies there. The principle is the same in the next world, but thought Over There has a more immediate and direct effect than it does here on Earth.

If a spirit person focuses his mind on a place and 'homes' in on its image he will be transported there, faster than lightning, faster than sound, faster than light — once he's perfected this idea of thought-travel.

Of course, Earth transport is duplicated in the Next World for all those who desire it. If you fancy sailing down a canal on a boat of a lazy afternoon, it will all be there for you. But of course you'll still have a very real spirit body in the Hereafter with all of its limbs perfectly intact, so you can take stroll or a walk, or you can go for a run.

Continuing with Thought: could you explain to us your own thoughts on prayer?
Prayer is a stream of spontaneous thought, born of

desire in the heart of the person who is praying.

A person who prays is opening up his own soul, raising his mind and then linking it with an ever-lasting flow of inspirational thought, spiritual healing energies and the regenerating power of the God-force. Because The Great Spirit's energies are ever waiting to pour down into us, I see prayer as a soul-exercise through which we can receive our own guidance, and our own healing from our Creator. That's the main purpose of it. Of course, we can also send out prayers to request help for others.

Do you believe that God hears our prayers?
Oh yes, undoubtedly. I believe that God is not a person but a Life-force, a Consciousness, a Great Spirit; and I believe that we're all linked to this Great Spirit and that we are integral parts of the Cosmic Parent. We are all God's children – and therefore we're all brothers and sisters.

When someone prays, the prayer is carried along on a wave of thought and it's usually picked up by other small portions of God's Spirit; that is: by our loved ones in the spirit world. The spirit people who care for us and watch over us will then do their best to answer our prayers on God's behalf.

Let's move on and consider the area of personal relationships. If a woman marries twice, which husband will she be reunited with in the spirit world?
The answer is: both of them, either of them, or neither of them. It's entirely up to her. 'In the Kingdom of Heaven there is neither marriage nor

giving in marriage,' and that is true.

The only power that can bind two souls together is the power of love.

Provided that two souls love each other, they'll find each other in the next world, and they will remain together. If the woman loves both of her husbands she can see them both.

If she's drawn only to one of them, she will see only him; or it may be that all three persons will decide to go their separate ways. But, because life is everlasting, they can still remain good friends.

When we lose a loved one, is that person always with us and at our side; and would he or she know about everything we do?
Oh, no. The spirit people aren't always beside us and neither are they aware of what we're doing all of the time.

The world of spirit exists at a higher vibrational frequency than the Earth, and they're busy Over There: they're rendering service. If they want to know what's going on in our lives, they have to make an effort to tune-in to our thoughts, and we would have to do likewise in order to contact them.

Provided that attunement is made, each world will know what's happening in the other.

They visit us frequently, but they're not always aware of everything that goes on here.

So when the spirit people communicate their survival to us, either through you at one of your large public meetings or through a medium in a private consultation, are they always successful?
No, they're not. In many cases they *are* successful,

I have to say, but contact between the two worlds should always be regarded as an experiment.

Mental mediumship – the linking of two minds across two worlds – requires a precise telepathic attunement to take place; it is a joining of two minds on a wavelength of thought and love, and there are many hidden factors which could either hinder or assist the forging of this contact.

It's rather similar to the way in which TV and radio waves are continuously passing through our atmosphere: we can't receive them or translate them unless we're tuned in to their particular wavelengths, and even then we need an electronic set to pick up their signals. In mediumship, there has to be a medium who is sensitive enough to pick up the thoughts, voices, and images that are being transmitted to him by communicators in the world of spirit.

Just as radio and TV sets can go wrong, so can a medium's reception be impeded. It isn't easy for the spirit people to reach us; however, many of them are reasonably successful.

Communicators who push themselves forward to get their messages across are more likely to succeed, whereas the shyer ones will sometimes stand back and I may have to encourage them by saying, 'Come along, now, let's have your message. I'm willing to listen to you.'

And, of course, the medium's sensitivity – or his lack of it – must always be taken into account.

The spirit messages may be reaching us, but are we developed or sensitive enough to register them clearly?

Some of the most poignant and tragic cases you must come up against may involve the deaths of children, because this seems to make little sense to us here on Earth. Are you able to give any news or comfort to grieving parents?

Yes, I am. Everybody survives the grave – even miscarried and stillborn children. The spark of Life is there in a child: a spirit body is within its form, and although the physical body may be lost — even while the mother is still carrying it — the child will be born into the spirit world, and there it will grow and mature.

There is no death – the child is still alive.

A lot of people believe that a child has to belong to a religious faith, or that it must be christened or baptised into a particular religion in order for it to live after death, but that isn't true.

We are all linked to the Eternal Spirit of God, and because of this we will all survive death, intact.

God won't overlook a little child just because it hasn't been confirmed into a particular faith: that's theological nonsense.

Does the child still grow up on the Other Side?

Yes, right up to the full bloom of youth; right up to a time of maturity when they feel settled and happy. And of course they will regularly visit their parents on Earth; and because of these consistent journeys they will never forget their mothers and fathers.

In the dream-state at night, all parents' spirit bodies can move out into the spirit world and they can reach their children, meet and love them, and speak to them.

The extended family in the Beyond will take care of the little ones for us.

Let's consider another important area now. Do we all have spirit guides or guardian angels?
In a way: yes, we do. There's a prevalent belief that every person has one particular spirit attached to him or her right throughout Earthlife, but I don't entirely agree with this.

We're personally responsible for governing our own lives no matter which world we live in.

There are many people on the Other Side who are interested in us, and who are attached to us by ties of blood, relationship, or simply by spiritual kinship. We do have people watching over us, but not necessarily, I think, one particular person.

Staying with the topic of spiritual influences for a moment: an area that's been written about a great deal is that of poltergeists. What exactly is a poltergeist?
The German word *Poltergeist* roughly translates as 'noisy, or troublesome, spirit'. These are souls who have passed over but who are still bound to the Earth by their desires. 'Where your treasure is, there will your heart be also'.

If a spirit man is very materialistic and covetous of his possessions, these are his treasures, and that is where his interest will be: he'll stay close to the Earth, next to his heart's desire.

Sometimes, poltergeists can physically move objects, but they can't accomplish this without first drawing upon the psychic power of the people in the house — mediumistic people must be present.

In my experience as a medium, and having worked with researchers and psychologists, I've discovered that poltergeists aren't responsible for causing much of the trouble they're blamed for. A great deal of this kind of phenomena often doesn't originate in the spirit world at all – it's usually generated by a child or a young person who has reached the age of puberty.

A young person's hormonal levels can suddenly increase greatly, and then their auras — the electromagnetic fields of energy surrounding their bodies — can throw off immense psychic energies which can physically move objects in the house.

Staying with spirit energies: most people have heard of spiritual healing, and of course you yourself are a healer. How does it work?
Spiritual healing is composed of powerful spirit energies that emanate from God: these pass through the healer, and then radiate into the electromagnetic auras of the patient.

Healers often think of such energies as a love-force or as a correction-force that comes *from* spirit, *through* spirit, *to* spirit: from God the Great Healer, through the spirit of the healer, and into the spirit of the person requiring help.

It's an exchange of energy; and doctors on the Other Side, along with spirit guides and their assistants, help mediums such as myself to transmit these energies to the sick and suffering, wherever they may be.

In recent times, the British Medical Association granted doctors permission to refer their patients to spiritual healers, provided, of course, that the doctors maintain overall responsibility for the welfare of their patients.

At the root of spiritual healing is the power of Love, and I think it is probably one of the greatest gifts that anyone can possess.

Do we need to have faith for this healing to work?
No; it works because it's a psychic science; it works because the power originates in God's Spirit, and because we are Spirit, too.

Spiritual healing comes to us through a series of natural laws, but if you *do* have faith, this certainly helps the healing to work. It's reported that the Nazarene, when he healed people, said, 'According to your faith be it unto you'. This means that if you do possess faith, and you believe that the healing is going to work, then you will start up a wonderful self-healing mechanism within you. Your mind will kick-start your body to commence healing itself, and this power will work in concert with the healing energies coming to you from God through the spiritual healer.

If people require spiritual healing they should find recognised practitioners who are registered nationally. Your doctor may be able to refer you to reputable spiritual healers.

But spiritual healing works because of Love and God, and because it's a psychic science — so you don't really need to have faith.

If someone were to visit a healer, what could they expect?
They would probably meet a gentle, kind soul whose motive is to serve. Healers usually possess a

depth of compassion and a genuine love for suffering humanity. They'll invite you to take a seat, talk to you, and when they begin the laying-on-of-hands they might simply touch your shoulders or hold your hands — that's known as contact healing. Or they might sit alone, or in a group, keeping you in mind while sending out healing to you by thought and by prayer — that's known as absent or distant healing.

There's been quite a lot of study on spiritual healing: some people don't respond to it and death occurs. Have you any thoughts as to why that should be?
Yes; nobody passes until the time is right.

Even when a person is receiving spiritual healing, if the soul is ready to move into its next stage of development and growth, through the natural laws which govern it, then its time is up and that person must pass over.

But it should be remembered that death isn't the end of life, it's the beginning of an adventure in the next world.

Spiritual healing can relieve pain, and bestow a more dignified passing on the person who is about to pass over.

Staying with medical topics for a moment, what about people who've lost a limb in this world, or who suffer from some kind of physical deformity?
Will they still be deformed after death?
No. The spirit body exists in perfect health: it is an etheric vehicle made up of energy vibrations. Whatever you do to the physical body, you cannot

damage or make ill the spirit body. So if someone has lost a leg, for example, it's only the physical limb that has gone: the etheric limb will be unharmed in the spirit body.

That's the Law.

What about people with mental difficulties and special needs: how do they fare in the Beyond?
Such difficulties arise because there is something wrong with the brain. The brain is a kind of fleshly computer that registers the mind through the power of the spirit, which then manifests this as action in the physical body.

If the brain malfunctions, this doesn't mean that the mind is affected: the mind is perfect. The brain holds the problem; but once the brain 'dies' and the person passes over, a balance is struck. Over There, a handicapped person will possess more freedom of expression. At the end of the day, there's spiritual compensation for anyone who is suffering in this way.

Let's talk now about the controversial subject of reincarnation, which states that a soul can be reborn as a different personality. What are your thoughts on this?
Obviously, I'm not the Great Spirit, so I don't have all the answers: but, with God, I believe that all things are possible – therefore, reincarnation is possible.

I can't prove that to you, and I believe that a lot of souls who say they've been reincarnated would also have difficulty proving it to you, because there are lots of alternative theories available which can explain away the belief in 'previous lives'.

The soul, itself, undertakes to incarnate; no one Over There orders it to do so.

The souls who come back, are souls with a mission. I think Mother Teresa of Calcutta was a wonderful example of an old soul who took up a mission to come into the world again to show us what the power of love can do. I think the same about Martin Luther King in America — he was an old soul who came into the flesh again to finish the job which Abraham Lincoln had started, that of helping to free black people.

You teach that God is a Great Spirit. Why do you think God allows so much suffering in this world?
I don't think of God as a person or as a vengeful deity who wreaks havoc on people He doesn't like, and who pours love on those whom He does. God is a Great Power, a Great Spirit that encompasses a set of natural laws which govern the Universe; and one of the most important laws is possibly the Law of *Cause and Effect,* which many scientists accept.

We put out Causes through the expression of our thoughts, words and deeds, and eventually we will reap the exact Effects of these energies.

I think suffering is the Effect of possibly a number of Causes that we've put out into the world. Suffering occurs because we transgress some of the Universal Laws, under the umbrella of which we all live.

If we put ourselves in harmony with these laws of nature, we'll gain inner peace and radiant health; and if we don't, we'll create inner disharmony and disease may follow.

Suffering springs from our misalignment with the wonderful laws that govern health and well-being.

Do you, then, believe in the devil?
No I don't: priests and theologians invented this mythical creature to try to resolve the problem of 'evil' in the world, and to keep their followers firmly under their thumbs.

Man has the power of the Spirit of God in him, and through his freewill he uses this power to create beauty or to destroy. It is the exercise of man's freewill that causes havoc on the Earth.

Incidentally, I'm not very happy about that word 'evil': I always think about misguided souls rather than evil souls. And of course, *like attracts like*.

The only 'devil' I believe in, is man himself.

If man looks into the mirror either he'll see the cruellest animal that has ever stalked the Earth, or, if his vision is different, he'll see a wonderful part of God's Spirit which can love others, care for them, teach them and help them.

Another topic now – we've all heard of people undergoing major surgery and being pronounced 'clinically dead' on the operating table, and then they suddenly come back to life and report they've undergone an out-of-the-body experience, having travelled down a tunnel or into an all-engulfing light.

What do you think actually happens in these cases?
Quite simply, a person's consciousness exteriorises in the spirit body and then it leaves the physical

body, just a little way, and later returns and brings back a message. The all-engulfing light many such travellers see could be the light of the spirit world, which is brighter than our light on Earth. As for travelling down a dark tunnel: I don't think anyone is certain about what this is.

Some people think it's a mental representation, a symbol: being freed out of darkness and projected into light, the traveller's mind may be picturing this experience symbolically as a tunnel.

However, a lot of people who've had an out-of-the-body experience return with the absolute conviction that they are never, ever, going to die; and their lives are usually changed for the better.

But some people believe the journey is created by the subconscious mind, which is beginning to prepare for death. What do you think about that?
That's a possibility, but lots of people who've had this experience have come back to life in this world, and they're still here.

If someone referred to you as a fortune-teller, what would be your reaction?
Mediums and fortune-tellers exercise totally different skills.

Mediums are not fortune-tellers; mediums link with people living in the next world, but fortune-tellers have no such link – they are pure psychics who read your mind, your aura, or your circumstances.

Regrettably, many people visit fortune-tellers and pay them large sums of money simply to be told everything they already know.

Mediumship produces communication with discarnate entities, but fortune-telling produces a purely psychic reading of your mind and circumstances.

If a full-scale nuclear war broke out and destroyed the Earth, what would happen to the spirit world?
Nothing at all. You can't destroy Mind or Spirit: they are indestructible, immortal – they cannot be harmed. The spirit world would still be there.

As you glance forward, Stephen, can you ever envisage a time when there will be no more war in this world of ours, and a time when mankind will live in peace?
Only when individual souls birth the idea of peace within their hearts, and then actually live it out in their lives with all the love that they possess — only then will peace reign on Earth as it does in Heaven.

*

That concludes the text of the tape, but following on from the wide interest generated by my work I'll now tackle some of the more unusual, and sometimes quite personal, questions which the public has asked me during my tours.

Let's go live into the theatre:

Does abstinence from sexual activity help the soul to realise its Greater Self? Has it helped you? Are you celibate?
Everything has a purpose, and we wouldn't have

been born with sexual characteristics if they weren't important in helping our soul-natures to evolve. Abstinence from sexual intercourse is a personal choice. Some mystics have chosen, and have publicly advocated, this path for various reasons; but I haven't. To deny one's sexuality and its obvious impulses could cause deep psychological problems.

I'd advise moderation in all things.

And no, I'm not celibate; though there've been times in my life when I certainly felt as if I was!

In your book, In Touch with Eternity, *you said 'people can be irritating': isn't that a rather unspiritual comment to make?*

No, it's the truth.

What does being 'spiritual' mean? Surely one mustn't be a liar or a hypocrite in order to be 'spiritual'? To obtain a firm basis for progress, first and foremost we should be honest with ourselves.

We can't lie to ourselves.

I can love and respect the God-spark of Divinity within every soul, but sometimes the way in which this light is shaded or partly obscured by the personality often leaves much to be desired.

There's a very true saying: it's easy to be an angel until somebody ruffles your feathers; and sometimes, especially if workloads are stressful, I don't think I'll ever fly again!

Stephen, as a devotee I've followed your work and teachings for years now, and gained much benefit from your lectures, your discourses, and your demonstrations, but I'm particularly interested in your growth as a person. Your first three books have shown three very different Stephens. Why is this; and which one is the real you?

None of them is the real me, sir. I am to be found nowhere in my books because they're just records, a collection of memories that record the growth of a personality through its life experiences — but I am not that persona or 'mask'.

The real person — the soul, the essence of my true self — lives beyond personification, thought and emotion, and it transcends clumsy words and descriptions, as does yours.

We are all Spirit.

If you are not a 'who', then what are you?

Just like you, I'm a part of God, the Great Spirit; a consciously aware reflection of the Universal Mind. But the difference between us may be that I have realised this, and perhaps, as yet, you have not.

If you come from God then surely you can convey something more important to the world and its Thought than our survival after death?

We all come from God, but I'm currently engaged on a carefully prepared mission which I agreed to undertake before my birth; at the moment, this part of the message incorporates the teachings of soul-growth delivered through mediumship.

I was most interested when you wrote that within relationships once Respect is gone, the relationship is over.

What exactly did you mean by respect?
Respect means allowing another soul the time and space to freely express itself, to be given the kind of unfettered freedom that you yourself desire.

Respect asks nothing for itself because it doesn't give, in order to receive. Making a big show of respect to someone in 'higher' authority over you is nothing more than fear or cunning, masquerading itself to gain you future rewards.

In any relationship, real respect means having a sensitive appreciation of the intrinsic right of other individuals to express their feelings, their opinions, lifestyles and thoughts, according to their levels of development.

A man with respect doesn't condemn others for being different from himself; so I'd place respect hand-in-glove with toleration, unconditional love, and graciousness.

When respect is missing in relationships, what exists in its absence? Surely: turmoil, bitterness, shallow judgement, and a myriad physical and psychological barriers that curtail the free-flowing thoughts and activities of others.

There can be no real happiness amongst all this.

It's better to live alone in peace and freedom than to suffer all the soul-crippling indignities that a lack of respect breeds. If the delicate flower of respect withers away, then true spiritual love could not have been living within that relationship — for if love had been there, respect wouldn't have died.

So would you advise any couples who are at loggerheads to stay together for the sake of their children, until their youngsters have grown up?

I can't make decisions for others — we're all personally responsible for ourselves — but surely it's better for children to mature with one balanced and emotionally stable parent, rather than exist in a home poisoned by anger or rent with frustration, ceaseless bickering and argument?

Is it right you teach that we know when we're going to die?
Yes, just as you knew when you were going to be born; and this information resides in your Higher Self.

But if we know what our future lives will be like, having mapped them out during our sleep-time existence, what's the point of incarnating when we already know the outcome?
Knowing it, and *living* it, are two quite different experiences.

How can people who are trying to be spiritually minded ever be happy in this sad and ugly world, Stephen?
Happiness has little to do with the 'outside' world, or with anything or anyone else that seems to be 'outside' of ourselves, and more to do with what is living *within* us.

Happiness is purely a state of appreciation.

Everything is passing; all things are transient, except you, the inner being: your consciousness will remain for ever; so, your most important task is to set yourself right, to realign yourself with the Universal Laws, emotionally and psychologically.

Instead of building castles in the air and wasting

energy chasing fanciful desires — forget all that; instead, take a long, cool and objective look at what you already have around you in your life.

Make a comprehensive worklist: write down and identify everything that's breeding misery and discontent in your life, then systematically remove each of those obstacles, if you can.

After this, you'll feel much better because you'll be subject to less stress, and you'll experience a greater sense of freedom.

Removing the misery in your life cleanses the mind, and it's from this stable position that you can count your blessings and go forward to build a much brighter future.

Should a person who is spiritually searching for God and Self, or for the meaning of existence, forsake society and the world to become a hermit, to live alone, or to go into some sort of closed religious order to find answers to his questions?

Not necessarily, for all the answers lie within the Self; and by this I mean: the solutions will be found within your Eternal Consciousness, within the Essence of the Great Spirit's Life-force, which pulses deep within your mind.

Within the Self we can also blend our minds with spiritual inspiration and receive helpful guidance.

Even during strenuous activities, we can achieve inner peace.

But whether we stay in society or not, we can't escape the fact that we're all very necessary to one another.

We like to think we're independent beings, but in fact we're all interdependent.

In the light of this, what does running away gain us? Who was it that built the hermit's mountain cabin? Who beat out the nails from hot metal? Who formed his steel axe and hammer? Where did the recluse obtain his clothes?

You can't deny the material world with one hand, and then with the other buy your food and clothes from city merchants.

No man is an island; we need each other. The very chair you're sitting on was first fashioned by someone's thought, and then it was skilfully materialised.

Every situation, whether great or small, must eventually be faced; and all problems must be challenged and solved through personal effort. But all these solutions are already living within your Higher Self, living side by side with their causes — and what the questioner must do, is find them.

So we should remain amongst people while we're seeking out the Spiritual Way?
You can be in the world, but not necessarily of it.

Surely it's better to give service than to ignore humanity's cries for help? We have an eternity in which to solve our problems.

I especially like your spiritual poetry. Are your poems given to you by outside intelligences or are they all of your own making? And will you be publishing them in volume form?
My poetry is inspired and born in different ways, sir, but generally it springs from my own mind.

I'm pleased you enjoy it, and I hope to publish a collection in the future.

You talk a lot about loving, caring and sharing, but you don't have children and you say you aren't interested in personal relationships, so what can you possibly know of love?

Because they've read my books, many people assume they know me, sir.

Hundreds of correspondents have written to say they feel I've been a part of their lives for years — but this is, perhaps, sentimentalism, and simply an emotional reaction to my life and work.

Only those who are intimately connected to me might know me; and only they know who they are.

As a very private man I do find your question rather personal, but nevertheless I'll answer it.

I most certainly know what it is to give love freely from the soul, unconditionally, with no strings attached. I've also been extremely fortunate to have felt deeply loved in return; and, of course, like many others, I've suffered several losses.

So life hasn't passed me by.

I'm just an ordinary man with sometimes very powerful needs, desires and thoughts, just like you.

How Deep is the Night

How deep is the night
how still the air
how silent is the sleeping city
how empty is this room
   since you went away.

Alone in the silence,
  I remember when our nights were filled
   and the air was living-bright
    and the city's sleep passed unnoticed
    in a dark room, full of light.

But now, you've gone –
I know not where —
  and the night is void with loneliness
  and all that's left
  are flickering mem'ries
  galloping across the lighted hills of my mind
   watering my sight –
   but I'll never be blind.

  ...Tonight, my breast is still,
     inside a velvet darkness...
  deepening the night,
   and emptying the air,
    now that I breathe it alone...

Stephen O'Brien

Behind everything,
   through everything,
      within everything,
         is the Power of God –
            which is Everything...

13

Journeys of the Soul
*A Spiritual Odyssey of Freewill
and Predestination*

Take an imaginary step with me and, just for a moment, visualise God in the form of a human being (as a man) instead of in the form of a Great Power.

God sits down and gathers together one hundred six-inch wooden rulers and glues them onto a very large hardboard base, both horizontally and vertically.

Soon, He has created a solid, quite complicated maze: one hundred wooden rulers are joining, interlocking and creating dead-ends in an almost impossible to solve puzzle, rather like the many famous tree-mazes found in the grounds of English country mansions.

God finishes His work, fashioned by His own hands under the direction of His own mind, and then He places the wooden maze on the ground.

Gazing down at it from a great height, He knows there is only one entrance into the maze, and only one exit on its opposite side; and from His objective viewpoint He is able to see not only the place where any traveller may enter, but also all of the dead-ends that he may encounter on his journey through the complicated maze – and God can also see the only possible way forward which leads to the exit.

Satisfied with His work, and content that the pattern has now been set and placed on solid Earth, God sits back and awaits the arrival of a traveller who will be the first investigator to try his luck in the complex wooden maze.

Soon, a little white mouse happens along the road and suddenly discovers the entrance to the maze; but at first, he doesn't recognise it as a place of many pathways, so he steps confidently inside; but after turning a few corners he soon feels hopelessly lost among the high wooden walls. The white mouse is so small and fragile that the walls of the maze dwarf him: he cannot see over them, around them, through them, or above them.

All he knows is that, as he glances forward, there appears to be a set of possibilities in front of him, several different roadways from which he might choose in order to escape. So, he puts his best paw forward and travels along his chosen pathway, one which he has selected through the power of his own freewill.

But way up on high, God — the Maker of the maze — gazes down from His privileged position and clearly sees that the road which our traveller has taken will ultimately lead him to nowhere but a dead-end.

God already knows that the little mouse will have to eventually retrace his steps and then try another pathway until he will discover or finally stumble upon the correct route forward and out.

God knows that all the effort which the mouse will put into this brief investigation will add to its experience of life, and that this information is not immediately available to the traveller.

Meanwhile, the mouse shuffles along and turns down blind alleyways and around corners that seemingly lead nowhere, or into interesting diversions which will teach him many valuable lessons and will keep him travelling forward with interest and vigour.

But then, after many disappointing failures and many unsuccessful attempts to escape, and much anger and frustration, the little traveller suddenly delights God because at last he reaches the correct pathway that will lead him into freedom.

But even as he walks it, the mouse doesn't yet recognise it as the roadway which leads forward and out.

But God, observing from His high vantage-point, sees all, and He rejoices.

This the pattern of the journey of your soul.

God is your own Higher Self.

The solid ground supporting the maze is the Earthworld, in which you now exist.

And the maze represents the tangled web of life's experiences which your soul has planned and set down.

The many pathways in front of you may well be several different lifetimes.

The traveller – the little white mouse – is you, in your present physical consciousness, exercising what you believe to be your own freewill.

The way forward into freedom is your release back into the Spirit Realms from whence you originally came.

Now read the story again, but this time with the added knowledge that hidden within it there is an All-knowing, All-powerful Great Mind or Spirit Consciousness which created every single element in this spiritual odyssey — including you.

14

The Living God

'Is there some kind of God?' hundreds of people have asked me; and down the centuries billions more have pondered on this important question:

'If there is a loving God, then why doesn't He intervene in times of tragedy when we need Him; and why doesn't He clearly answer our prayers?'

Furthermore, countless believers are particularly perplexed when atheists demand of them, 'Where was your compassionate God during the Holocaust in the Second World War when millions of people were murdered in cold blood? If your God cares for humanity as much as you claim He does, why didn't He stop this slaughter?'

Many religious people find it impossible to answer these difficult and thought provoking questions; but solving these problems could well be one of the most important steps we may ever take in our journey of soul-evolution. After all, if there is a God who will, as some authorities teach, lovingly 'reward' or cruelly 'punish' us, then we ought to know something about Him in order to ensure our long-standing personal happiness.

On the other hand, God might not exist at all.

If you are an atheist — someone who doesn't

believe in a God – you may still find this chapter interesting because in it I shall address a number of these difficult questions and offer some answers in a way that some people might find surprising and unusual.

Let's start by acknowledging the fact that many believers today seem so discontented with their idea of who, or what, God is that they are leaving the orthodox religions in their millions.

Since 1999, the Church of England has declined to publish its attendance figures because they are so embarrassingly low, and they are continuing to fall daily.

The media have also reported that believers in the Roman Catholic faith are 'haemorrhaging' from its ranks at an alarming rate.

Today, around 90% of the English population do not attend any church.

Why is this?

The answer is simple:

Across the world more and more people are being educated, and it is this light of knowledge which has caused a worldwide religious revolution.

Thankfully, the days have gone when people were told to simply 'have faith' and were instructed never to question their religion's teachings – and we must applaud the fact that the Christian Church no longer has such a crippling stranglehold on the minds of its adherents, as it did in the ancient world and in the Dark Ages.

Yet even today, in some underprivileged countries where education standards remain low and living standards are woefully inadequate, millions of citizens are still held in the vice-like grip of some form of orthodox theological or superstitious belief. In these societies, people are actively discouraged from questioning orthodox thought; but, in my view, those who blindly follow the dictates of others may never come to realise the true nature of the Infinite Spirit, which — for want of a better name — man has called God.

During my own spiritual quest, I've discovered that this Mighty Creator is a Power whose Essence is found within each one of us, and that we can unveil or reveal Its Presence through undertaking a simple process of self-enquiry:

Man Know Thyself.

Many people who wish to step boldly into such a personal investigation may first need to recognise that their present disillusionment about God is probably caused by their past ideas of what they believed His Nature to be; following this realisation, they can then try to discover what the true 'personality' of God is.

Now, let's take some positive steps towards a better understanding of the Creative Spirit...

To start this journey, we must first be willing to surrender any preconceived ideas of what we may think God is, for unless we can release our deep-rooted opinions and personal biases we will not be in a position to welcome any new concepts.

We must also recognise that in this limited space we're undertaking the immense task of trying to understand a vast concept which may very well be beyond all possible human understanding.

Countless attempts have been made by man, who is finite, to comprehend God, who may be Infinite, and many of these have inevitably fallen short of uncovering all of the answers.

Perhaps this is why God has often been called 'The Ineffable One': something, or someone, which remains fully inexpressible and which defies description.

The Creator has also been thought of as a vast *Consciousness,* as a source of origin of the soul, a *Sense of Being,* or as a state of *Living Experience,* rather than something we can easily categorise with our intellect or with language.

Nevertheless, let's press ahead and see if we can understand this mysterious Being.

In order to unveil the nature of God, we will have to begin by assuming that He exists. The idea of a mighty deity has fascinated billions of questioning minds over countless millennia. Human beings have always felt that 'somewhere' there might be a powerful 'something' or 'someone' that is existing through, or at the very back of, Life itself.

'We could not have originated from nothing,' many people reason. 'Nothing comes from nothing – so there must be "something", some kind of "Power" from which we sprang.'

For many people, this is a reasonable assumption; so, for the moment, let's go with it, and start our quest by giving a universally fair and generally acceptable statement of what many questioning believers have conceived God's nature to be.

This statement will present us with a common-ground supposition from which we can then work forwards. And the statement reads like this:

Somewhere, seen or unseen, there may be some kind of Eternal, Infinite, All-powerful Influence: a

Consciousness, a Spirit, or a Presence that is pervading every facet of existence. This Single Power seems to have a measure of responsibility for creating, governing and maintaining the order and running of Life in this universe.

It may well express emotion and mentality, and It may appear to be involved, either personally or impersonally, with the lives of Its creations.

Most religious people would probably find the above statement both reasonable and acceptable.

We can now investigate some of these claims by following the prophet's advice to 'seek and find', and we'll begin by applying some simple philosophical thought.

Down through the centuries many great minds have wrestled with the idea of the existence of a Superior Being. For these intelligent people, the phrase 'you must have faith in God' was simply not acceptable; and it still isn't for many of today's thinkers, who require evidence, reasons and facts to support the existence of a supposed Supreme Power.

Philosophers, atheists and agnostics counter religious assertions such as 'There is a God' with challenging questions like, 'Before you can state "There is a God", you'd better explain exactly what you *mean* by the term "God".'

At first glance, the phrase 'There is a God' sounds like a simple statement of fact, as though we might be saying, 'There is a tree'. It appears to be a straightforward sharing of factual information – but is it?

We can see and feel the tree, we can cut its bark

and obtain enough material evidence to justify its objective existence. What's more, others can copy our actions and get the same results.

But it might prove difficult to obtain objective evidence of God's existence — and this is where all the problems start.

When believers come up against this logic they sometimes quote religious teachings because — for them — these carry the stamp of authority.

But philosophers challenge them again with, 'You haven't explained what you *mean* by God' — to which the eventual end-of-argument reply is often, 'God is a Power in which we must have Faith.' And this, of course, plunges us into very deep mystical and intellectual waters; for what is Faith?

Such a question inevitably leads us away from objective facts and back into the misty realms of inner conviction.

Non-religious people, of course, declare, 'Faith in a God is not enough: I want you to prove His existence to me' — and at this point we seem to return to a classic circular argument, for how can you prove the existence of God?

Nevertheless, let's see if we can take some steps towards resolving some of these questions.

Working from our previous statement of God's probable nature: if such an Infinite Being exists, He can have no boundaries because His infinite *State of Being* could not be limited by any lines of demarcation; for as soon as we place limits around Infinity it would immediately become Finite.

By the very definition of 'Infinite', which means 'endless', such an everlasting God must be an eternal entity, an entity that will last for ever.

This would mean that God would be an Infinite Presence: an immortal, everlasting Being whose Spirit is everywhere; which in turn would suggest that everything which has consciousness, and which appears in the vast arena of Life, must be living or vibrating within the Essence of this Infinite All-pervading Presence, or Power.

Something that is eternal could not have had a beginning; and by the very definition of the word 'eternal', it will never experience an end. So, the Origin of Everything was probably in existence before Life as we know it appeared on the planet.

Unlike physical man, who has a limited awareness of what is around him and within him, a limitless Infinite Mind would be aware of everything that is existing within Itself, within Its Universal Spirit. It would be conscious of every single thought and of every life-form which is existing within its vast Self.

Such a mighty power would be omnipresent — that is to say: it would be present in all places at the same time. It would be omnipotent — which means all-powerful; and it would be omniscient — which means all-knowing.

These qualities seem implied in the teaching attributed to the Nazarene: that God knows of the smallest sparrow's fall.

So, the power of this God-Spirit gifts to each life-form a common link: there is a part of Its Universal Force uniting, and running through, everything in existence.

If this is true, then all of the religions man has created, which, on the surface of it, seem to be quite separate belief systems, are now revealed as sets of beliefs which have been created, and which now function, within the Essence of the One God.

What at first seems like a diversity of religious form and belief, is in fact a Unity of belief: there is only one God, but many pathways that will lead mankind back to the knowledge of this Single Supreme Source.

The All is in the one; and the one is in the All.

If the followers of the many religions of the world truly understood this principle, religious tolerance would be instantly established and no more wars or bloody crusades would be fought in the name of the Almighty God. A new day would dawn for mankind, and a mutual respect would be established.

But to continue our investigation:

One of the Nazarene's teachings claims that God is 'a Loving Father', moreover 'Our Father', and this implies that God is a caring entity; and we have already established that this caring Spirit *is within us, now*.

If this is so, then a vital link between God and mankind has now been realised; and because of this intimate link, God is *personally involved* with each of His creations, even if they've assumed Him to be distant and disinterested.

For the believer, God now becomes a powerful and immanent presence that lives within each heart and mind, within each soul and spirit.

And if this God is an all-knowing entity, as we have supposed, and It also contains within It the minds and lives of all of Its creations, then It must be fully aware of every emotion and every feeling generated by every human being, every animal, and every other life-form.

This, of course, strengthens the idea of a God who is a caring Parent; and it is now an easy step to assert that God must therefore possess *consciousness, sensitivity, awareness, feeling and emotion,* because we ourselves possess these attributes – surely, we can only possess these qualities because they are already existing within the One Power from within which we take our conscious awareness and our very life-power.

It couldn't be otherwise; for we, who are human (and who are called the Many), couldn't possibly manifest anything which hadn't first originated within our Primal Source (which is called the One).

By observing the world around us we can see that all sentient creatures are divided into two genders, and this also applies to several life-forms in the vegetable kingdom; therefore, if the all-pervading Presence is at the back of every manifestation, He or It must be an androgynous power; that is: a Power within whom both the masculine and feminine aspects of creation are reflected.

In the past, it may be that people conceived of God as a masculine entity because man's physical power often exceeded that of woman's, and therefore he seemed to be the leader. In other words, man 'created' the idea of God in his own masculine image.

But within an androgynous Spirit, both sexes are afforded equal status; so, perhaps we should cease calling God 'He' and start referring to Him as 'It', for God is now seen as a Father/Mother principle.

However, to avoid confusion for the moment, and purely for convenience, I'll continue using the pronoun 'He', even though our reasoning has indicated that the Infinite Spirit cannot possibly be a glorified finite male.

Now let's take a look at the controversial issue of man's much-treasured freewill.

If The Great Spirit's Mind-Power, and therefore His Thoughts, together with His Creative Will, are flowing through His Spirit (and subsequently through each and every one of us), does this mean that He is controlling and directing every life?

Some simple logical deduction may indicate to us that, indeed, God's Thoughts would seem to be at the back of man's thoughts, for the Many cannot exist without the One; and if this is true, then where is the power of man's freewill now?

Surely, if nothing can exist outside of God, mankind's actions now seem to be mere reflections of the One Creative Will, as it moves through the lives of the Many, who are inextricably bound up in the Mind of the One.

Could this be the hidden meaning of the religious prayer, 'Thy Will be done on Earth, as it is in Heaven'?

Some people might strongly disagree with this, and they would offer a different interpretation, but my purpose here isn't to strengthen established beliefs but to question and discuss them.

One of the main objections to the loss of man's freewill, in favour of all his actions being brought about by the overriding Will of God, is what the philosophers call 'the problem of evil' or 'the problem of pain, injustice, cruelty and tragedy' that is so prevalent in the world.

The basic argument goes like this: 'An earthly

loving father wouldn't allow his child to suffer, and would do everything in his power to cure his little one's sickness and assuage his pain. Why then, does God, the so-called Almighty Heavenly Father, stand by and allow tragedy to hurt His Children in the human race without taking any steps to prevent it? Why doesn't God rid the world of this problem of evil? Doesn't He care?'

The answer to this problem is implicit in the question.

The mistake that many people make is to assume that God is Love, alone, and that no other emotion or force could possibly exist within His Being.

But God cannot be Love, alone.

If we, who are the lesser, are capable of immense cruelty (and we are certainly capable of this), we can only express this force because we have obtained the power to do so from the One who is our Originator, and who is our only power-source.

This thought may not sit well with orthodox religious people...

Without doubt there exists in the world a very painful and dark energy which is being expressed through violence, hatred, anger and so-called 'evil'; and, in recognising this, we face directly the problem of suffering, and the reasons for it.

To resolve this issue we must cease to think of God only as a loving entity, and begin to think of Him (or It) as *an imperfect and evolving Consciousness*: as the One Spirit which is slowly evolving through the living experiences of the Many lifeforms that It has created.

If this concept is accepted we begin to understand that man's ceaseless struggle to develop and unfold his mind, his character, and his soul, through the daily trials of his existence, is taking place because the Spirit of the evolving God is expressing Itself through mankind's actions.

Once this idea is accepted, the causes of the difficulties in our lives may be better understood – behind all of our struggles a purpose is operating: *evolution*.

As creatures living within the Spirit of God, we are marching forward with Him, side by side, towards the ultimate goal, which is to achieve Perfection.

If all of our assumptions are so far correct, what then would be the point of our praying to this God, if the Kingdom of God (or the Kingdom of the Spirit) is already within us? In effect, wouldn't we be praying to ourselves?

The simple answer is *yes*; but there are other factors to take into account.

When we turn our attention inwards we may become more aware of the Power from which we originated; we may 'touch base', so to speak, and there we may reinvigorate and refresh ourselves by freely drawing upon our Creator's energies and inspiration.

Religious people claim that their prayers seem to sustain and reaffirm their Faith; and they also feel that by 'linking up' with God they feel much closer to their Maker.

But prayer isn't always a self-centred request: many petitions are sent out for the good of others, or for world peace, etc.

Let's now take a closer look at prayer:

Prayers are subjective desires, born of emotions that are firmly rooted within the mind of a personality, within which the Infinite Spirit exists; and this Infinite and Omniscient Spirit would foresee not only the rising of each soul's request, but also the outcome of its desired actions.

Bearing this in mind, would God want to answer our prayers?

I believe the answer to that is: yes.

The Spirit of God could answer each prayer through the services of some of the many creatures He has created. He could use discarnate spirit personalities in the Beyond to answer our prayers — people whose minds are existing, or vibrating, at roughly the same frequencies as the person who is praying. He could also use Earthly people like ourselves to bring about results.

This, then, could be God's way of 'personally hearing' and then 'personally answering' each of our petitions. The spirit people confirm this idea, and this explains why our 'answers' are often slow in materialising, because our spirit friends have to work through the complex spiritual laws governing communication between the two worlds.

I can remember an instance of one of my own prayers being answered in this way.

It happened one cool August evening, at the end of a hot summer during which I'd felt at a loss as to where my next steps on Earth would take me. At such difficult times I've always turned to seeking within, and I've often walked on the gently rolling Welsh hills and mountains to be utterly alone with myself; totally alone with God and His invisible Angels.

On that summer night, the stillness of the verdant landscape beckoned me like a silent hand and I ascended to the top of a mountain, just as sunset was falling. Strolling quietly amongst the wild flowers I let my thoughts run free; then I settled on an ancient grey rock that was set deep into the terrain, and closed my eyes in thoughtful prayer.

To truly pray, I believe we must sink deeply into the soul-nature of ourselves and try to touch the spiritual fountain of never-ending healing strength and inspiration which springs from the One Source, and which reaches us through our Higher Selves. Inspiration is ever waiting to pour into our souls from the wellspring of God's Spirit, whenever we touch more closely the Living Power within us.

Floating within the cool velvet darkness behind my eyes, I quickly lost touch with earthly thoughts but I could still hear the distant calls of skylarks mingling with the sound of the evening breeze. After sending out my requests, I became absolutely still, and I mean *really* still: the kind of deep inner stillness that belongs to those whose minds are uncluttered by ceaseless thoughts which impel them from one anxious psychological displacement activity to another.

In the twinkling of an eye, the mists of the spirit world rolled aside, and as the gossamer veil between Heaven and Earth began to vaporise all about me, there came a shining golden light.

With my eyes tight closed, I watched the glowing cloudbanks gradually gather together in a circle around me — and within them appeared the hazy forms of shining spirit men. From the next realms, five white-robed, luminous beings tuned in to my mind. They had the appearance of elderly grey-bearded sages, and they radiated the most incredible sense of soul-stillness and powerful wisdom it's ever been my privilege to experience.

One of these wise beings spoke to me with his thoughts, but his words seemed clearer to me than the distant cries of the skylarks.

With compassion he said, 'You will not be left comfortless, for the way ahead will shortly be made known to you.'

Suddenly, the pressure of my anxieties lifted from my mind; and the glowing forms slowly faded from sight, as though someone had dimmed a light switch, and I was once more alone, back on the violet mountaintop.

Within a few days, this sage's prophecy was fulfilled and my pathway became much clearer to me – and thus my prayer was answered.

By communing with the Spirit of God within me, I received not only personal spiritual healing and strength, but also the guidance of wise souls from Eternity; and I fervently believe that this kind of comfort and aid is available to everyone.

Such immediate results, however, don't always occur: experience has taught me that they usually arrive in their own good time, and not in ours. The God-Power operates through channels of Its own choosing, according to Its own Creative Will, and within the scope of Its own time-scale and Its Natural Laws; and these Divine Laws, which are integral parts of God, govern us in every aspect of our thoughts and feelings, no matter what we might think of them.

The answers come when we are ready to receive

them — and not before.

We don't have to wait until a mythical Judgement Day to receive our so-called 'rewards' or our 'punishments'. The Supreme God, whose nature we are trying to uncover, monitors and 'controls' every life via His Natural Laws. He has no need to judge us in some final celestial court, because judgement is an ongoing part of evolution.

Judgement is an inward process which personally involves the Creator within us — and this continuous judgement is delivered in each individual life via the inner voice of its own conscience; and this 'still small voice' of conscience may well be a 'vocal' reflection of God's Laws, which in turn is coloured by the state of our own mental evolution and moral standards.

In this very limited space, having now explored some of the more difficult ideas about what we think the nature of God may or may not be, what conclusions can we draw?

Is man alone?

Is mankind the result of a haphazard hotchpotch of chemicals which happened to fuse together in the distant past? And if he is: who or what created those chemicals in the first place?

Was it God?

Does God exist?

For those who fervently believe God does not exist, few arguments will win them over.

But what about the rest of us?

Is there anything that we can see, feel, know or experience, which would substantiate, or at least indicate to us, the nature or existence of a Divine Spirit?

Is there anything which might convince us that there could be an All-powerful Consciousness which is aware of us, has created us, and which seems to be evolving within us?

I think there is...

Gaze up into a dark night sky filled with millions of twinkling stars that are invisibly held in their places by mighty forces unknown, then try to imagine the immense distances between them. All the brilliant suns visible to our naked eyes are glimpsed through our own amazing galaxy, the Milky Way, which might contain upwards of a hundred billion stars — and this is just *one* galaxy in a universe which has a possible hundred billion other galaxies within it.

Pause for a moment, and allow the immensity of that incredible thought to register...

Now hold in your arms a newborn babe and look into its clear eyes; marvel at the beautiful light glinting within them, and feel the movement of its wonderfully complex little body as you embrace it and caress its soft skin.

Then contemplate the miracle of its conception and birth: how the amazing foetus with its plasma, blood, sinews, bones, nerves, organs and tissues, formed inside its mother's womb — seemingly without her conscious aid — then marvel at how the child made its entry into this world. Ponder also on how, after the passage of time, this child will develop into a separate personality, quite uniquely its own.

It's amazing to think that since the dawn of time no two people have ever been created the same...

Then stand on a cliff and stare in humility at a deep red sunset, or at the purest violet dawn, and try to appreciate the wondrous beauty of their radiant colours. As clever as we think we are, we can't touch these colours, accurately reproduce their vivid hues on canvas, or even attempt to create such magnificent natural vistas. We can only ever be passive observers of the beauty and majesty contained within the magnificent natural world.

Even the very thought of how these scenes are perceived by the 'mechanics' of the human eye is incredible. After receiving millions of vibrations of light, the nerves and cells of the eye convey them to the complex brain which, when linked to something mysterious called the mind, is able to translate them and present them as images to our sight.

The very thought of trying to create these intricate processes almost takes our breath away.

And the next time you sit down to eat, remember the planet where your food came from. Visualise your mighty Mother, the Earth, as she ceaselessly turns on her unseen axis, revolving to a mathematically precise time-scale while remaining invisibly suspended in space, and all the while being lit by an ever-radiant sun which has burned its energies for countless millions of years, without mankind lifting one finger to aid these natural phenomena.

If the very thought of bringing into being these wonders isn't enough to indicate to us the presence of a Mighty Creator, then let's think again about Nature – and as the seasons follow one another with unbroken regularity, let us try to comprehend the origin and blessing of life-sustaining rainwater as it quenches the grateful crops we've planted. Even with all of his current scientific prowess, man cannot manufacture the raw materials from which water, or the seeds of our foods, originated.

Nor can he sculpt the living forms known as trees, or mould with his hands the multifarious oxygen-generating plants, perfumed flowers, or even one single blade of bright green grass. These wonders exist entirely independent of man's will, and it's certainly beyond his power to create them or to bless them with that strange and mysterious pulsing gift called Life.

Then stop awhile and be awestruck by the power and unbridled energy of the Earth's great oceans as they incessantly ebb and flow; these tides have perpetually moved through countless millennia: their waves were lapping sandy shores long before mankind came into being, and they'll continue to bathe this little planet long after he's left it.

And since time began, man has been puzzled by, and yet still he contemplates, such immense issues as the origin of his conscious awareness, and the mysteries of time and thought, and even by what could be the force that keeps his heart beating – but final conclusions are still beyond his grasp...

And when next someone holds you so close that you can feel the warmth of their breath on the nape of your neck, and the beating of their heart as it mysteriously and spiritually conveys to you its deep and wonderful power of love, the explanation as to how this is occurring will still evade you.

But the wonder of it all is this: we are aware of these experiences, and can enjoy these inexplicably thrilling emotions and ecstatic feelings as they resound somewhere unseen, deep inside the centre of our souls, in the very heart of our innermost selves.

Let us then be thankful for the shining jewel of consciousness which has been given to us so freely and mysteriously, and which grants us this awareness of our thoughts and feelings.

And here are some more challenging questions to those who still do not believe in a Creator God:

Is there someone amongst you who, simply by taking thought, could bring into being out of thin air any one of these remarkable manifestations?

Stand up the man who can snap his fingers and instantaneously create a parallel universe to our own, and then fill it with multifarious forms of life and radiant energy.

Name the clever scientist who has the power to bless inanimate forms with the mystery of a Living Mind.

And who among us can fully explain the depth of our feelings as experienced in the presence of freedom truth, beauty and love?

Is there one person alive who is capable of governing, with perfect mathematical precision, a mighty universe so vast that human beings cannot even see the 'end' of it?

Man remains silent...

There is no one who can accomplish any of these incredible feats.

Man, who considers himself to be intelligent, is unequivocally governed (and stunned into silence) by the majesty of every one of these miraculous powers.

Man can only try to understand the power of the Pure Consciousness that resides within him, and seemingly also 'outside' of him. Man can only realise that, in truth, he cannot of himself create anything – he can only adapt what has already been created.

These are humbling thoughts.

Against this background of seemingly impossible challenges and astounding feats, it's easy to see why countless human beings have acknowledged their humble position in this universe. And it's easy to see why billions of people have willingly embraced the existence of some kind of Creator-God.

Yet, because of the immensity of the concepts we've been discussing, man has often misunderstood this Cosmic Power, which could be the reason why he has so often misrepresented it. The Great Spirit of Life has been frequently belittled and grossly degraded by man's tiny imagination.

In his ignorance, man has obscured the Essence of God with futile rituals, stifling creeds and unnecessary dogmas; he has used his limited thought to create the idea of a 'universal human father', in order to ease his own sense of insecurity.

But behind all this, the Eternal Spirit has unerringly continued unfolding and evolving through the expression of His Consciousness-Being.

Untarnished, unbroken, and unchanged by the feeble imaginings of mankind, He forever expresses His omnipotent Creative Will, regardless of what human mentality has ever believed or has ever done.

Countless mortals have been 'born', have 'lived', and have then transformed their energies and have 'died' — but God, the Supreme Power, in His magnificent vast universe has remained in existence, slowly evolving and functioning in perfect balance and blissful harmony.

Some parts of the Spirit of God have advanced further towards Perfection than others, further towards Perfect Love and Perfect Thought, but other parts of His Spirit – that is: mankind, the animal kingdom, and other life-forms in the world as we know it – are still struggling along, desperately trying to catch up with, and then to emulate, the more advanced parts of God's Spirit.

And this is the reason why there is evil in the world: the whole of mankind has not yet advanced enough to express the natural compassion that is already being radiated by the more Perfect parts of God's Spirit.

To conclude this glimpse into God and His existence, I would like to record my own part-mystical, semi-scientific personal view of what I consider to be the true nature of our Creator; only this time, when referring to the Eternal Presence I shall address 'Him' more correctly, I believe, as 'It':

The Great Spirit is an eternal all-pervading Life-force.

God is the One Life, the Only Power, the One Mind, the Single Energy; the One from out of which have sprung the Many, which are forever

contained within the boundless Infinity of the
One.

God is the Everything, and the Nothing; God is
the Absolute. It is an omniscient, omnipotent,
omnipresent entity of Pure Consciousness that is
not bounded by any limitations of time or space,
for It has created' these 'illusions' within Itself.

It exists within, through, and around everything
that we know, and everything which, as yet, has
eluded our discovery.

All universes are held within the Mind of the
One, and they, plus all other things which exist, or
vibrate and manifest Life within them, are
thought-forms 'created' by Its evolving Consciousness; and these thoughts are held within Its
Image-Making Mind and within Its Feeling Spirit.

No life-form could exist anywhere, in any
universe, unless it had first been 'born' within, or
had 'evolved' itself out of, the Spirit of the One.

God conceived us: we belong to God.

We are Children of God.

The Great Spirit is our Father and our Mother,
and It is personally involved in each of our lives;
a portion of Its Spirit is beating within our very
minds and hearts.

God is an androgynous power that holds within
It the thought-forms of both sexes, the male and
the female, and each manifestation of Life possesses 'positive' and 'negative' aspects of energy
simply because it was 'born' within the Essence
Itself.

God is vibration and movement: sound and
silence; stillness and activity; all darkness and all
light; all beauty and all ugliness; all depth and all

shallowness: the Spirit of God consists of duality.

Both Destruction and Creation are held within Its Power, as is the ability to Sustain life.

God is a Living Experience.

Our Primal Source is filled with sensation, sensitivity, awareness, emotion, thought and mind, and can best be described as Pure Consciousness — as can all of Its manifestations, which are but pale reflections of Itself.

Even seemingly insentient objects possess the gift of Life.

The Pure Consciousness is in a state of perpetual evolution and unfoldment, and therefore all life-forms, which are continuously functioning within The Infinite Presence, are slowly helping It to evolve Itself by developing their passionate natures through the experiences granted to them by the One who is All.

It accelerates Its evolution by experiencing the personal circumstances of every life, by experiencing all of the suffering, as well as all of the joy, which each soul contributes to Its Parent.

Such character-building experiences encourage all of God's creatures to diligently seek, and then to eventually find, Its central Divine Spark, which is a Power that is embedded deep within them.

Man's spirit is struck from a Divine Spark of God's Spirit; he has been 'thought into being' within his Parent, and consequently will feel drawn to 'return' into what he considers to be his true home: the 'Perfection' of his Creator.

Man is constantly travelling towards self-realisation, and it is only through this process that God's Presence may be made known to him:

he must realise God within his mind, and establish within his thoughts a deeper and more personal awareness of his Creator's Spirit.

Throughout eternity we will express the will of this Supreme Spirit in each of our existences, and we will forever seek a closer union with It, and try to gain a fuller understanding of Its Parenthood and of Its beneficent Healing Power.

The Great Spirit is the governor of all worlds, within and without, visible and invisible. God is the arbiter of all destinies, and It achieves this guidance through Its own immutable natural laws which govern every facet of existence, everywhere.

These all-embracing, unalterable rulings are so mathematically precise in their operation that every Cause will undoubtedly produce its exact and corresponding Effect, which becomes — in its turn — yet another Cause; and this process will continue into Infinity.

Through the Law of Attraction (Like Attracts Like), It ensures that the circumstances for conflict, challenge, and therefore for soul-growth, are drawn within the orbit of each of Its creations, attracted there by God's own Thoughts, which are living within the life-form itself, in order that The Parent might evolve. (For example: Love attracts Love; Fear attracts Fear.)

If we align ourselves correctly with the universal laws we will obtain harmony (or ease) within our composite being; but conversely, our misalignment will result in disharmony and disorder (or disease). And these universal laws cannot be defied or abrogated, or overruled.

The Infinite Central Mind cannot be persuaded through any kind of 'vicarious atonement' to comply with our finite human desires, which are merely smaller expressions of Itself; but our prayers may be answered by some of Its other discarnate spirit-world denizens, or by other life-forms, or by us ourselves, according to Its all-powerful Creative Will.

God's Creative Will constantly manifests Itself by operating through Its laws in every plane of life: in the physical, emotional, mental and spiritual planes of being.

The One expresses Its Will and manifests Its Power by continuously pressing through the thoughts and feelings of the Many, no matter where they exist.

Its Will will be done on Earth, as it is in Heaven.

Because mankind is forever linked to the One First Cause, to the Great Spirit of Life, opportunities to spiritually evolve within the Parent are forever available to him, and also to all of God's other creations, which includes the souls in the animal kingdom.

We are in God, and God Is in us.

We are Children of the One Light.

The Infinite Spirit of Consciousness-Being is our First Cause and our Last Effect; It is the All that ever Was, that Is now, and It is everything that ever Will Be.

The Spirit of God is our One Reality: It is our Fullness and our Emptiness; and we cannot be where the Divine Presence is not.

The Great Spirit Is the Alpha and the Omega – the Beginning and the End.

258

And this is the One Living God.

We Belong to the Stars

From ancient stardust we are made:
   galaxy-children birthed afar;
   mentalities castawayed,
   invisible to the naked eye,
   uncountable, unweighed,
yet beating like the heart of an avatar
as every life-note's played.

We belong to the stars, you and I,
fashioned by Living Breath long-since:
   from a timeless nothing
   sprang liquid thought
   which breathed and burned
   genetic fingerprints.

An Infinite Spirit exploded Its Mind:
dispersing suns and sentient clouds;
   warming blood and sprinkling souls
   as stardust gifts
   through hands of stone
   and hearts of flint.

From only One came the All that Is:
an Oversoul breathed out Its Thought;
   and back to Alpha we must return —
    heartaches,
     journeys,
      starlight dreams –
       from beginning to end
        the soul will yearn.

Stephen O'Brien

15

Heal Yourself
with Light and Colour

'The Great Spirit, God, is filled with Light and Vibration which will heal your complete being,' said the spirit doctor's gentle voice, late one evening as I sensed several Other-World visitors standing around my bed.

This experience happened at a time when my nervous energies had been depleted by excessive touring and too much mediumistic work.

And the spirit doctor was perfectly correct: after carefully following his instructions and drawing upon the radiant Light-force, exactly as he'd suggested, powerful vibrations penetrated every fibre of my being and replenished my body's energies, which then set me on the road to perfect health again.

You, too, can heal yourself with light and colour.

Because regenerating light-waves are continuously radiating from the vibrant Essence of the Living God, they're ever available to us.

Untold hidden Power resides within your psychic being and displays Itself in a personal radiation of dazzling multi-coloured lights, which are known collectively as the human aura; and much has been written about these auras, these electromagnetic fields of energy which surround all living and, seemingly, inanimate things. In fact, extraordinary photographs of everyday objects (ranging from loaves of bread to keyfobs) have revealed remarkable psychic images which show 'forked-lightning' sparks radiating from them. These pictures, taken by the method known as Kirlian photography, are so commonplace now that they've even appeared in popular magazines and daily newspapers.

Not surprisingly, when a spiritual healer's hands are photographed with a Kirlian camera, the pictures obtained are far more impressive, and the brightly coloured sparkling lights extend much further than normal into the surrounding atmosphere – and they're extremely vibrant, which reinforces the idea that healers are tapping into, and then channelling, some of the Cosmic Power.

One man who pioneered a way of seeing some of these soul-lights was Dr Walter John Kilner (BA, MB Cantab.) who joined the staff of St Thomas's Hospital in London in 1869 and worked there as a surgeon and physician. His main interest was in electrotherapy treatments and he was appointed director of the then innovative X-ray department. But he caused a world sensation when he formulated the Kilner Screen, through which some of the lower-frequency human auric lights could be viewed.

His fascinating research was published in 1911 in a popular book called *The Human Atmosphere*, which, because of its success, is still available today. If you want to further your studies of these

fascinating subjects, your local library will probably stock books about Kirlian photography and Dr
Kilner's discoveries.

Cosmic Light and Sound consist of *vibrations,*
and therefore these energies are at the very root
our existence: the Spirit, or Life-force, of everything feeds upon them; and without these vital
emanations, nothing could exist.

Perhaps the most visible of these universal
power-supplies is our own sun. Its energy re-
sources are immense and its vibrant light helps to
give birth to, and then to regenerate, everything on
Earth. The sun is the ultimate source of all our
physical power (and a part of our spiritual power,
too), without which no life-forms could have
evolved on Mother Earth. So it's hardly surprising
that ancient man worshipped this mysterious and
glowing orb.

But hidden within the sun's health-giving energising rays are much more essential but 'invisible'
forces, which can be seen clairvoyantly.

Furthermore, our bodies, both physical and
spiritual, are continually absorbing these essential
psychic emanations: there's a mighty reservoir of
vibrating energy freely available to us, and all we
need to do is to more closely attune ourselves to it.

Later on, I'll be sharing a simple 'healing by light'
exercise with you.

But first: why do we need this alternative health
therapy? Well in many respects, today's humans
live unnatural lives: in our modern world we are
surrounded by thick concrete walls that keep out
God's regenerating sunshine; and through the
pursuit of money, many people feel trapped inside

a hectic, hyper-stressful rat-race that puts pressure on them to buy the latest luxuries as well as the basic necessities.

Added to this, there's the considerable stress of bereavement which, because of man's ignorance of the laws governing life after death, can adversely affect his mental and emotional health; a fuller knowledge of the universal law of survival after death would undoubtedly help him to cope much better with the painful loss of a loved one.

The psychic vibrations of grief, which are often seen by clairvoyants as dark grey clouds of gloom and despondency in the aura, can throw the whole physical body into disharmony. Bereaved people often punish themselves through their own self-pity, which is exactly what a great deal of grief is revealed to be (when truthfully examined, after all their tears and emotions have dried up).

But the certain knowledge of an eternal life allows people to wish their departing loved ones well and gives them the freedom to graciously let them go, in the full knowledge that although their familiar physical presence can never be replaced, their souls live on.

The problem of grief arises because it has its root in the emotional centre of man's ego-self, in the part of man's mind that is known as the bodily consciousness, which, because of its sole interest in its existence in the physical world, asks, 'What am I going to do now?' or states, 'I feel lonely and empty inside — I can't go on living,' etc.

Although these are quite natural reactions to a painful loss, when objectively examined these statements have no real truth in them.

These fears are centred in the ego-self, or in the 'I-thought', which is the major cause of nearly all of man's physical, emotional, mental and spiritual disorders.

The I-thought is the most easily registered portion of the conscious mind, and it springs out of, and is intimately connected to, the material body. It is the I-thought that gives rise to physically-centred emotions and desires such as: *I want, I must have, I am happy, I am sad* — plus a multitude of other emotions, including those felt during the grieving process as mentioned above.

The I-thought is a mind-mechanism that tricks the soul into believing 'I am actually this physical body' — when, in fact, you most certainly are not: you are a soul, registering *through* a physical body.

You are much greater than your body, you are limitless Consciousness, and none of the I-thoughts can apply to the fundamental parts of you; that is: to your Mind and your Spirit, which are your eternal aspects that transcend all the impermanent phenomena of the physical world.

When seeking health it is important for us to remember that any serious disturbances in the mind and emotions will undoubtedly mirror themselves as illnesses in our physical bodies.

Bodily illness (disharmony), and bodily health (harmony), are often caused by mental and spiritual soul-conditions.

To attain health, man needs to balance all the subtle life-forces of his body, mind and spirit.

Just look at what we punish ourselves with today: our foods are chemically grown, unnaturally prepared, fast-frozen, or boiled so much that every ounce of goodness evaporates long before they reach our stomachs. They also contain several chemical additives, which health-conscious people avoid like the plagues they might well be.

On deeper esoteric levels, 'dead' meat also contains toxins from the slaughtered creature's system and the psychically impregnated horror of its frightening death, which is powerfully impressed within every cell — this negative energy remains psychically 'alive' in the tissues, and it can then become 'programmed' into the human body that consumes it.

For the same psychic reasons, no spiritual healer would advise anyone to wear animal fur. But even man-made clothes today are tightly-woven to block out from our skins as many revivifying sunrays as possible.

Common tapwater is chemically treated, and the air we breathe is so badly polluted in some countries that it showers down as yellow acid rain which is strong enough to rust iron lampposts and mark the paintwork on cars.

On top of all this, billions of people worry needlessly about things that shouldn't concern them at all, which often gives rise to deep soul-anxiety, which in turn prevents them from obtaining rejuvenating and restful deep sleep.

And each morning, all over the world, alarm bells ring and rudely wake up millions of people, then propel them into a highly stressful, helter-skelter rat-race to undertake jobs they really don't want to do, but feel that they must do, in order to earn their daily bread.

Then there's the different kind of suffering and

misery of all those who've been made unemployed because of struggling economic systems: many such folk are left wondering how on earth they're going to financially support their families.

A poor diet, bad hygiene, sluggish constipation, gluttony and overweight cause people further health complications. Another two problem areas are smoking and drinking; but despite government health warnings about the dangers involved in these life-threatening habits, millions still insist on daily destroying their physical health and well-being.

Other disturbances, such as the stresses within emotional relationships, cause people immense problems, too: these are far too numerous to list, but worthy of mention here is sexual frustration.

The sex-drive is powered by a vital life-force, which, if not adequately expressed, can cause serious imbalance in anyone's life.

People create all these problems (and many more) directly or indirectly, and yet they can't understand why they don't feel too good!

It's a living wonder that some people still have the strength to draw breath, let alone to be healthy in today's crazy society, which, I'm afraid, is sick – some have even said 'rotten', and it's hard to disagree with them.

When illness strikes people down, they tootle off to the doctor begging him to make them well again when, in fact, gaining and maintaining wellbeing is their own personal responsibility. But, sadly, we seem ever ready to lay the blame for our ill health at anyone's feet, except our own.

So what's the answer?

Is there anything we can do to start realigning ourselves with the natural laws of health and harmony again?

Well, yes there is.

We can start by studying all of the above mentioned points, and then correcting them.

I must also stress that physical exercise is a great health boon. I take a good deal of it, both in a multigym and in rigorous aerobics classes. There's nothing like working up a sweat two or three times a week for a few hours, trimming off the fat and building up the muscle, and getting fit at the same time. After all, exercise is one of the body's natural ways of cleansing itself.

Even if you're elderly, or aren't as mobile or able-bodied as others, gentle physical movement will improve your blood's circulation and maintain your body's efficiency. I know a few people who are wheelchair-bound, but they keep themselves trim by daily exercise of their upper torsos.

My own routines, in addition to a vegan diet and no alcohol, have kept me in radiant health; I'm now at my ideal weight, carrying little excess fat: my lungs and heart are healthy, and I've never smoked in my life.

Every health-conscious person knows that two of the nastier side-effects of being too heavy for your height and build are heart disease and blood pressure difficulties, and if we're honest most of us will admit to eating more food than we need. But vast numbers of people still ignore this basic law of health, and they keep digging their graves with their teeth.

I feel sure everyone would benefit by taking a

one-day liquid fast every so often, or by going on a short liquid diet to help purify their body's toxin-laden tissues. Why not be sensible: ask your doctor for advice and then get started on a healthier life style from today onwards.

If your body could speak to you, I wonder what it would say? In over ninety per cent of us it would probably scream for mercy at the top of its voice.

But are we listening?

Your body is the temple of your spirit, the vehicle through which you express yourself in this world: it's *your* temple and the upkeep of its health is *your* responsibility.

To help you to achieve optimum health, you can obtain much self-help literature from your doctor or from reputable websites on the Internet; so, I'm going to concentrate now on alternative corrective therapies, on some help that you may not be able to get at your local surgery. I'd like to highlight some of the simple esoteric (or hidden) aspects of health contained in the wonderful healing properties of light and colour.

Spiritual healers like myself place implicit trust and faith in the curative effects of light and colour, simply because we've had them proved to us so many times. But we're not alone in this belief: today, even the medical profession recognises that light, and hence its reflection — colour — radiate amazing healing properties that were previously ignored by modern medicine.

For example, scientific research has shown that when people suffering from angry mental distur-bances or deep-seated emotional traumas are placed in a room bathed in violet light, they become strangely calm, and sometimes they fall asleep.

Whereas this might surprise many people, healers have always advocated the use of violet light for quietening the mind, for these energy-rays vibrate at the top end of the visible light and colour spectrum and are often known to produce a light-headed and sometimes 'silencing' effect in the mind. This is why sunbathing with an ultraviolet (UV) lamp can be harmful if undertaken in prolonged doses: people can easily fall asleep and get badly burned from over-exposure to these violet rays.

I remember when I got home after one stressful tour, I stripped off, put on a violet-coloured knee-length T-shirt and wore nothing else all day. By that same evening, its powerful colour effect had calmed me down and fully 'balanced' my systems.

Nowadays, even hospitals are realising the importance of healing by colour and are redecorating their drab grey or white wards in much brighter shades to cheer up the patients' senses.

Such livelier energy-vibrations have been proved to encourage speedier recoveries, and this is good news, for, as with any spiritual healing or other alternative therapy, light and colour treatments should go hand-in-glove with conventional medicine, and not be exclusively replaced by them.

But before we can try to heal ourselves with light and colour, we need a basic understanding of exactly what these terms mean, and only then can we correctly use them to promote good health:

Light

Light is an energy waveform that is radiated by luminous bodies, and these vibrations are conveyed through the invisible ether of space in waves that spread out and travel at the phenomenal rate of approximately 186,000 miles per second.

The seven colours of the rainbow are frequently called the primary colours, but in a stricter sense the primary colours of light are really three, and these are: red, green and blue-violet.

However, if you mix these three shades of light in the right proportions they'll produce white light.

You can see the print on this page because the paper absorbs every kind of light-wave *except* the ones that are 'vibrating' at the same rate as the particles that form the creamish tint of the paper, and those of the black ink: these two light wavebands are reflected away — which is why you can see their colours and read these words.

Colour

Colour is the name given to identify the various sensations with which light at different rates of vibration affects our eyes.

Think for a moment of a red rose: it's a mass of vibrating atoms of physical matter which is absorbing every kind of light-wave except those of the lower-frequency red vibrations; so these are reflected back off its surface and into our eyes, and we then recognise these wavelengths as the colour red.

In terms of colour pigments, there are again

three primary colours, but this time they are: red, blue and yellow — and these can't be produced by mixing together any other colours that you can think of. However, by blending together these three primary colours, many other tones and shades can be obtained.

The crux of understanding light and colour is this: *everything is vibrating*.

Light and colour can heal us because, just like them, we are also a form of 'spirit life-force' (or soul-matter that is in a state of constant vibration) and this is the common connection that links everything together.

Colour and light, and sound and vibration — they're all basically made up of the same moving and 'alive' spirit energy.

Also in common with light and colour, each part of our physical bodies is a group of atoms that is vibrating at varying frequencies: flesh and bone are two different types of tissue that have different consistencies because their atoms are vibrating at slightly different speeds.

Everything that is us — the mind, the soul, and the body — is continuously vibrating, and therefore all other vibratory fields can, and most definitely do, affect us. If you doubt this, just think again of how the sun's rays can burn your naked skin; and what is sunlight but *energy-rays in vibration* which, when shining on your body, affect the rate of vibration of the particles of your skin at the point where the two meet.

We feel warmth because the atoms of the sun's energies are quickening our skin particles.

And the same principles apply to colour: if you

stand in a room painted in a deep-red rose colour you'll be bathed in the light-frequency known as red, and this low rate of vibration will certainly affect you when it meets the vibrations of your body, mind and spirit.

Everything in the universe is interconnected and nothing is really independent of anything else.

The properties of light and colour influence the vibratory state of every particle of us, and therefore they can dramatically affect our state of health and wellbeing.

Light can either aid or hurt us.

Sunlight is beneficial in sensible doses, but concentrate it into laser light and it can kill.

In medicine, 'post-operative shock' is a rather nasty side-effect caused by the misuse of light during major surgery — but I can offer the medical profession some simple, light-therapy advice to alleviate these effects: the intense white lights in operating theatres are one of the main causes of this condition. White light is so highly active — so full of powerful energy vibrations which contain all the colours of the visible spectrum within them (as a simple glass prism experiment reveals) — that it can regenerate and also excite protoplasm, which can psychically disturb the delicate balance of tissue-structures and sensitive organ cells in the body's darkest recesses, which have never before 'seen daylight'.

If surgeons illumined their patients in a mid-green light, post-operative shock would be reduced because the colour green falls right in the middle of the known spectrum and therefore it promotes a balancing and harmonising effect.

In essence, we human beings are made up of light, sound and vibration, and these energies can either be our saviours or be our destroyers. Rightly understood and correctly applied, light-therapy could stabilise all aspects of our physical and psychic being.

But wrongly intensified and incorrectly applied, as in the case of a powerful laser warhead, light can physically destroy us.

That's why it's so important to choose the right colours to wear next to your skin. The wrong colour-frequencies may lower your vibratory fields (and possibly aggravate any medical condition you might have), but sensible and carefully selected colours could radiate more positive energies, which can help to correct or promote general good health.

Chromotherapy (colour and light treatment) can have a profound and direct, esoteric (or hidden) effect on all the visible and invisible bodies of man.

The cosmic properties of light, colour and sound penetrate the psychic being to its deepest levels and can create harmonious vibrations within the spiritual matter that makes up the complex set of inner soul-bodies, which every one of us possesses. By mentally visualising selected light rays and then psychically drawing them into yourself through your willpower, you may recharge and harmonise not only your soul, but also your body, mind and spirit.

Harmony creates health and ease; disharmony creates disorder and dis-ease.

Here are some general guidelines on what kind of effects colour and light might induce when either light rays or coloured clothes are placed within the vibratory fields of your aura.

The Principal Light and Colour Shades and their Possible Effects

Red: stimulating
Orange: vitalising
Yellow: quickening
Green: harmonising
Blue: peace-inducing (pain-healing)
Indigo: purifying
Violet: silencing
White: regenerating

Other Popular Colours

Black: strengthening
Grey: neutralising
Rose-pink: soothing
Brown: stabilising

In the above list, the seven colours of the visible spectrum are placed in rising order: from red, which has the lowest vibratory rate, ascending to the violet rays, which possess the highest frequencies.

A quick glance shows what effect each colour might bring; it's then a simple matter of wearing that shade, or shining that colour of light, over the areas where you feel treatment is necessary.

For long-lasting benefits, why not treat yourself to some daily colour-healing therapy by redecorating your surroundings?

Pay particular attention to your bedroom because

one third of your body's life will be spent in being bathed by its colour vibrations. Remember: even in a totally darkened room the colours will still psychically vibrate.

Choosing your colours, of course, is a very personal decision, and what works for some people might not work for others; so try some experimentation. But keep in mind that while it's true to say that each colour can have a different effect in the realms of emotion, soul, and mind, etc, the basic meanings of each colour remain roughly the same.

I'd advise you to stay with your chosen hue until you can feel the benefits of the treatment for yourself.

Remember, too, that each colour also possesses a *negative* effect, and that this usually radiates from its darker and muddier tones; so it's quite important to choose the brighter, more positive and pleasant shades for your treatment, and to avoid the more garish and brash tones.

For me to give this subject the breadth and depth it deserves I'd need to write a complete book about it, of course, but here are some of the main and more widely accepted qualities of the positive colours and their possible beneficial effects:

Imagine that a man has one broken leg. Under the plastercast his muscles will daily lose some of their strength through lack of use. His encased muscles are nothing more than a mass of physical matter vibrating at lower frequencies than his normal leg's muscles, which are more active, fitter and healthier, and therefore their vibratory rate is faster. To clairvoyant vision these two sets of muscles will show marked differences in the psychic colours (or vibrations) they're radiating into the man's aura.

In order to regain an efficient vibratory rate, the weaker set of muscles will obviously need exercise, coupled with a sufficient intake of proteins and vitamins, but they can also be helped towards regeneration by colour treatment.

The colour of the white plaster and bandages is in itself a regenerating hue, but, in addition, the man could wrap a red cloth around them to stimulate tissue renewal; then after a while, he could exchange this for an orange-coloured cloth to help to revitalise his cells.

The slower vibrations of his weak muscles would eventually 're-attune' themselves or 'speed up' their frequencies to approximate the vibrations of the orange light-waves; and this would aid the man's body to use its proteins and nutrients to rebuild his tissues. Eventually, harmony could be re-established and maintained by using a green cloth or by bathing the injured area in green light-waves, until full activity and health is restored.

There's a great deal we can do to help ourselves whenever we're ill; we should keep in mind that everything has an influence on us, whether seen or unseen — it's as simple as that.

If you have arthritis in the legs, then why don't you choose some green clothing to try to balance out the vibrations in those regions?

Or if you suffer from a nervous debility, or are 'highly strung', then why not select a light-blue garment to generate a sense of peacefulness over your solar plexus? Your solar plexus is situated just above your navel, and it's recognised as the seat of the central nervous system; and there's also an important psychic powerpoint over that region.

The shades you select from the list, of course, must be alive and bright, and not be dismal and dingy, for the very dark and murky hues can often have an adverse effect on you because they don't convey as much positive power or vibration as the higher tones do.

As a general rule: the lighter the shade, the higher the vibration, and therefore the more beneficial the effect will be.

Negative colour shades can do us the grossest disservice. I once helped a young man who had a long history of mental illness and nervous depression, and when another healer and I called at his modest flat we were appalled by its décor.

The confined rooms were dark and dingy, and were daubed with low-frequency, miserably drab and murky colours: there were muddy browns, blacks and depressing clashes of cloudy purple-reds in abundance. None of the colours mixed, matched, or complemented one another, and the overall effect was one of confusion, garishness and misery; and these disharmonious vibrations affected him every day.

The state of this man's mind had unquestionably projected itself outward and reflected itself in the depressing colours with which he'd chosen to surround himself.

I now have an amusing picture of you lowering your book and furtively glancing at the walls out of the corner of your eye!

And why not?

As a matter of interest, how do you think you and

your home fare with regard to the healing effect radiated by your décor?

Before taking a more critical look, here's another general rule which, if actioned, will help to promote harmony and wellbeing within you:

A calm and balanced mind is the cornerstone upon which a contented and healthy lifestyle is built.

It's essential to maintain an inner tranquillity if you want to achieve all aspects of good health; peace of mind and a degree of mental serenity are vital ingredients. And you must also establish equilibrium within your mind and emotions; after all, the mind controls the body, and each area of your being will reflect upon the others.

Many mystics believe that the Essence of God, The Great Presence, can be located in many virtues but that the realisation of God beats in Absolute Stillness; and that if we wish to know peace, our own mentality should harmonise with this essence of tranquillity, because we're forever linked to this Eternal Mind.

Show me someone who doesn't worry, who takes regular exercise, both physically and mentally, rests and eats well and sensibly; someone who loves the silence and also listens to finely orchestrated music; someone who delights in the beauty of poetry and in the challenge brought by new and invigorating thoughts, and enjoys the majestic tranquillity generated when appreciating the powerful psychic energies of the countryside; someone who has a sensitive heart which has a true understanding of the feelings and thoughts of others, and therefore acts accordingly with graciousness;

show me someone who does everything in moderation and who is as happy in his own company as he is when in a crowded room; someone who is thoughtful and kind, and who is therefore rendering selfless service to others; someone who truly loves others unconditionally, enough to let them go, and set them free, if necessary; someone whose character contains the good soul-qualities of patience, toleration and compassion, empathy and sympathy for all, which includes love for those creatures who inhabit the animal kingdom, and therefore he doesn't poison his body and degrade his soul by eating flesh foods; someone who expresses a genuine respect for everyone's right to speak, think, and act freely, and who has purged all the negativity of bitterness, regret, anxiety, and hatred from his own soul — and I'll be proud to shake the hand of a healthy human being.

But how many such people do you know?

More importantly, are you such a person?

Now here's the simple light-therapy visualisation exercise I promised you earlier. I hope it will help you to alleviate the crippling effects of stress, or pain, and that it may promote general good health and balance in the four main areas of your being: in the physical, emotional, mental, and spiritual aspects of yourself.

The pressures in my own public life are sometimes so immense that I've often used this, or a similar, visualisation technique to re-establish peace and strength within me.

It's quite easy to do; it's safe and beneficial, and it can be practised at any time of the day or night. To get a full grasp of its format it's best to study it well first — and then, why not try it out? You might be surprised by the results.

A Basic Light and Colour Therapy Visualisation Exercise
for Promoting Balance in Body, Mind and Spirit

Sit entirely alone, in comfort, and preferably in a semi-darkened or low-lit room.

Whatever your situation, make sure you won't be disturbed: put out the cat or dog, cover the budgie's cage and place the telephone in a distant room; close the windows and draw the drapes, because you're going to relax...

When you feel calm, affirm to yourself by speaking out loud, 'This time is for me, and for no one else.' And then let it be so.

You can lie down if you wish, because it won't matter if you fall asleep — in fact, you'll gain more benefit if you do. Many people choose their bedroom as the ideal place to dismiss the rushing and noisy world because they feel more at ease there and better able to travel within themselves to reach a state of mental tranquillity. But it's up to you.

Loosen any tight clothing until you feel comfortable and, if you can, softly play some of your favourite classical or mystical music, very quietly in the background. It doesn't matter what piece you choose, provided that it soothes your mind and doesn't cause you unnecessary aural stress; it should sound relaxing and be able to promote within you a wonderful feeling of being utterly at ease with life, with yourself, and with everything around you — for this is the mental and spiritual state you're going to seek.

Now lie down, or sit back, and listen to the peaceful harmonies of the music; there is great healing power in sound vibrations, just as there is in light.

Gently close your eyes, shutting out the world, and with vocal positivity reaffirm to yourself again, 'This time is for me, and for no one else.'

Then be quietly aware that it's now time to bid farewell to all of your unnecessary bodily tensions — soon they must gently ebb away...

Recognise every tense muscle in your body; be fully aware of each area of tension that you can sense, and then quietly say to yourself, 'All my tensions are now floating far away from me...'

Address each part of your body, one at a time: first gently tense your feet, then instruct them to fully relax. Then, after they've released their tensions, move on to the muscles of your legs: tense them, and then relax them. Then think of your hips, waist, stomach, chest, shoulders, arms, hands, neck, head and scalp — one area at a time, and repeat the same tension and relaxation techniques.

Take plenty of time; and if you still feel tense when you've completed the set, go over it all again until you feel fully relaxed.

Pay particular attention to your stomach area (over your solar plexus), and to your neck and throat, where a great deal of tension frequently gathers.

When each part of your body is perfectly at ease and feels completely swamped by peacefulness and rest, draw in some gentle breaths, a little more deeply than you would normally.

Then, breathe much more deeply than usual, drawing your breath right down into depths of your lungs.

Then relax...

Now quietly, but positively, affirm with your voice, 'My body is relaxed and at peace with itself. Stillness and peacefulness are pervading my entire mind and being...'

And then consider visualising the following scene, which is designed to bring you the beneficial effects of colour healing:

Imagine that your mind is a pool of still water, unmoved by the breeze on a hot summer's day. Clearly see this — visualise it on the inner screen of your mind's eye. Gaze into this calm pool. Look into its clear crystal depths and notice how the small silver fish, dart to and fro at play. Put your hands into the pool and feel the velvet coolness of its refreshing waters on your fingers. Then say to yourself, 'Just like this still pool, my mind is calm; it is peaceful, tranquil and serene...'

Then, in your mind's eye, lie back on a grassy bank near the pool and gaze up at the bright blue cloudless skies above you, and especially at the white sun that shines brilliantly in the electric blueness.

And with each gentle breath you take, breathe in this white, regenerating sunlight, just as if it were air. Imagine the light as a breath of life, and breathe it deeply into your lungs.

Indraw its strength, and fill your body with its vibrant healing energy.

And when you exhale, breathe out of yourself all

your anxieties and cares — *and let them go*.

Be aware of this release of tension as you exhale. Once more be conscious of the blue sky and the coolness of the nearby water. Then breathe in the sunshine until you can see that all of your body is filled with its radiant and golden/white light.

See every atom of your body sparkling with the brilliance of the healing, regenerating light, and tell yourself, 'White light contains every colour of the rainbow. The white light is healing me, refreshing me, energising and cleansing me. I am all Light.'

Repeat this a few times until it becomes, for you, a reality.

Then languish back on the green, grassy bank and enjoy the warm sunshine, deeply sensing the quietness, tranquillity and serene calmness of the summer's day, and the restfulness of your peaceful mind, which should now be totally devoid of chattering thoughts.

Then affirm to yourself, 'I will remember this peace; I will keep it alive inside me. It will live within my life; it will remain with me in every second of every day — and nothing will disturb its healing effect.'

Acutely sense this state of deep tranquillity, and intimately bask in the peace which passes all understanding. Know it; enjoy it; be it, and again tell yourself that you'll retain its calming effect throughout your daily life.

And then, when you feel you've relaxed enough: open your eyes; gently wiggle your fingers and toes, and sit up slowly.

Come back to Earth and set about your everyday life again; but try to keep this inner stillness at the back of all your daily routines — no matter what happens.

And remember: it doesn't matter if you fall asleep during this visualisation — you will still be refreshed and will feel regenerated.

This is just one of the many simple but helpful and invigorating healing by light and colour exercises which have been with us since antiquity.

Many basic treatments like this have been passed down into the public domain, but others of a more profound and esoteric nature have remained veiled in secrecy, and have been revealed by Spiritual Masters only to their personally-known initiates who attended the ancient mystery temples of long ago.

However, much of these great souls' timeless wisdom and spiritual knowledge has thankfully been preserved and is now coming to light again in what's been described as the New Age, which is a time of Enlightenment in which the old ways are re-establishing themselves.

Man has moved out of the Age of Pisces, and into my own birthsign, the Age of Aquarius, and in this New Epoch much more of man's ancient spiritual knowledge is reappearing, slowly filtering down from the Realms of Light beyond the Earth and into today's world.

In fact, 'Light' is the term frequently applied to the spirit teachings we can receive when we're in mental attunement with wise and evolved discarnate minds.

During my countless out-of-the-body excursions I've travelled deep into many of The Kingdoms of

Light in the next world, and have been privileged to meet some of these ancient souls.

Leaving my physical body sound asleep in bed, I frequently achieved 'lucid consciousness' during my many soul-journeys, and I can clearly remember — and am now about to relate — some of the occasions when I met my spirit guide, known as White Owl, and benefited from receiving such timeless wisdom...

...from the place where stars are born and die
  comes the light that infuses the mind of man

from the centre of the heart of a cosmic soul
  comes the breath of life which beats in all

from the fathomless depths of timeless space
  comes the shadow-dance of a future now

from the tiniest speck of planetary dust
  comes the birth of a world as yet unknown

from the middle of the human spirit
  springs eternal life...

Stephen O'Brien

16

Ancient Wisdom

I

...Gradually I became conscious in my spirit body somewhere in the next world, outside what seemed to be a place of learning. When I saw hundreds of people moving up and down some marble-like steps into a huge impressive edifice, I instinctively felt this was going to be a fascinating astral journey.

The people were all dressed in different coloured robes which were created from a self-luminous spiritual light, and which seemed to be a part of themselves.

Standing beside me was my spirit friend, White Owl, resplendent in violet-coloured raiments that reached from his shoulders to the green-and-blue marble-flecked floor. I was attired in similar fashion, but my robes were of an electric blue colour.

Everything in the vicinity was so very lucid and 'alive', especially the magnificent building in front of us.

'This is one of the many Halls of Learning in this sphere,' informed my guide. 'Let us go inside.'

'Delighted,' I smiled, and we moved up the pastel blue-veined steps and into the first of several massive halls.

The walls and floor were made of some kind of cool-feeling stone, and I intuitively felt that this material had never been quarried: these premises around us had been created or 'built' by many minds.

There were no ceilings; and as I passed underneath the vast archways — they were about five hundred feet high — I noticed that the walls were open to a cloudless sky.

But before I could question this, White Owl instantly read my thoughts and answered in his own deep thought-voice, which I heard clearly within my mind, 'There is no need of roofing in a sphere where rain is unknown.'

I understood, nodded and smiled, and we walked further into the heart of the enormous hall.

Decorating the walls on either side of us were large murals, which seemed to have been hand painted, or perhaps it would be more precise to report that they 'felt' as though they'd been hand painted. The interesting scenes depicted a number of eras in man's history: some of them showed prehistoric times and contained friezes of dinosaurs and other now-extinct beasts, the like of which I've never seen on Earth.

And I remember thinking to myself, 'There must be many more old animal bones to dig up back home on Earth. Some of these species haven't been discovered yet.'

'Take care,' advised my friend, 'for too many thoughts of Earth will draw your spirit body back there quickly, and this journey will be over.'

I immediately checked myself, and changed my mind. 'Who did these?' I asked, indicating the beautiful works of art on every surface.

'They are thought-pictures, moulded, or created, by artists out of the ether which responds more directly to our thought-power than your physical matter does. These scenes are progressing upwards in time through the various ages of man, as you can see.'

Then we seemed to walk along, or rather 'float' along, further into a pale blue marble-effect room, and I was immediately struck by the change of atmosphere projected by the pictures displayed there.

'But these have transcended our current time back home,' I said, surprised to be viewing what seemed to be a part of man's future.

'And what is *current time*?' asked my bemused friend.

'Well, the late twentieth century.'

'But you did not originate in the twentieth century – that is merely your current Present. You belong here, in this world, which exists in time-lessness.'

'But I just left the late 1900s to come here for some nightly tuition.'

'So it seems, but that is not how it really is. Your physical body belongs to a certain point in the stream of time, but your Spirit cannot be contained within one time-conscious personality.'

'Yes, but–'

'Your ego — the thinking part of yourself; that which identifies itself with the personality and fleshly body known as Stephen O'Brien – this ego is speaking these thoughts, but the Greater You seems to be silent. The real You is an intrinsic part of for ever.'

I understood what he meant, but clarified it further by asking, 'Are you trying to show me how these pictures of man's future were created?'

'Yes. The time-stream can be met by an incarnating spirit at any point which it has earned the right to touch. But these artists are not fleshly, and are merely copying what seems to you to be man's future. To them, however, it is an ever-present Now because they can touch the time-stream wherever and whenever they wish: they are not limited by clumsy physical vision, and their minds can span eternity.'

'We've discussed this before,' I said, 'that the future, the past and the present are all happening now, together, simultaneously, but people who are "trapped" on Earth in a three-dimensional physical world are only aware of a small portion of their consciousness, which they consider to be their Present.'

'Yes, and here on these walls is a glimpse of what, for you in the twentieth century, is yet to come. But these images will imprint themselves on your mind, Stephen, because we'd like you to share some of them with others.'

I nodded, then gazed more intently at one of the horrific scenes that were being projected onto the surfaces about me, a strange picture which seemed to have a certain movement and a degree of life all its own. 'These times are terrible,' I groaned. 'The destruction and carnage are vile.'

'As you see, man has a great deal more to learn. Always he tries to dominate and to destroy. Look there, and see the annihilation of these lands before us... This is the result of greed and of the misuse of political power. And here is the man whose selfish desires will be satisfied.'

And upon the wall appeared the form of an officer, whose skin was olive-brown, and whose short, swaggering body and gait radiated a sickeningly arrogant atmosphere. I took an instant dislike to everything about him. I noticed there was a large white letter 'S' on the back of his green fighting-jacket, which was set alongside some odd yellow serpent-like motif; and he carried a kind of pistol in his hands, with which he was indiscriminately shooting dying soldiers all around him on a battle-field. Each time another victim died, the self-righteous smirk on his moustached lips was frightening to witness.

'I've seen enough,' I groaned, turning my head away from the sickening bloodshed.

'Very well; let us move to the next room.'

And this we did — where much less disturbing times were being projected upon its walls.

Before my eyes now, it seemed to me that the Earth had been so badly ravaged and polluted by man that I was witnessing some future scene of rural reconstruction: hundreds of people, who were dressed almost like peasants, were busy re-structuring the peaceful but savaged countryside.

Men, women and children were tilling the soil by hand — I saw no machines — and were then placing into the earth containers of what I sensed were helpful and harmless organic chemicals. I think they contained some kind of advanced soil-medicine, which was being administered to try to re-establish the ground's fertility — for all around them in this farmland (which must have stretched out for a good hundred miles) not a single blade of green grass was growing.

I was acutely aware that the productive soil had been damaged by man's shallow scientific folly. His war weapons had raped Mother Earth and had turned her into a wasted no-man's land of shell-holes and toxic radiations, which had poisoned much of her land until she had become a dead place of no growth.

'When will all this occur?' I asked.

'After the devastation,' said my companion with a note of deep sadness in his voice, 'after the time when a manic lust for power and greed will have run riot through the minds of a small group of tyrannical men who will have sought the nations for their own. As you can see, there are three key personalities involved.' And he pointed at another surface where I perceived these three officers in counsel: one was a fighting-on-land expert, another specialised in air warfare, and the last was an expert in battle tactics of the sea. The land expert, who was known as 'the butcher', was the officer whose image I'd seen earlier.

As I listened to their vile plans for perpetrating further carnage and destruction, I slowly shook my head in disbelief; they intended to seize more land, on which they then planned to 'create a new and genetically streamlined human being'.

I was stunned into silence.

'Man has much to learn,' commented my teacher.

'He does indeed,' I sighed.

'Come, Stephen; we will move to another area...'

II

We entered a large room that was covered by some sort of transparent ceiling which, in itself, was another kind of projector-screen. Placed neatly all around the five walls were colourful couches, chairs and chaises longues. We sat on a yellow silky-covered divan, and in silence we peered up at the translucent dome.

Soon, another dozen or so students of all ages joined us, and a stillness descended and enveloped us, creating the kind of anticipation one feels in a cinema just before the film is about to start. In fact, it felt just like a night out at the movies, only we were surrounded by bright daylight.

In this gathering of varied nationalities, I sensed there were some present who held a keen interest in science; many of these people, I thought, had studied this subject on Earth, and I also 'knew' that they were newcomers to spirit life.

'Correct, on all counts,' confirmed my friend.

Strangely enough, I was aware, too, that some of these students were not yet 'dead': like me, they were out on astral excursions while their physical bodies slept, and this was another lesson in their spiritual education. In fact, I saw several spirit guides among the crowd, accompanied by their mediums; and I psychically knew that one robust young man was still attached by the silver cord of life to his fatally injured physical body, which was lying in a deep coma back on Earth.

Suddenly, the pleasant diffused light within the auditorium dimmed a little, and our attention was drawn upwards towards the dome. All at once we were looking not at a celluloid film being projected onto the ceiling, but at a breathtaking dark night sky: above us was a vibrant starlit scene which was somewhere in deep outer space, but we could see it as it was at that very moment.

My psychic awareness told me this wasn't some staged reconstruction: it was a real event, and we were gazing at this magnificent view through some kind of 'living telescope'.

'What you see is now occurring in a faraway galaxy,' said a man's deep voice, which reached us from out of no particular place – there weren't any speaker-systems, the voice just 'arrived'.

Then my guide's thoughts came to me, and I'm certain that no one else heard him say, 'There are souls out there, now, whose mind-images and thought-transmissions are being projected back here to us. And this is what you see before you. Are you fascinated?' he smiled.

'Yes,' I replied with my thoughts; and we were then presented with 'A Journey Through the Stars', in which mysterious and fiery constellations of distant universes unfolded before our gaze. It was a highly educational and scientific programme, with no further spoken commentary being delivered, but nevertheless many 'silent' facts, figures and statistical information were inwardly communicated to the listening crowd.

We learned how the galaxies and stars had been made, and how everything that exists was first conceived as a thought in the Mind of God, the Great Spirit. Each manifestation, we were told, had within it a Divine Spark that consistently encouraged it to seek a closer union with Its Essence, and to ultimately recognise its destiny. This would be accomplished — so the narrator's thought-voice said — only after humankind had progressed through aeons of spiritual unfoldment.

Each teaching point was conveyed to us by a living picture that was being projected from somewhere in a distant universe, as perceived through the eyes of the special band of spirits whose task was to illustrate this lecture.

The educational instruction placed much emphasis upon the fact that mankind would attain spiritual progression only through conquering his challenges and soul-hardships, only by plumbing deep down into his soul; and during those testing times he would discover his latent strengths and abilities. Man must overcome each hurdle in the pathway of his evolution, our instructor told us, in order that he may move ever inwards towards the attainment of ultimate spiritual Perfection, and then he'll gain more knowledge of God.

As well as being informative, this presentation was packed with excitement and it was much better than a visit to a planetarium — it was more vital and far more interesting. This was no dry and arid theoretical talk — it was compellingly 'alive'.

In fact, it was so interesting that I've no idea how long we stayed in the hall, but after the lecture concluded and we all filed out, I couldn't resist an amusing remark to my guide. 'Lovely film,' I said, 'but I didn't think much of the popcorn!'

He grinned broadly, and we passed through into another area of the Hall of Learning...

III

We soon joined another group of intelligent youngsters who were seated in an informal class, which was discussing universal religion, morality, philosophy and ethics.

Sitting quietly at the back of the tutorial we listened to their quite profound conversations, which seemed to be far beyond the normal mental capacity of ordinary sixteen-year-olds; but then spiritual development in the Beyond can take place more rapidly than it does on Earth.

As the bright youngsters threw some mind-boggling questions at their slim and youthful male teacher, White Owl must have sensed some deeper vein of subconscious thought about to surface within the group, for he leaned across and softly whispered to me, 'Listen very carefully to what transpires; it might interest you. You may not agree with all of it, but the experience could be enlightening.'

Then a stocky, short-haired lad (his hairstyle resembled a newly-shaven, brown peach) raised a new topic by discussing the spiritual teacher known as Jesus of Nazareth.

'Surely, what he meant,' he continued with youthful vigour and conviction, 'is that if someone struck you hard on one side of your face and then you hit them back, you'd be behaving no better than they were: you'd be expressing anger and releasing more of it into the world. But if you resist anger, then you'll have learned more self-control.'

'And what conclusions do you draw from that, Shaun?' asked the olive-skinned and dark-eyed teacher.

'Well, that anger begets anger, and that in the presence of this there can be no true peace and reconciliation between souls. It seems to me,' he added thoughtfully, 'that the important point here is self-unfoldment.'

'I agree,' chipped in a blonde girl, who was a very serious and studious-looking type.

Then the lecturer, whose youthful looks belied what I sensed was an ancient mind, added his own comments, 'The Nazarene's teachings had nothing to do with any set religions of the day, and neither were they intended to create new sects. His words and teachings are concerned with the Spirit, and were inspired by what some men call the Holy Ghost.'

'It was a barbaric age,' said the attentive blonde girl.

'And the people needed a concept of God that might counteract these traits,' chimed in the short-cropped youth. An invisible Father who was loving, rather than a wrathful deity, suited their minds and helped them to progress towards a fuller realisation of what the Great Oversoul Is.'

'Yes,' agreed the affable teacher, 'but the bulk of the Nazarene's teachings have barely survived on Earth; emotional dust and crippling mental dogmas, creeds and rituals have been so tightly woven around them that modern-day man often misinterprets his spiritual truths, and blots them almost from view.'

'I agree,' said the boy, as his teacher continued: 'But as I told you last time when we discussed these issues, there will shortly come a "find" of several ancient documents on Earth which will bring to light more of these pristine truths.'

'When exactly will that be, sir?' asked the blonde girl, stealing the question from my mind.

'Quite soon,' he answered calmly. 'Specialist guidance is currently inspiring several Earth-minds to uncover these relics, but it takes time to influence the slow mentalities of incarnate men and women, as you know,' he said, 'and also: the time must be right, as fixed by higher authorities. When mankind is ready, the writings will be discovered.'

A giggle rippled through the classroom, and I sensed they knew quite well that if this 'find' were to be made too early, certain men with vested interests might try to suppress the wisdom contained within it.

The lecturer continued his theme with quiet authority.

'All of Jesus's teachings were about developing the Self and realising the God within. He taught, did he not, of learning how to know and govern the character and the mind — the importance he placed on motivation and soul-intentions shines through all of his parables. By achieving soul-growth, he said, one would become aware of "the Father within".'

'But God as a father is such an outdated concept,' said the questioning girl.

'Yes, but spiritual teachings must be acceptable to

the cultural history and mode of thought of the generations who are receiving them, so that they're palatable,' answered the teacher. 'But humanity is now ready for much wider views, greater and more accurate revelations of the truth. You cannot teach a toddler the kind of pure mathematics you've learned here.'

'Well, you could,' said Shaun, 'but it's highly unlikely it would understand it.'

'Quite.'

Then another hand shot up at the back of the room. It belonged to a quiet girl of possibly fourteen, who had jet-black curly ringlets and deep brown eyes.

'May I ask why you refer to truths,' she challenged, 'because truth surely has an absolute reality only within the mental constructs and understanding of its perceiver?'

'Now there I'd have to disagree with you,' said the lecturer, 'because we can all hold *opinions*, but absolute truth is something very different — it exists no matter what we might think of it. There's a world of illusion separating these two. All the spiritual truths I've taught you in these classes have come from the stories revolving around the Nazarene and his teachings; I was a follower of his. In fact, he helped me rather a lot, but that was a long time ago now.'

There was a respectful silence amongst the group; everyone glanced at his neighbour, impressed by the humble way in which the teacher had expressed himself.

I was going to ask my guide a question, but he anticipated it and raised a silent finger to his lips and then pointed it at the man. So I stayed silent and listened intently, sensing that more interesting points were about to emerge.

The lecturer continued, 'It was never the intention of the spirit known as Jesus in that particular incarnation to create an organised religion, or to gather together a set of dogmas and creeds. What his teachings revealed were spiritual truths, and these are what must be extrapolated from the many myths and mysteries which have been built up around him by some of his over-zealous followers throughout the centuries.

'As an ordinary man, born in the normal way into a large family, but descending from the royal line of King David — and hence his title "the King of the Jews" — he became a powerful prophet and mystic.

'He was an exceptionally evolved soul, born to achieve a remarkable spiritual mission.

'Of course, the Judea of that time was under an iron-fisted Roman rule, and the Jewish nation continually prayed for a messiah — for a much-needed deliverer — who would be its prophet-king, who could wield the might of legitimate royalty and also establish the Teachings of Righteousness.

'To these ends, Jesus was trained for both roles; but his mystical and spiritual education among the Essenes, who were a band of white-robed healers living in semi-closed communities at that time, set him well on course to be hailed as their Teacher of Righteousness, which title he was eventually given.

'As an acclaimed leader of the peace-loving and scattered Essene communities, he encountered several problems with another band of political activists — the people we discussed in our last class, who were known as the Zealots, and whose prime aim was to overthrow Roman rule by brute force, with the spilling of blood if necessary, in order to cleanse the holy land and return it to God and righteousness.

'Naturally, the Zealots wanted Jesus to be their commander-in-chief, but he refused because his highly evolved soul set him against such barbaric acts.'

'He preferred the Way of Peace,' said Shaun.

'That's right. But amongst these Zealots was one known now as Judas, a dissatisfied mercenary who eventually became his life-threat, as I'm sure you know.'

'But what about the miracles, sir?' asked the curly-haired girl.

'Such signs and wonders all conform to the natural laws, and the Master perfectly understood these. We must remember that when we speak of the Nazarene and the example of his life, we are talking of an ancient being whose spiritual progression is legendary in these spheres. His body may have been that of an ordinary man, but he was certainly not an ordinary soul. In His teachings He often referred to his physical temple as "The Son of Man", and to his spirit as "The Son of God".

'And his immanent Spirit of Love is still here, in these very spheres around us. It also still lives within compassionate hearts on Earth, in souls who desire to serve any of their fellows who are in need.

'The Christ-light, as revealed through the many stories, parables and allegorical tales that have been gifted to mankind, is ever available and willing to touch and aid all those who attune themselves to it when they try to help unconditionally any other beings who might be struggling along their difficult roads of spiritual progression, out of the darkness and up into the light.

'The Christ-like beneficent healing guidance and inspirational power can reach the hearts of these people only because they've set their feet firmly on the path of service to all, for Love's sake alone.'

The whole class quietened, drinking in the depth of his implications, and the respectful silence lasted a minute or more. As for myself, I was enthralled, and was so impressed by this lecturer's obvious and transparent honesty, and with the sincere way he delivered his truths, that I wanted to stay longer and hear much more.

'But come,' said White Owl, 'there are more places I wish you to see.'

So we retired quietly, leaving the group of youngsters engaged in further vigorous, healthy and open-minded debate, which centred on whether or not religious organisations were needed on Earth.

I commented to my friend as we left, 'Their teacher was a very kind soul,' I said, 'and he seemed to know a great deal about the Master's teachings and ancient Judea. What's his name?'

'They call him Paul,' said my friend, as we walked on to our next port of call...

17

Silent Sentinels

I

...From within an all-engulfing blackness, my psychic vision suddenly faded into consciousness just as my guide and I were standing together in a bright spirit sphere somewhere near the foot of a magnificent blue-grey mountain, down which clear crystal streams were freely running.

Gazing all around me at the majestic views of the spirit world, I had my breath taken clean away by their sublime beauty.

During this stage in our astral journey I'd regained awareness in the middle of one of our many discussions, as we were walking along a river's edge lined with rising banks of brightly coloured wild flowers.

'This is lovely,' I remember saying, breathing in the scented air.

'Yes, these borderlands between the astral worlds and the higher realms are particularly pleasant,' responded my guide. Then, after we'd enjoyed more of the glorious sights, he resumed his previous topic of mankind's gradual progress through evolution.

'For many centuries man has been losing his sense of priority. By taking refuge in self-created religions, his insecure emotions have clung for too long to a dusty and outdated past. In science he has advanced quickly, but his soul still lingers in the backwaters of spirituality, and much of the realisation of his origin and of his eventual destiny is still veiled from him, by none other than himself.'

'Is there anything I can do to help?'

'Oh yes; there is always service to perform,' he smiled, after which his brown eyes were strangely stilled, as though he were contemplating something profound, something so deep that I wasn't skilled enough to read his thoughts.

'Name it,' I said.

'First, walk with me a little way,' he replied, 'for there is something I'd like you to see.'

And we moved out over the verdant riverbank as though we were 'floating' in the air on a gentle summer breeze, and we crossed over the stream. We drifted quickly towards the opposite bank where we stood under the wide and spreading branches of a very old and friendly oak tree. I say friendly because it radiated a sense of great age and, strangely enough, a feeling of wisdom, as though it had seen and touched the countless human minds which had rested beneath it, and as if it had both experienced and absorbed their many interesting life-stories.

'This is one of my favourite places,' said my guide, leaning his bare back against the wide trunk.

Brushing a lock of long black hair from his forehead, he gazed up into the clear blue sky, as I gently sat beside him. Both of us were wearing dark blue loincloths, which allowed the sun's rays to vitalise us.

'Many people have walked and talked here,' I said, reporting my awareness.

'Many,' he echoed, 'and this ancient tree knows every one of them. I often sit here when I need to contemplate. I find these surroundings ideal when I wish to read the records.'

'What records?'

'The collective thoughts of man, the sum total of everything that has ever been, from the beginning of time as we might know it, right through to the end, they say — though I have never been able to mentally reach that point. Amongst such beauty as this, which lightens my soul, I can fully relax and glean what men once were, what their desires for their tomorrows might be, and, indeed, what some details of their future pathways might be. I have done that several times with your own life, and with mine.'

'But how? Is it something to do with the tree?'

'No, we two are just old friends, Stephen; and this area is conducive to my making such a mental effort,' he replied, patting the rough brown bark as a man might congratulate his faithful dog for retrieving a thrown stick.

There was a long, thoughtful pause while we took in the breathtaking beauty of the landscape all around us and listened to the soft rustling of the oak's leaves above us.

'May I read these records with you? Will you

show me how?'

He turned his compassionate face in my direction, and in a quiet voice said, 'Just close your eyes, and think of the sun.'

I obeyed, leaning back as we both dismissed visual contact with the countryside — and straightaway within the screen of my mind I was looking at some kind of huge and mighty multicoloured whirlwind, rotating at a very slow speed.

It was so frighteningly powerful and absolutely magnificent that the very sight of it thrilled and silenced me. I was mesmerised when I sensed its awesome living energies, which were living lights that contained within them every known rainbow colour, plus dozens of others I can't even describe because I've no words to convey their sight or feeling.

Although the tremendous cyclone seemed to be moving in ethereal slow-motion, as I watched it swirling, suspended in space a huge distance away, I intuitively knew that its true velocity was incredibly fast.

Overcome by its magnitude, I was conscious that it contained every thought that had ever been born, acted upon, spoken of, or dreamed of since the beginning of time as we know it.

This revolving power was filled with the evolution of man's mind and with every one of his feelings, as if his thoughts and ideas had been attracted to each other by magnetic forces, or by gravitation, and they were now endlessly spiralling around and around, but still living, and full of sentience and meaning.

As it thundered and sparked with intermittent

explosions of light, it seemed to instantly convey to me an immediate sense of mankind's countless heartaches and losses, his laughter and dreams, hopes, desires, black hatred and bitterness, as well as all of his unbridled anger and the pulsing of his profound human and divine love; in fact, everything he'd ever experienced...

I was humbled, captured, exalted, overawed, and struck dumb and by its eternal omniscience.

'Do you feel the power?' whispered my guide.

'Yes I do... Yes, I can see it...'

'Then gently join your mind with mine, and I'll help you to tune in to these energy-fields, because there is something I want you to experience. Be still now. Be as still as you dare, and then blend with me.'

With reverence, I eagerly obeyed his instructions to the letter and released my willpower into his care while watching the vast cyclone, and at the same time calming myself within. I seemed to occupy two states simultaneously: I was a deeply fascinated yet somehow indifferent observer of the hypnotic lights.

'What must I do now?' I questioned.

'Just be still... for not everyone possesses this skill; I shall make the effort for you — but stay with me, mentally, and you will see what I will see.'

So I remained absolutely quiet, exercising the kind of perfect trust that spirit guides request of their charges at such times. And then it happened – I was no longer viewing the whirlwind, for it had vanished, and in its place there appeared some strange scenes.

At first it seemed that I could see a distant part of

man's past, but then I realised my mistake, for into my mind there came an overwhelming awareness that the miserable pictures rolling out before me now were a part of the Earth's future, and not of its history.

Before me there sprang into view an island surrounded by grey and lifeless shallow waters. There was no blueness in the seas, and the sky was coloured fiery red; and a dense and murky yellow atmosphere pervaded everything in sight.

The sun looked like a huge, bright red balloon; it was large but swathed in misty cloud formations. Then I instantly knew there was no more life on Earth; it was a sudden realisation that man had long since become extinct, and what was now left was all that I could see: the fragile, crumbling ruins of some shattered cities scattered here and there at short distances from the seashore.

Then out of nowhere a man's deep voice seemed to say, 'It is finished: it is over. He is foolish; he is gone...'

And without warning, these scenes quickly shifted away and I saw nothing more...

My eyes were wide open and White Owl and I were once again seated under the benign oak tree. I rubbed my forehead, stunned by the tragic end I'd viewed.

'Come,' said my guide, breaking my sense of isolation; and, standing, he took my hand and all trace of sadness immediately dissolved as the image of the mighty cyclone of Collective Thought was replaced with a feeling of joy. 'Now we can go on our journey,' he said.

'Where are we going?' I mumbled, brushing

invisible cobwebs from my face and standing beside him.

'To meet some people — if indeed I can call them such — who are not from Earth at all, not from its past, nor from its regrettable future which you have just glimpsed...'

When he squeezed my hand the freshness of the flowering riverbank swiftly disappeared like early morning mist in bright sunlight, and I was immediately caught up in the spirit, and the next thing presented to my vision was the familiar background of deep outer space.

We were both moving forward at an incredible rate, travelling onwards, way up into a black night sky with planets and stars scattered all around us. It was such a welcome change from the great melancholy I'd just known and, thinking back on it now, that's probably why he'd planned this short flight.

'The Universe is so silent,' I marvelled at last, utterly overwhelmed by its peaceful grandeur, as I always am when I take these journeys through space.

'Yes...' he replied thoughtfully, 'stars are born and then they die; planets rage with power, unleashing mass destruction in atomic explosions; and yet, behind all this there remains Tranquil Stillness, apart and away from everything that moves — and this is the Spirit of God.'

'God dwells in silence,' I agreed, 'and it's impossible to escape Its all-encompassing embrace.'

He smiled and we 'flew' on — if that's the right way to describe two beings who were horizontal with their heads pointing forward towards a myriad glittering constellations.

For quite a while words were unnecessary and silence was all we needed; silence, and moments filled with visual splendour. We simply watched and experienced, and observed in wonderment the vast night sky and the transcendental beauty of the stars set in infinite blackness.

It was a wonderful experience, quite beyond description.

Then I pointed a finger towards a distant galaxy where a supernova explosion was taking place. It seemed so close that I felt I could have touched its dazzling power; but I said nothing and just indicated, and White Owl's gaze followed my arm and we beheld the disintegrating sun. Its sudden burst of energy was immense, streaming forth light, gas and debris all around it; and yet there was nothing to hear but silence — not a single physical sound reached my ears, but the sight stirred my soul...

'See there – to the right,' said my guide's thoughts, and I noticed another cluster of faraway stars within clouds of gas shaped like a horse's head, and inside this atmosphere there seemed to be a feeling of 'life' as we understand it on Earth.

'We have arrived,' he said.

And the next instant we were swiftly descending through a yellowish cloudy atmosphere above a planet. No words, I think, could accurately convey the peacefulness that surrounded everything there.

Quite quickly, we approached the firm mustard-coloured soil, which easily bore our light weight, and we breathed in the crisp fresh air, which seemed more vital than that of the higher worlds we'd recently left.

Gazing around us on all sides, I could see impressive, high green mountain ranges, and we seemed to be standing within what could have been an enormous crater; it was several hundred miles across, and we were located near its centre point.

'Where are we?'

'To give you a name would be meaningless,' he said, 'its phonetic sound would not register properly in your mind.'

'Try me,' I joked; and he did — and he was right. I can't even remember it correctly now, let alone pronounce it.

'I am taking you to meet a group of souls who have been friends of mine for a long, long time,' he said.

We then walked forward towards the dead-centre of the cavernous crater where I could see there was some kind of glass-like shaft, leading down to beneath the planet's crust. It seemed about fifty feet across, and upon arriving at this translucent, rainbow-coloured 'stepway' — memory fails me. Either I was put to sleep for a while, or possibly my mind has been blanked of information which mustn't be recorded...

II

...My consciousness returned when White Owl and I were in the middle of an impressively large, glass-like cavern, lit by a diffused but bright peach-coloured light that seemed to have no central source from which it was created. We were both standing beneath what I knew to be the surface of the same planet's crust.

Bathed in this odd light, I sensed that the atmosphere contained everything in it: like the whirlwind of Collective Thought, the very essence of hundreds of thousands of minds and characters, the memories of countless lives, and the multifarious life-stories of innumerable souls seemed to be 'living' around us in the atmosphere. That's the only way I can describe it.

'Their collective thoughts are strong, are they not?' smiled my teacher, who'd been carefully monitoring my reactions.

'Yes; but I don't know where I am,' I returned innocently, 'or what I'm registering.'

'Although this is a new experience, you have drawn the right conclusions,' he enlightened me, for he was obviously aware of my quandary.

'Be still, and tell me what you feel, Stephen.'

So I gathered my awareness and tried to sense more acutely the fine vibrations — and my findings startled me.

'Oh, I... I'm in the presence of... great wisdom,' I said, all at once humbled by this realisation.

'So you are,' he replied, his eyes glancing forward to where, just in front of us, something odd was occurring...

About six feet away — it sounds silly to give such a finite measurement, but that's what it felt like — a short distance ahead of us there came a glowing, bright yellow-and-blue cloud of self-luminous light which started to gently condense and swirl, and undulate like the soft rippling of a still pool of water after a pebble has been dropped into it.

Within this cloudy mist I could see no visible

form of a man, but nevertheless I sensed 'he' was there: this seemed to be a male presence, and he was someone very old and wise indeed. He was also someone for whom speech was unnecessary, I felt, and I assumed that this light-being, with whom we might converse, couldn't actually speak.

'Correct,' said my guide, 'but watch, and listen.'

And then, quite by surprise, a deep and resonant voice issued forth from the glowing cloud:

'Greetings again! It has been some time since we last communicated so directly with one another.'

'Far too long, my friend,' returned White Owl in his distinctive but gentle thought-voice.

The cloud-personality, on the other hand, sounded like an ancient sage whose tones were low and tremulous, as though quivering from great age.

My guide spoke by thought, but this tremendously evolved being, who I'd incorrectly felt couldn't talk at all, was in fact producing perfect objective sound.

Then it suddenly occurred to me that what I was hearing was the cloud-being's mind, and not his voice at all — yet his thoughts were so much clearer and better formed than my own or those of my companion.

Then the voice seemed to 'turn' in our direction and the column-like mist was now about two feet in front of us. It was about eight feet tall and two feet in circumference, and all the while it was softly blurring around its indistinct edges, and it didn't really hold one constant form.

Each time it spoke, small explosions of peach-coloured light flashed and then instantly dissipated in the region where the head and shoulders would have been, had it been a human form. It addressed my teacher again.

'I am glad you have come; I knew you would, and have transmitted my thoughts to that effect,' it said, and then out of the blue it suddenly *changed its voice* to that of a cultured woman's low and mellow contralto tones.

'We knew your curiosity would get the better of you.'

And then *a third voice* of a younger male spoke from it, as if answering my evident confusion:

'We are Many,' he said, 'and yet we are only One.'

Thoroughly nonplussed, I held my silence while studying this luminous misty column, which seemed to gather itself up off the ground to a height of about five feet, to form a rough circle of itself: a complete, three-dimensional, yellow-and-blue hovering sphere, suspended in the atmosphere, measuring about six feet or so across.

'I'd thought you couldn't speak,' I ventured, somewhat hesitantly.

'We cannot. We radiate thought,' said the warm-voiced woman. 'Your own mind clothes it in symbols that you can comprehend.'

'We have no language,' said the deep-voiced resonant sage, 'we have no —'

'— means of physical communication,' interrupted the young tenor-male tones. 'We are Many and —'

'— yet we are only One,' completed the sage.

'Is there something you wish me to know, or do?' I questioned, knowing that this kind of spirit experience usually has a purpose behind it.

They obviously sensed my preference to hear the cultured warm tones of the woman, for that was who replied.

'Yes,' she said, 'we have watched you for many centuries now...'

I knew she meant *mankind*: the Earth and its people, and not me personally.

'How interesting it has been to see the rise and fall of so many nations,' she continued, 'the vanities of great ruling powers, and man's scientific strides forward, towards his ultimate destruction — only to rise again like a giant flame from the ruination of bloodshed and despair.'

I maintained a humble silence, but my thoughts wouldn't keep still and I wondered if she was referring to the legendary lost continents of Lemuria and Atlantis.

'How valueless are names,' she exquisitely intoned, obviously aware of my thoughts. 'But the rise and fall will be repeated.'

Then I wondered why on Earth she was communicating this to me, and whether some 'secret' implications had somehow failed to register in my mind.

More peach lights flashed in the centre of the cloud as her gentle voice broke my train of thought.

'The rise is slowly climbing towards its zenith, but the fall this time will be great... Man has not learned. He has not —'

'— *learned*,' finished the young male's sad tones.

Gathering my senses and trying to understand, I leaned forward and addressed the living mists.

'Have you — any of you, or all of you — an

identity?' I asked.

'We are many,' replied the resonant old sage, 'and yet we are so few.'

I took it that the cloud of voices meant they consisted of one individual made up of multitudinous 'separate' personalities.

'We are in the presence of intelligence,' the woman said smilingly, as if she were grateful for some mild amusement.

But my vanity was short-lived when White Owl said, 'There is a greater purpose for our presence,' after which the Cloud of Knowing resumed speaking in the woman's tones.

'We have visited your planet many times, and sent our guidance to numerous prophets and seers. Millions of inspired men and women have been encouraged by us to march forward and progress,' she said. 'But what now concerns us most is harmony. Humankind finds itself in a state of deep disharmony.

'Man must first be in harmony with all aspects of himself (in body, mind, spirit and soul), and only then can he ever hope to achieve harmony with the rest of the universe and with other forms of consciousness.

'As with us here, consciousness can be totally aware of itself only when there is one harmonious accord between its many intrinsic parts. Although we seem to be Many, we are but One — and this is, and always has been, our message.'

And in that moment a thought-flash lit up my mind: she — *they* — meant that all the nations on Earth should join together until every mental, emotional, spiritual and physical barrier which currently separates them is utterly dissolved. Then peace would be born.

I felt privileged to instantly sense the mission of this luminous cloud of witnesses.

'There is no separation or diversity,' she intoned, 'in Reality, All is One. And we are but Silent Sentinels,' she added, as if reading the questions in my mind, 'unseen on Earth, except for the rare manifestations of our presence and power; unheard, except within the minds of our chosen ones. And now we require further access to man.'

'I think I follow,' I said, 'but what can I do?'

'Tell man that the way has already been made known,' she replied in her warmest response yet — at the same time conveying to me that an acute awareness of their Mind and Its presence had 'appeared' innumerable times in Earth's past. Throughout history many seers had witnessed such glowing clouds and spheres; and disembodied voices had accompanied other marvellous signs and wonders, as frequently recorded in religious and mystical writings through the ages. 'But they failed to understand us,' she said, rather forlornly, 'and made us into a God.'

'And worse than this, a vengeful God,' joined in the resonant sage, echoing much of her pathos.

'But we are not,' said the young male. 'We are somewhat more aware of God than they, but we are not God Itself; and we are not vengeful, but thoughtful and loving.'

The sage continued, 'Tell our friends on the material plane to seek advancement firstly in all the inner sciences — in the study of the inward path of the soul: in soul-discovery. Remind them of our message, which speaks of seeking self-realisation, of seeking the God within themselves. Ask them to love themselves, to care for others and to think seriously of their tomorrow's consequences, which will result from their actions today,' advised the deep-voiced ancient.

Then the young man added, 'Again we state that the purification of thought and the sensitivity to feeling is the way to progress — but most of all: create a heart that loves,' he said compassionately.

Then in perfect unison their three wonderful voices blended and intoned, 'Yes: the pure heart which loves can prevent the fall, after the rise.'

'I'll tell people,' I said, with quiet conviction.

And at this promise, the spherical cloud of voices shimmered like a dazzling, living pink light, shot through with peach-coloured sparkling stars: there were hundreds of tiny explosions within it and its electrical substance seemed to bristle with joy.

Then White Owl gripped my right hand much tighter, and suddenly my spirit sight left me — it vanished like a feather pulled into a whirlwind.

18

Psychic News

*(Extracts from a feature interview by journalist,
Rita Smith, published in Psychic News,
London, Saturday 8th August 1992.)*

Medium Launches New Book and Tour

Medium Stephen O'Brien is all set to embark on his sixth UK tour this month, which coincides with the publication of the third volume of his autobiography, *In Touch with Eternity.*

His two previous books — *Visions of Another World* and *Voices from Heaven* — sold over 10,000 copies in the first two weeks of their publication.

Following what the medium described last year as 'worrying contract disagreements' with his previous publishers — he claimed that they were denying him 'editorial control of the text' — Stephen's latest paperback is being published by Bantam Books (Transworld).

Speaking on behalf of the publishers, Transworld editorial representative, Brenda Kimber, said, 'Bantam was absolutely delighted to acquire Stephen O'Brien's latest book. Although his many gifts inevitably bring him many pressures, Stephen is always the complete professional. He is devoted to the people he serves. It has been a great pleasure to work with him.'

The book describes Stephen's work as a medium and contains many fascinating glimpses of life in the spirit world, including vivid accounts of visits to the higher realms with his guide, White Owl.

'These visits to the spirit world took place over the years,' said Stephen. 'Education is the key. Mediums are called upon to uplift and educate. It is an ongoing process. As you uncover one truth, so others are crying out to you to be found.'

The medium also tells how on one occasion his consciousness 'touched the past', and he was actually able to see his mother and himself as a child in Swansea.

'It was a time-slip,' he said. 'I was able to be present while the family day was going on. I believe if I had spoken to my mother she would have been aware of me.'

The medium commented, 'All my life sceptics have been pitted against me. It doesn't matter. A fact is a fact whether you believe it or not. I don't believe there is a life after death, I know it.'

Asked how spirit guides reacted to working with the media, Stephen responded, 'The spirit world will work with anybody who has got a willing heart and whose motivation is right. We are the limitations to their power. They would basically prefer conditions for contact to be absolutely perfect, but I have been working publicly now for about twenty years,' he commented, 'and have never had those conditions yet!'

Stephen said he wrote his books, 'in order to

share my experiences with people', especially with those who knew little or nothing about mediumship.

'I have never believed in preaching to the converted,' he explained. 'I cannot see the point of it. The good news we have is for the people.

'Spiritualists already have it.'

The message relayed by his spirit helpers would, he added, 'remain long after the messenger is gone: and that's the way it should be.'

'Mediums,' he maintained, 'have the power to change lives. The purpose of mediumship is to touch and awaken the soul of mankind. I think once the power of Spirit has touched the heart and mind of a human being he can never, ever, be the same person again. A magnetic link has been made and we are reminded of our true source and essence. Slowly and surely it opens up a channel of power through our Higher Selves to the spirit world and to God.'

The medium's tour manager, Jeff Rees Jones, told *Psychic News* that Stephen would be 'travelling to twenty major cities across Britain, demonstrating his mediumship in city halls and theatre complexes.'

On this latest tour, lasting from August to November, Stephen will be visiting venues in England, Scotland and Wales.

'These tours are very gruelling affairs,' Stephen commented. 'Living out of a suitcase is really no fun. It is often a quite lonely, work-filled time.

'The intense stresses from both the public and the press can be quite crippling, especially for such a quiet man as myself, who prefers solitude to concentrated media attention.'

Describing himself as 'fit as a fiddle', the medium said he had 'undertaken concentrated physical exercises and a special vegan diet', which helped him shed 14 lbs. 'I now weigh just under a neat 10 stone (9 stone 12 lbs.),' he added. 'It's all worthwhile when you see, perhaps, a mother's smile as she receives a meaningful message of survival from her young child on the Other Side.'

Asked whether he expected harassment from born-again Christian fundamentalists on his tour, the medium replied, 'I expect a few – my life wouldn't be complete without them!

'Nothing is forced on anybody,' he pointed out. 'We should never think that we're in the business of converting anybody. We are here to serve. My meetings are all about love. They're also about encouraging people to develop the good soul-qualities of peace, harmony, toleration and brotherhood.'

'Personal sacrifice,' he explained, was involved in 'delivering the message of the Spirit. If you have promised the spirit world you will serve, you have to give whatever you can, and not dwell too much on your own feelings.'

19

'I Heard a Voice from Heaven Say...'

My bags were packed, my suits were pressed and my cat, Sooty, was left with friends while my super-fit, brimming-with-vitamins body crouched in readiness on the starting block, facing another round of national tours.

My manager, Jeff, had the starter-gun and — *bang!* — we were off.

Rushing headlong at full pelt, city followed city and meetings flew past in a continuous blur as I rocketed from one end of Britain to the other, stopping briefly only here and there to make some guest appearances on TV and radio programmes, which I'd been contracted to do.

The first surprise came when my telephone slot on Britain's popular live daytime TV show, *This Morning,* broke the national record for the series. I'd done the usual talk followed by a nationwide phone-in on psychic happenings, and within twenty minutes so much interest was generated that the switchboard was jammed with over 1,800 telephone calls. This was my second appearance on *This Morning,* hosted by the popular British presenters Judy Finnigan and Richard Madeley (known to British viewers as Richard and Judy).

I'd been invited back because after my first visit, as well as their viewing figures quickly increasing, something unusual had happened.

On that occasion, the studio had encountered 'some weird goings-on'. I was conducting the phone-in when, out of the blue, a young male caller suddenly accused me with, 'You don't believe in the same God as the Christians.'

I looked into the camera and said gently, but emphatically, 'There is only *one* God' – and upon the instant, millions of television screens blanked out right across the United Kingdom. For the next four minutes the TV channel lost vision and sound throughout the country, and to this day their technicians are unable to account for the power drain.

Next morning, of course, the tongue-in-cheek *Daily Star* tabloid provided the answer by declaring to its readers that, 'Medium Steve spooks up the TV works!'

'Your spirit people certainly know how to handle a difficult situation and turn it to their advantage,' said a friend.

Incidentally, the *Daily Star* later ran an amusing feature asking its readers to choose their 'Perfect Christmas Guest', and a wide selection of celebrities frolicked amongst its columns. There was the actress Joan Collins, about whom a man from Derbyshire penned, 'Her steamy presence would keep everything on my table hot.' There were also invitations to such famous singers as David Essex and Dame Kiri Te Kanawa; and the actress Susan Hampshire made an appearance, as did Nanette

Newman; and one of the public had unexpectedly invited yours truly to lunch! A woman from Sheffield had written in saying, 'My ideal guest would be medium Stephen O'Brien. We could have a three-way conversation with my late beloved mother, to ease this painful year without her.'

I was touched — and I'm sure her mum *was* with her; at least, when I read her letter I prayed she would be, and that she'd make her presence warmly felt.

The impact of both television and the written word is enormously powerful, and an interview with Frank Bough for Sky TV — which was repeated several times — illustrates my point. A friend's brother, who was working forty miles offshore on an oil-rig in the North Sea, saw me and Frank chattering away about psychic matters at four o'clock in the morning! It's incredible to think that while I was tucked up fast asleep, oil-riggers, along with thousands of other insomniacs and late-shift workers, were listening to my opinions.

On the same programme was the actor Jack Wild, who as a young man had played the Artful Dodger in the musical film *Oliver!* While he was on air promoting his latest role in *Robin Hood, Prince of Thieves*, with Kevin Kostner, his fiancée and I were chattering away in the green room, and it turned out that she was very taken with my work and was so thrilled to meet me that we missed Jack's contribution (!) — so I apologised and gave her one of my autographed books.

Then I was off again onto a seemingly never-ending road: more cities followed in quick succession; and at another TV station I met one of the newest young British pop groups, and we shared some laughter and a little professional advice. They were called *Take That* (a group of physically motivated, and often semi-clad young men) and they were being filmed dancing frantically to their latest release. Quite new to the British television scene at the time, one of the boys, the singer Robbie Williams, seemed rather anxious. 'Don't worry,' I said, 'the public'll lap it up.'

'Do you really think so?' he asked enthusiastically, interested in what he may have thought was a clairvoyant prediction.

'Oh yes,' I said, 'just keep shifting it all about and shaking everything back and forth, and smile a lot and they'll love it!' And of course, they did: the group got to Number One with their song 'It Only Takes a Minute, Girl,' whereas, in fact, the record itself was nearly three minutes long, as one of them pointed out. But at least my comments broke the tensions of filming and we all had a good laugh.

But there was quite a different backstage reaction when I appeared on Ulster TV, in Ireland, with the author David Icke, the singer Michael Ball, and the popular British comedian Terry Scott, who was undoubtedly fascinated by psychic abilities. No sooner had we met in a swish hotel's restaurant than Terry, then aged sixty-five, grabbed both my hands tightly, pulled my face to within a few inches of his (our noses were almost touching), and stared at me while commanding, 'Now — look into my *eyes*! Go on — look into my eyes and you'll *see*!'

'Yes,' I said, a little nonplussed, 'the eyes are the windows of the soul,' I added, somewhat confused.

'I know as much as *you* do,' he stated with obvious conviction, instantly releasing my hands and leaving me dumbfounded.

However, I felt more sympathetic towards David Icke, who'd received much unfavourable publicity when the press claimed he'd said he was 'the Son of God'. Mr Icke maintained that he'd said nothing of the kind, and he took this media opportunity to reiterate that he was *a* son of God — as indeed we all are, for God's Spirit is within all of us. Of course, some bright spark at a newspaper had caught a whiff of a possible sensation — and that was that.

The other guest on the show that night was the singer Michael Ball, and we chatted about his British entry for that year's Eurovision Song Contest, which was to be judged in the following week. He seemed apprehensive about having his every reaction scrutinised by millions of people across Europe as the votes were telephoned in. But I was amused to hear his secret plan. 'I've got it all worked out, Stephen: when the juries start ringing in, I'm off to the toilet. And I'm not coming back unless we're winning!'

I didn't have the heart to tell him I felt the British song wouldn't come top: but, to be frank, I think he'd already suspected this. And we were both correct.

People often write to me about my mixing with celebrities and they say gushing things like, 'Oh, it must be *wonderful* to meet such famous stars, Stephen.' But honestly, they're just ordinary pleasant people. I'd go so far as to say you'd walk past many of them in a supermarket if they didn't have their make-up on.

Mind you, it's sometimes hard to realise that many of these glittering celebrities, who'd always seemed so far removed from my everyday life when I was a lad, are now my company in the media spotlight.

Ain't life peculiar?

My other TV contributions, such as the one on BBC1's live programme *Summer Scene* also caused quite a stir in the country, especially when after this particular interview I delivered a message to an elderly lady in the studio audience. Her 'dead' father made contact.

'He tells me quite emphatically,' I said, 'that there were family connections to the Rhondda Valley.'

'Yes, years ago,' she confirmed.

'And he's come here today with Liz.'

'That's my mother-in-law,' and she raised an eyebrow.

The next snippet could have proved quite embarrassing; we were on live national transmission and I really didn't know how to say what I was hearing, so I just trusted in God and delivered it straight from the shoulder.

'He says you're into your second childhood,' I ventured.

'Oh yes, I'm *there*!' replied the delighted woman, happily agreeing with her father, who then sent her his love and told her never to feel lonely because his caring presence was often at her side.

As well as many whistle-stop TV appearances — some of which I refused to do because of their disrespectful content — I lost count of how many radio stations I whizzed in and out of in the United

Kingdom.

On the airwaves, dealing with awkward telephone questions, sceptical interviewers, and an often grateful listening audience, are all now part of my public persona; and although it's true that the media have received me favourably over the years, I've never enjoyed being interviewed, photographed, or filmed. But I fulfilled all of my contractual obligations and dealt with the stresses as best I could.

Many autographed copies of my books were frequently offered as radio competition prizes, and one cheeky disc jockey even admitted to using *In Touch with Eternity* to balance the uneven legs of his favourite chair! But then, what am I here for, if not to serve?

Another amusing incident happened at an unmanned, down-the-line radio studio, which is basically a small padded room where the guest sits alone, forlornly staring into a single huge microphone, while he wears a set of headphones and waits (hopefully) to be connected to another radio station in a distant part of the realm for a live interview. I say hopefully, because I've done many such interviews that sent faraway producers into panic attacks when communication-lines broke down. The incident that makes me smile happened when I was plonked in front of the ominous black mike, patiently praying for a link down the headphones with the BBC in Ireland, when everything (as usual) went wrong.

I wanted Ireland, but the mysteriously clicking line suddenly produced a masculine, rather posh-sounding English voice, who addressed someone he believed was a famous British newscaster:

'Hello! Calling Michael Buerk in London!' he announced triumphantly.

'Foiled again, Moriarty!' I returned. 'This is Stephen O'Brien in Wales, waiting for a line to Ireland, and listening to Radio Scotland on his headset!'

'Oh gawd blimey!' came the surprised reply. 'Hang on, mate, and I'll see what we can do!'

Thankfully, I did eventually get the right connection, with just a few minutes to spare before my live slot.

Radio, of course, relies solely upon the voice, and sensitive people can register much of a man's soul by listening to him speak. After my talk to the Irish people, the renowned film actor Peter Cushing followed on with an account of how he sincerely believed that his beloved wife, Helen, who had died, would be waiting for him in the next world. Mr Cushing struck me as a very sincere man, and I hope my words about the certainty of an afterlife for everyone helped and comforted him — for he was quite right: he and his beloved wife will be reunited in a much better world beyond this one.

My own voice, however, took on much jollier tones when I vibrated my vocal chords on the new BBC Radio 5 channel. The *Rave* programme had asked me to direct my comments at its teenage audience who, they said, wanted 'to be entertained, so keep it light'!

'Oh, I'm such an old fogey,' I quipped — but I did quite well, I thought; which was quite a feat, really, when you consider that the youthful host referred to me as 'Stevie-poohs' throughout the interview.

And a similar kind of delivery was requested for BBC Radio 1's top show *Steve Wright in the Afternoon*. The infamous 'posse' of cackling actors, who frequently clap, whistle and jeer at all of the guests, were most amused when I told Steve that survival was for everyone. As a matter of fact, on that day the 'posse' were a few members short owing to influenza, so I ended up being asked to clap and whistle at myself with the rest of them, just to make up the noise!

After every TV or radio appearance, of course, the public's interest is always considerably regenerated and, as a result, press features are frequently requested.

When the *TV Times* ran a story on psychics and mediums helping the police, I was particularly pleased they were gracious enough to quote an important point which doubly underlines the private nature and the sanctity of communication:

Stephen O'Brien said that while he has helped people holding high office in this country he would never disclose who or why.

Asked how mediums can help the police Mr O'Brien explained, 'We may be given an article of clothing or a missing person's watch. That article is the psychic-key to the person, rather like a house-key. Or we may be taken to the scene of the crime, where we pick up a psychic snapshot of the circumstances surrounding the event.'

Stephen ended by saying that once, at a sitting, a girl who had been brutally murdered manifested. 'She didn't want me to contact the police so I took no action,' he said.

'It's like a doctor's confidentiality — you don't betray a trust.'

A high media profile, of course, also encourages professional people to write, and hundreds of work offers continued to arrive from UK organisations, and from other countries, too.

Interesting invitations to tour Rumania, Hungary and India have all been recently offered. A few months back I was even asked to fly to Germany where my hosts would accommodate me in their castle on the banks of the Rhine if I would demonstrate survival evidence to a group of twenty Catholic priests, all of whom were working in a hospice for the sick and dying.

But I declined. My time in Britain is usually so taken up with writing and travelling that I've been forced to refuse most offers. 'I'm afraid there's only one of me,' I've replied, 'but so many of you.'

However, I did accept one evening engagement at a Waterstone's Bookshop in England, in Canterbury, on the night before one of my public meetings. Interest ran high and all the tickets were sold a few weeks in advance. I followed in the footsteps of such notables as the Labour Politician Antony Wedgwood Benn, and the fiction horror-writer James Herbert!

But from the moment I entered the building, strange things started happening to the electrics: they dimmed and flickered and then the entire top floor where I was to lecture was suddenly plunged into darkness.

The assistant manager came pelting through the crowd. 'Is this something to do with you, Stephen?'

he gasped.

'Not that I know of,' I said innocently, 'but it's happened before.'

So we all trooped down to the still-lit ground floor, where the staff hurriedly cleared away book-tables and I stood on one of these while a hundred and twenty people sat down on the carpet, up on the stationary escalator, and on the stairs. I gave the audience a test to gauge the strength of their psychic abilities, followed by what I hoped was an interesting talk on the very marked differences between psychic work and mediumship. I concluded the workshop with a book-signing session; and a lovely time was had by all!

I've autographed thousands of books over the years (I usually just sign 'Stephen'); and I still get lots of practice at the end of each theatre meeting.

But I've done other memorable signing- sessions, too, such as the one at the renowned Atlantis Bookshop in Museum Street, London, at the invitation of Tim Haigh, the editor of *Psychic News* at that time.

I've also been known to startle sales assistants around the country when I've made surprise visits to local bookstores while on tour.

After *In Touch with Eternity* was released upon an unsuspecting world, even more letters than usual poured in from everywhere you could think of, by land, sea and air. My weekly postbag swelled with hundreds of interesting epistles. People said they were spiritually moved by the book, grateful for it, and then asked me when the next volume (this one) would be published. So many wonderful letters of kind support and encouragement arrived that I was overwhelmed by the public's love, and I soon discovered I couldn't cope with the amount of replies.

It took months to clear the backlog, and if some readers received short answers, please forgive me, but I'm only one man, and the demand seems to increasingly outweigh the supply.

Letters ranged from praise to acerbic wit, and from the hilarious to the deadly serious; and I even had offers of marriage or 'delicious and tantalising cohabitation', from people of all ages and backgrounds — and from both sexes, I might add.

One perfumed envelope looked rather promising: it was a charming letter from a lady somewhere in deepest England (modesty prevents me from naming her town). On reflection, I think I must have one of those 'Please would you take me home, feed me, and then put me on the mantelpiece' faces, for she — like several others before her — was offering 'a lifetime of unbridled passion and wedded bliss'.

All very well, you might say, but in addition to making some very lewd and unprintable suggestions, the poor soul also made the silly mistake of enclosing a recent photo of her ample, but cuddly self. I couldn't help smiling when I remembered an old British comedian reading out some similar fan-mail on TV many years ago, and how wittily he'd dealt with it. He said something like this: 'And here's an interesting note from a leggy Miss Fanshawe from London: "You'd better marry me, or else: snapshot enclosed". Well, Miss Fanshawe, having seen your photo, I think I'll marry Else!'

Other parcels arrived containing gifts from all

parts of the world. Even my cat, Sooty, had a weekly dose of her own adoring fanmail. I'm sure she's most touched.

She's been delighted to receive scrumptious 'delicacies' from the Orient, kitty toys, and even her own personally hand-knitted woolly pillow with silver stars, bright cloth flowers and colourful little plastic animals attached to it. This splendid array of creatures had amusing stickers glued on to them, labelling them as 'Clairvoyant moo-cow', 'Psychic alligator' and 'Over-sensitive hedgehog'.

She was absolutely thrilled with it, especially when she realised that her edged-with-fringes tinkly-bell dream-pillow had been stuffed full of sensuous catnip. Madam thought she'd died and gone to heaven, or else it must have been her birthday.

But the funniest thing about this gift was its description. 'Please find enclosed one intergalactic space-flight and activity mat. Would passengers please belt themselves in and refrain from standing while the mat is in flight.'

I found this very amusing, and even more so when later on, another note came from Sooty's admiring fan saying, 'Thank you for the photos of an ecstatic Sooty on her space-mat. I shall treasure them always and I'm now frantically knitting her a launch-pad, cockpit and joy-stick!'

And I had plenty of my own excitement to contend with. Although my whistle-stop public appearances continued to exhaust me, they also gave me the opportunity to present the message of survival to many thousands of newcomers to the paranormal; and for this, I'm very grateful.

It seemed strange for someone like me to be appearing at such bastions of the British entertainment industry as the much-loved City Varieties Theatre, Leeds, one of the world's most famous music halls, where I've happily worked to full houses on several occasions.

The building has a charming Edwardian presence all its own, which was best captured by BBC television's *The Good Old Days* music-hall programme, when the show's compere Leonard Sachs greeted the colourful audiences, who were attired in old-fashioned clothes, by introducing the world renowned show with some very flamboyant phrases.

When the stage manager told me, 'The chair you'll be sitting on was the late Leonard Sachs' seat,' I had an amusing idea. As soon as my meeting began I delighted the audience by mentioning Leonard and heartily imitating his gusto as I loudly declared, 'Perhaps I should start by saying: Good evening, ladies and gentlemen! And welcome to this phenomenal and supernormal extravaganza of mediumistic and psychic impressions which involves — chiefly *yourselves*!'

And the audience loved it.

The City Varieties stage is quite tiny when compared with some of the opera platforms I've appeared on, and other stages like the vast Wembley Conference Centre in London. Backstage at Leeds you have to keep doing gymnastic double-bends and constantly ducking your head while ferreting your way through a rabbit warren of small corridors, because the ceilings are incredibly low.

How on earth the British female impersonator,

Danny La Rue, manages to get through these minuscule stairwells in full bustle, voluminous skirts, and furs, without losing a few sequins or a feather boa must be one of the modern miracles of the British entertainment industry.

It's spooky to think that while I was delivering spirit messages at my Voices Management meetings there, I knew that the very boards under my feet had been trodden by the famous feet of such renowned stars and entertainers as Gracie Fields, and the old-time comedian Max Miller, and the eternal saucy songstress Marie Lloyd; as well as by modern-day British comedians like Ken Dodd, Larry Grayson, and practically anyone else you can think of who's famous.

But Voices Management doesn't organise all of my venues, of course. *Psychic News* asked me several times to appear at their special events, and two of these were called 'Mediumship '91, and '92'. These were public meetings to celebrate the newspaper's sixtieth anniversary, as well as to raise funds for it, and to bid farewell to its departing editor of ten years, Tony Ortzen — while at the same time welcoming its new man, Tim Haigh.

A glittering array of notable lecturers and popular sensitives worked in some London theatres to raise funds; and one of the venues was London's Mermaid Theatre in Blackfriars. Every seat in the house was taken, and a planeload of sixty people had jetted in from Denmark, just to be there.

No sooner had I arrived than two ladies pressed a bright bouquet of flowers into my arms, 'With blessings of light and love'. Such kind gifts and cards from the public are often left at stage doors, and they're very much appreciated. (My sincere thanks to everyone who gave them.)

At these London events, I worked alone, and also with my colleague, psychic artist, Coral Polge, who drew the spirit communicators' portraits, which were then projected on to a large screen. The following compilation of *Psychic News* reports brought to its readership in seventy countries a sense of the evidence given, and they begin with the spirit return of a young lad called 'Steven'.

During the afternoon a double demonstration of clairvoyance and psychic art was given by Welsh medium Stephen O'Brien and well-known psychic artist Coral Polge.

Coral began to draw the portrait of a young man. 'He had hair like thatch, very thick,' she said. 'He died with a head condition. It would have been quite sudden.'

Stephen then picked up the link.

'A terrible tragedy,' he stated. 'He passed quickly. It involved a car and four people. I think I'm with someone up in the balcony. Who is Brian?'

Mrs Bloomfield, the recipient, recognised Coral's drawing. 'It was the name Brian that clinched it,' she said later. 'That is Steven's father's name.' (Steven was the lad Coral was drawing.)

Explaining why he had been presented in profile in his portrait, the communicator said through Stephen O'Brien, 'I'm giving you this side because the other side was so badly damaged in the crash.'

The medium said that Steven had chosen to be drawn in this position because there was a photograph of him just like this, belonging to his father, Brian.

'The communicator,' said Stephen O'Brien, 'has just said, "Susie almost joined us. She's still here: but she came into contact with the windscreen."'

Coral, still busily completing the portrait of young Steven, commented, 'Also, somebody must have had broken legs in that accident.'

'Correct,' replied Mrs Bloomfield. 'Susie had been hurt in the accident; she had broken her legs and nearly passed over. That was absolutely right!'

Stephen O'Brien then relayed this message for the communicator's father.

'Hold my dad; kiss my dad, and tell him I'm very much alive. And I'm sorry, Dad, for worrying you so much.'

Commenting on the accuracy of the messages she had received, Mrs Bloomfield said, 'It was incredible!'

Another communication was given from a woman called Ellen, who must have had great difficulty in getting about. Stephen proceeded to give evidential information about her to the recipient. Then came, 'She's telling me to remind you about the ferret. Do you understand? Did a ferret go down someone's trousers?'

'I understand,' said the recipient, amid much laughter, 'but the ferret went *up* the trousers, not down!'

Stephen then went on to relay the message, 'She's saying she has a baby that you lost with her, a boy.'

The mother was delighted to hear the words, 'Your son is really glad he belongs to you, and not to the lady who has recently betrayed you,' he added.

'I could wring her neck!' the woman exclaimed.

The mediumship continued as the drawing of a rather stern-looking, elderly woman appeared on the screen, and Stephen said that he could hear the hymn 'Rock of Ages' being sung. 'I feel she had strong connections with the Salvation Army,' he said. 'I hear the name of Mrs Powell. She's one of the old school from many years back.'

The woman was said to have had 'a big family, and just fell asleep when she passed over in her eighties.'

The recipient confirmed this and that the Powell referred to was her sister, not herself.

'She's still a Salvationist!' laughed Stephen. 'She's telling you to hold on to your faith even if someone tries to ridicule you.'

Another recipient was told by the medium that a Mrs Cooper-Williamson — 'the name is hyphen-ated' she emphasised — was trying to help her with some figures.

'She's talking about adding up a column of figures which comes to all but £400,' said Stephen.

'Yes, that's me personally,' said the woman.

During the double demonstration by Coral and Stephen, the psychic artist drew the portrait of an elderly man, which proved to be the answer to a prayer for one member of the audience.

'I have a very tall, very angular man here,' said Coral. 'I get a great sense of loping along.'

Stephen joined in saying the next communicator had a link with the name Margaret Edwards. 'That's with me!' answered a young woman, after a pause.

'Will you watch the picture of this person as it progresses on the screen?' said Stephen.

Referring to someone named Lizzie on the Other

Side – 'She always called a spade a spade' – Stephen told the recipient, 'to put your foot down.'

'Why are you smiling?' asked Stephen.

'Because I'm trying to do that, but not very successfully,' came the reply. Later, the recipient — she came from Lewisham but did not wish to give her name — told how she recognised the picture as that of her grandfather. Although she knew the name of Margaret Edwards, at first she did not claim the message because it was someone on Earth, until she realised her uncle's mother was also named Margaret Edwards.

The recipient later told *Psychic News* of her feeling of isolation and how she saw the world as 'a hard, alien, and uncompromising place.' She had even contemplated suicide.

Almost at the end of her tether, she told how the night before the demonstration she had said to the spirit world: 'I can't handle it any more. I want a message of reassurance from Stephen O'Brien.'

Her wish was granted.

The young woman explained she had never seen Stephen before except on television, but after reading his books, she 'just felt he would be sympathetic.'

Of the message 'to put her foot down', she commented, 'It's true. If I'd done that two years ago, I wouldn't have the troubles I have now.'

That last example of how a spirit message averted a suicide attempt underlines just how private, meaningful and relevant the Other Side's evidence can be, but only to the person who is receiving it.

Sometimes, spirit messages can sound like nonsense to the public who are listening to them being delivered — *it is only the recipient of the link who can tell just how meaningful the content is*.

Survival evidence can be quite touching and poignant, or funny and amusing, and it's often packed with personal references and hidden meaning.

The spirit people seem to know just what to bring, exactly what is required to comfort, uplift and educate those who stand in the greatest need; but the mediums delivering these communications, of course, can frequently remain unaware of their important content.

There's one other message of love and consolation that sticks in my mind, and it came through at Dundee's Caird Hall, in Scotland. I record it now because I hope it may assist many people who have to face and cope with the difficult circumstances it mentions.

'I have your grandmother here,' I announced to a nervous young lady who was standing at the microphone in the aisle, patiently listening to her spirit communication. 'And she's singing the old song "In My Sweet Little Alice-Blue Gown". Oh, that was her name — she was called Alice!'

'Yes, she was,' came the tremulous reply.

'And she says that she passed over in a hospital bed.'

'That's correct.'

'But she was semi-conscious, in a coma, before she went.'

'That's right.'

'And one night, you and she were the only two people in her side-room: and when you were all alone with her, you held her hand, just like this —'

and I copied the peculiar handhold her spirit grandma clearly showed me.

'Yes, I did,' said the tearful girl.

'And she tells me you sat there and thought to yourself, "I wonder if my darling Gran can hear me, or see me?" Is that correct?'

'Yes...'

'Well, Alice now says, "You sang to me, too."'

'Yes, I did... I did sing to her.'

'She says, "You held my hand and smoothed my old wrinkled skin, and you sang so softly and beautifully to me: *When you're weary, feeling small; when tears are in your eyes, I will dry them all.*" You sang "Bridge Over Troubled Water" to your grandmother, my dear.'

'Yes, I *did* sing it. That's *exactly* what I sang to her...' she whispered emotionally through the microphone, wiping away tears as her grandma's touching recollections silenced the audience.

'Well,' I concluded, 'Alice says she loves you very much, and your special song to her really meant a great deal "to an old body like me, girl." And she's ending her message with, "And please, Stephen, please tell my darling: *Yes* — I *could* hear you, *and* I could see you, too."'

But her emotional granddaughter was quite tearful, and far too overcome to reply...

Despite my joy in conveying such poignant messages, delivered on stage in the quiet stillness of shadowy auditoriums, my life off stage has now become so terribly hectic that it often takes unexpected turns, and sometimes it gets quite exciting. I mean, how many chances in a lifetime does one get to visit Hollywood? After one TV chatshow appearance, a popular screenwriter telephoned me for advice about his latest project. It was a script based loosely around the successful psychic film *Ghost,* starring Whoopi Goldberg, Demi Moore and Patrick Swayze — only his new script was to be a comedy.

I dutifully read his plot and was offering my suggestions when he suddenly surprised me with, 'Listen, Stephen: if it goes into production, would you be our psychic consultant on the set?'

'Would I?' I said, raising my eyebrows. 'I'd be delighted!' — and I'm still raising them, and still waiting.

Well, we live in hope!

Speaking of which: one night back at the ranch — my old council flat where for nearly five years I'd been tortured by the incessant noise made by my dreadful neighbours, and I'd also suffered from their unruly bad behaviour — my personal hope of leaving the wretched place was fast flagging away.

As many readers will already know, at these premises I'd been beaten up and my old car had been vandalised several times. On top of all this, the police had made several drug-raids on the apartments of some troublesome young tenants in my block. I was now at the end of my tether and my patience had all but run out.

For the past eleven years, since I'd moved out of my father's house and into three different council flats, I'd suffered what seemed like a continuous horrifying nightmare from which I felt I couldn't wake up. Until...

In the early hours of one morning, just as I'd crashed into bed at around 2 a.m., dog-tired after being forced to listen to loud thumping rock music from a tenant's record-player, from underneath my duvet-cover I suddenly heard a voice from heaven say, 'We want you to know: you'll be moving soon.'

'Oh good grief!' I exclaimed — sitting up in the night, and modestly gathering the sheets around me.

'Pardon I, but did you just say *moving*?'

'Yes,' whispered the voice.

'Well, thank the Lord for *that*!' I replied enthusiastically, flopping back down onto the bed and snuggling under the sheets.

Then a momentous realisation suddenly dawned on me – *freedom*!

And I immediately sat bolt upright again and yelled back into the spirit world, '*And it's about time too*!'

20

Psychic Atmospheres

One morning, I made an important decision about leaving the troublesome city flats where my tour manager, Jeff, and I had lived next-door to each other for five years.

'Between tours, we're going to get new houses,' I said, 'and now's a good time to buy — people can't sell their properties and prices keep falling.'

Jeff peered over his teacup, nonplussed.

'Oh, and where's the money going to come from? There's a recession on, in case you've forgotten,' he said.

'Don't worry about that,' I replied cheerfully, 'have some faith. God will provide. My spirit friends have predicted a move for me soon, and I believe them,' I said.

'Well, these horrible flats are getting me down,' said Jeff. 'Yesterday some of the nasty tenants shouted abuse at one of my friends outside, and the Scotsman downstairs was beaten up by a gang of louts.'

'Neither of us will be here much longer,' I added confidently, 'the Other Side will see to it. Anyway,' I smiled, 'I got a letter from a lady in Gloucester today, and she said a spirit voice told her I'd now earned the right to have a quiet country house.'

Jeff raised a sceptical eyebrow and took another swig of tea, as I produced the note from my briefcase and read it aloud. 'I'm sending my prayers for you, Stephen, because as far as I'm concerned you've worked yourself into the ground for the good of others during the last twenty years, and you've suffered enough. It's about time God gave you the peace and quiet you deserve, especially after helping so many thousands of people who are searching for truth, like me.'

'Let's hope she's right;' said my manager, adding, 'we'll both start looking for houses in the morning.'

'And I'll use my sixth sense when we visit any properties,' I promised; for like thousands of other people, I'm quite sensitive to the psychic atmospheres of houses. 'When I see the right place, I'll recognise it straightaway.'

This conviction was strong because the secret history of old buildings has often revealed itself to me. I remember having a frightening experience when I was just twelve years old: our school went on a coach trip to an ancient Welsh castle and we had a smashing day out — until my friend, Mark, and I wandered off from the crowd and found ourselves near a small dark opening at the top of what looked like a spiral stone stepway.

'Come on,' I said, being a nosy parker, 'let's have a look down here,' and we descended the slippery steps, not knowing what we'd discover; but nothing could have prepared me for the psychic terror waiting for us at the bottom of the stairs.

With each step downwards, my young mind

sensed the walls closing in on it, and a tight ball of fear formed in my solar plexus. Suddenly afraid, I stopped in my tracks and yelled out, 'Let's go back!'

'Don't be stupid!' said Mark, giving me a sharp dig in the ribs with his elbow. 'Go on, Stephen! Keep moving!'

So, further down we went, until the stairwell opened out into a high grey-stone chamber about the size of a small house. A smell of damp moss filled the air, and as soon as I entered the room I immediately felt ill, as though my lunch was about to make a sudden reappearance – the sickening atmosphere spun my psychic senses around.

'Look up there!' said an agitated Mark, pointing to some rusty iron rings jutting out of the walls about ten feet above the slimy floor.

When my eyes found them I reeled against the nearest support, for all at once I psychically heard the cries of terrified men and women, yelling out in anguish and searing pain, and pleading for mercy and release. Their horrific blood-curdling screams seemed to resonate over my heart, which was thudding against my ribs.

I quickly tried to catch my breath.

'What's wrong, Stephen? You're as white as a sheet,' said Mark.

'Oh God,' I whispered, gulping to fill my lungs with clean fresh air, 'something terrible happened in here, I can feel it... There were people screaming and crying. It was awful... and it's something to do with those bars over there,' I said, pointing at the opposite wall where a rusty iron grid allowed a few rays of daylight to filter into the chamber. 'The people were petrified of that hole in the wall,' I said.

Then we froze to the spot, suddenly frightened by the sound of loud echoing footsteps descending the stairwell — but our fears quickly dispersed when our teacher entered the chamber with the rest of our twelve-year-old classmates.

I did my best to regain my composure, but was soon stunned again when our history master explained, 'This part of the castle was reserved for prisoners who were tortured here, boys.'

Mark and I glanced knowingly at each other.

'High up there, you can see some iron rings,' — and the class gazed upwards — 'traitors were hung from these, and they faced that grid over there.'

Everyone glanced over casually at the small barred hole; but when I caught sight of it again, my pulse raced away as I recalled the terrifying screams I'd heard.

'Outside the grid, there used to be a river,' said the teacher.

'But what was the hole for, sir?' I ventured.

'Well, it allowed the rising waters to completely flood this chamber, and to drown all the prisoners hanging from the walls.'

I was speechless, and didn't hear another word spoken by our teacher on the rest of that day trip...

Over the years, this kind of soul-power has intensified in me; and I intended to use this ability to register the hidden psychic impressions permeating the atmosphere of any possible future homes I would view.

Armed with confidence, one day (seemingly on sudden impulse) I drove down into the beautiful countryside of Swansea's Gower Peninsula.

Passing through several fishermen's villages, I eventually ended up gazing through estate agents' windows at picturesque properties and 'dream homes' up for sale. Unfortunately, they were all way above my price bracket, because my wages would only allow a modest mortgage.

I was very disappointed; the Gower countryside had always attracted me because its spiritual energies are so powerful: its old trees radiate extensive psychic auras and readily transmit their life-force to passers-by; and the country air, which is so much cleaner than that of the city's, is a great healer of the body, mind and spirit.

But I continued to search...

Then one day, while Jeff and I were looking at more pictures in an estate agent's window, I suddenly came across a small detached cottage standing in its own grounds.

'Oh, this looks lovely,' I cooed.

But I sighed heavily at the asking price, passed it by, and went to a café for refreshments.

But in the café, I quite suddenly received an overwhelming psychic impression.

'I'm going to see it, Jeff!' I announced emphatically — and this I did, straightaway.

When I got there, I fell instantly in love with the house. Detached and full of character, it was surrounded by magnificent huge trees, some of them hundreds of years old. It was set in natural woodland, and I was further delighted to see plenty of wildlife in the vicinity: squirrels, thousands of birds, cows, horses — and there was also a river, and a little brook nearby.

But best of all — there were no noisy next-door neighbours.

Even though the quaint house needed some work doing to it, its potential as a haven of rest was obvious. Just like that time years ago when, as a boy, I'd been able to psychically feel the terror of the prisoners which had been impressed within the walls of the castle dungeon, my sensitivity was now registering the atmosphere of the cottage — and a profound tranquillity permeated it. My mind clearly perceived this living vibration; even the ground the house stood upon seemed to radiate spiritual quietness.

Overwhelmed by its serenity, I immediately thought, and said out loud, 'This place is mine.'

Everything about it felt right; and, as strange as it might seem, I'd instantly recognised every stone in the building – and when I viewed the inside, each of the rooms was familiar to me.

Beyond a shadow of a doubt, I knew my spirit friends had guided me to choose this house during several of the astral journeys we'd undertaken in my sleep life.

I was also convinced that my inspirers had prepared the way for this property to 'fall into my hands', so to speak. As far as I was concerned, this place of peace had been specially set aside for me (coming, as it did, after many years of hard work and struggle) and I believed my spirit friends had been waiting for the right time for me to make this move. And the time was now: between my national tour dates, and just after my father's death.

I also realised that if I added together my savings and the money Dad had left me in his will, and then put down a deposit on the property, with the addition of a phenomenally high mortgage I'd just about manage to buy this house.

However, this move would financially clean me out.

'Never mind,' I thought. 'Surely, it's better to be penniless and to have a restful home,' I reasoned, 'rather than to suffer any more trouble.'

The decision was made instantly: I was going to get the house — somehow, *anyhow* – and that was that.

Furthermore, I wasn't in the least bothered about the possibility of facing the endless weeks of dreadful red-tape fuss that always precedes, and frequently delays, house sales in Britain; because within my soul I had an unshakeable faith that everything would turn out fine.

So I signed on the dotted line (which sent me up to my eyeballs in debt, but happy) and bought the house; and the first thing I did was to plant some willow trees in the gardens, and I named the cottage 'Willowtrees'.

I'll never forget the first night my cat and I spent there; it was marvellous.

Spring was in the air and the wild flowers had started to bloom, and summer was well on its way. As I lay in bed listening to the flocks of nesting birds giving their evening song, I smoothed Sooty's dear little person and said, 'We've come a long way, my girl. Whoever could have guessed we'd end up where we wanted to be?'

She gave a little snicker, had a comfortable stretch, and then relaxed.

After so many years of exhausting touring, I was

grateful to have found my new home, but also aware of the hard work that lay in front of me in order to meet the monthly payments. 'But at least we're here,' I said soothingly to Sooty, 'and God will provide. We wouldn't have been led this far without a purpose.'

She looked up at me, rather quizzically, I thought, as good as to say, 'Well, you may be where you want to be, old man, but you're flat broke!' — after which I laughed myself silly, then we both slept like logs.

In the weeks that followed, of course, both Fleabag and I began the long process of settling in and getting used to the old cottage and all its idiosyncrasies.

Because our new home is an electric-powered house in the country, it doesn't have its supply cables running underground as they do in the cities: here they run overhead on wooden poles, and this caused one minor emergency.

It happened one night during a freak storm when forked lightning and high winds suddenly brought down the power-lines, plunging me and Sooty into pitch-black darkness.

In the silver moonlight filtering through the windows, I caught sight of my eerie shadow flickering along the walls, as I fumbled through the kitchen drawer (stepping on Sooty's tail in the process) until I struck a match to light a candle. After this, for the best part of two hours, I crept up and down the stairs with my candlestick in my hand, like Wee Willie Winkie until the power was restored.

The following day, Jeff paid a visit and said, 'So, the spirit world's prediction came true after all,

Stephen: you've got your country house. You're very lucky.'

'There's no such thing as luck,' I replied, 'the time was right and it's all part of my life-plan. And anyway, you'll soon be getting your own place,' I announced. 'I can sense it approaching.'

And within two months, my psychic prediction proved quite correct. One day while out walking, Jeff spied a nice property in the city where the 'For Sale' sign had mysteriously fallen down and it wasn't even visible from the street.

However, *he* saw it. This made him think that possibly 'someone invisible' had knocked it over, which had prevented any prospective buyers from being interested in the house.

He arranged an immediate viewing and, just as I'd experienced in my own place, he instinctively 'knew' that this house had somehow been set aside for him. Visiting the property later, I fully agreed, and I, too, recognised its distinctive oak-panelled hallway with its most unusual 1930s ornate brass lamp, which had been fitted on to the stairway banisters. We'd both experienced déjà vu.

'I've seen this fixture before, in my dreams,' I said with conviction. 'I've been here in the astral world at night.'

'That's strange, so have I,' he confirmed. 'As soon as I saw that light-fitting and, in fact, every single room, something inside me clicked and I felt as if I knew the place so well.'

'Yes, I told you it'd be OK,' I smiled, looking around his new house. 'Welcome home,' I said — and my prediction was completely fulfilled when he moved in shortly afterwards.

'But I'll have to redecorate it from top to bottom,' he lamented, commenting on the drab colours of the rooms.

'Well, it could be worse,' I said. 'At least you haven't got large gardens to cultivate — like mine; they're vast and they haven't been tidied up for years.'

This, in fact, was a gross understatement, for the land at 'Willowtrees' was so overgrown that you could have re-filmed *Tarzan and the Apes* on it.

Then I had a bright idea: Adrian, one of my friends from England, was shortly to serve Wales by taking some mediumship services, so I got on the phone. 'How about giving me a hand with the grounds?' I asked.

'I'd really enjoy that,' he said, being a bit of a keen gardener.

So that summer Adrian came to the cottage for a week and, in addition to his spiritual work, in the sweltering June heat, he and I cleared the terraces and dug the flowerbeds, and basked in the glorious sunshine. We laughed and joked, sang and talked, and had a great time. We did a lot of hard work but it was one of the best weeks of my life.

The only bother we had was that whenever we tried to uproot old tree-stumps, suddenly — from out of nowhere — came hordes of horrendous prehistoric blowflies: they blackened the skies, then bit the living daylights out of us! We had lumps on our faces, backs, legs and arms — and at the finish, poor Adrian threw his shovel in the air and we both ran for shelter indoors until dusk.

A week later, my friend bid farewell to the razor-toothed midges and left me to finish the tasks in hand. But whenever I approached those tree-stumps, mysterious psychic signals must have gone out, and this time — out came the hornets! They were about the size of bumblebees and their piercing needlepoint jabs felt like TB injections.

So there I was: bitten all over, and still left with only half of the gardens partly dug, during one of the hottest summers ever.

But I didn't moan or grumble. I had a big smile on my face, for one of my long-standing dreams had at last come true.

I was happy, and I was where I wanted to be; contented in calm and blissful surroundings: just me, Sooty, dozens of those thirsty bloodsuckers, hundreds of tall green trees, and thousands of nodding daisies...

He maketh me to lie down in green pastures,
He leadeth me beside the still waters,
He restoreth my soul...

23rd Psalm

21

'Willowtrees'

It's high summer now. My gruelling tours and public appearances are thankfully over for this year, and night breezes are gently wafting over the tops of the sixty-foot trees surrounding the gardens here at 'Willowtrees' - my little home in the country, this little place of my own, at last.

It's been a sizzling-hot June this year; the radiant sunshine's never let up for a minute and throughout today the stifling heat scorched the grass all around. Dozens of bees have been flitting in and out of the wild flowers, and scores of birds have crisscrossed the sky in the bright sunshine.

I was glad when night fell, because it had been such an exceptionally long and warm day: it was the summer solstice — the longest day — so for the best part of it I wandered around naked in the gardens, mowing the grass and giving the massive trees a serious haircut. Then I oiled myself from top to bottom (literally) with sunscreen lotions and creams, and stretched out on an old blanket and toasted myself on both sides until nicely browned. It's been good to relax and unwind, to be finally far away from, and out of, the demanding media spotlight.

After my catnap, the grandmother clock in the library woke me by striking four and the breezes suddenly started to cool the air.

I finished tilling the soil, put away the garden tools, and called it a day as far as work was concerned; which was just as well, for by then my muscles were bronzed and my back was aching. All the bending, pulling, stretching, yanking and uprooting of unwanted shrubs and choking weeds had certainly taken its toll; so I gave myself a special treat.

I threaded the garden hosepipe up through the high branches of the big conifer tree, turned on the cold-water tap, and stood beneath the cool waterfall as it cleansed me of the long sweaty day, and washed away my gardener's pains.

It was absolutely gorgeous...

Then I slipped into some white boxer-shorts, poured myself a lemonade, sat on the verandah and surveyed the trees, and thought to myself just how fortunate I am to have such a peaceful sanctuary, at last.

At Willowtrees I can meditate in the quiet atmosphere, perfectly undisturbed, and fully recharge my psychic batteries between my hectic tours and engagements.

The clean, fresh air energises me, and makes me better fitted to go forward to serve others, as I promised the spirit world I would do, many years ago now.

A man has time to think in the country, its sights and sounds refresh his spirit.

This evening, high above me, I laughed at Sammy

and Sid, two acrobatic black bats who usually start their antics after the big owl in the woods has finished calling to his mate; those boys are a couple of good flyers. And I smiled at a chirpy greenfinch as he did his nightly skip from the willow trees into the stone birdbath for his wash-and-brush-up session, ready for the missus and bed.

This evening, I sat in silence and watched the last flames of the sun as they began dying away at just past 10 p.m. As darkness was descending, the bright evening star appeared, piercing the blue night, high above my beloved hills and mountains of Wales, and it was an incredibly beautiful sight.

As the sun disappeared from view, diffusing the sky and the faraway mountains with brilliant colours, I marvelled at the soft lights playing on the distant forests. Sitting quietly, awestruck by this astonishing beauty, I was aware of one pervading thought: stillness...

I truly love the depth and serenity of twilight, when the country seems to generate its own unique brand of silence, its own unique spiritual presence.

It profoundly stirs the depths of my soul-sensitivity.

And tonight, just as the first glimmer of stars peeked through a deep blue mantle, there came again this unearthly quietness...

It rolled in from the distant hills and gently swept across the fields, like an invisible hand bestowing peaceful sleep on every creature in its path; then onwards it went, undulating over grasslands and moving through hundreds of rustling trees, leaving in its wake — deep tranquillity.

The birds were the first to sense it: dozens of them suddenly stilled their songs, almost simultaneously; then, as if responding to some soundless call of the spirit, they flew to their nests, ready for slumber. (After all, they've got to be up early to whistle their dawn chorus at the sunshine, and to wake the man in the house.)

Whenever indigo night falls as beautifully as it did this evening, I can't help but think of the incredible aloneness of God, the vast infinity of timeless space, and the unfathomable depths of eternity...

But my reverie was broken by a noisy Sooty who came swaggering out onto the verandah, all smiles and furry trousers, looking like John Wayne after pulverising the baddies in a cowboy movie, and rubbing her fur coat along my shins and mewing for all she was worth — for her supper.

'OK. I'm hungry, too,' I said.

I could feel the night-air temperature dropping, so I scooped up Sooty in my arms and ambled inside, thinking about the blessing of sleep, and also about this book.

In the cool kitchen, I sat at the table and became very still, and sent up a quiet prayer of thanks to the Great Spirit for having been given such wonderful opportunities to share with so many people the spiritual truths I've discovered, during this, my intensely personal, spiritual quest. And I hoped that my words would continue to comfort and help others, for years to come.

And I reminded my spirit friends that, despite all the hardships I've suffered in this life, I still feel privileged to have experienced so many enthralling psychic adventures.

I recalled that since a child, my inspirers have never failed to daily advise and encourage me along every step of the way on my journey of self-discovery, on this exciting search to uncover and to fully realise the true Essence of Everything, whose name is Love.

Whenever I pray like this, as night falls, silent voices from eternity still deliver to me their gentle inspiration.

And whenever these angels (who were once just ordinary people) see fit to convey to me their further revelations about Life and its Meaning, I know it's because they want me to share their thoughts with others...

The Coming of the Sacred Night

Sunfall greets my quietest hour;
    stillworld,
    all around,
    inside, and out...

Shuttered doors
seal weary travellers aside,
as blessed day bows out to holy night.

Birds wheel against the purple lambent painted sky,
heartsongs a-fly,
and nesting chicks summon motherlove for warmth,
'ere darkness freezes folded wings
and dries up tired eyes.

Country night, in silence bathed,
descends o'er fields of sleeping mice;
owls blink awake,
but feather-pillowed children dance in misty haze,
   as I sit before my window-glass
   and King Thought
   flights of fancy takes.

Behold God's night,
   serene in beauty coolness;
behold the tender drifting air
   through hushing trees
   and shivering corn.
God's night has smoothed the wild asleep
'ere dark gives way to violet dawn...

Privileged are we
   to sit and freely drink of this;
and blessed are we,
   as if He had lowered down His lips
   and kissed our sufferings.

Blue country twilight deep
has pressed its mouth on mine.
   Worshipped Nimrod,
   true loveliness is not thine —
   it births from the soul
   of some beneficent God.

So fold your hallowed wings upon me;
enclose myself,
utterly loved in sunset flight,
by the deepest, holiest kiss of slumber —
the Coming of the Sacred Night...

*

If you enjoyed this psychic book, then you will enjoy reading Stephen O'Brien's other bestselling titles, and listening to his acclaimed teachings recorded on audio-cassettes. Books are available through all good Bookstores and Libraries everywhere; and signed Cassettes and Books are available from the Voices Mail Order Service, or on the Internet at:
www.stephenobrien.co.uk

Full details, and a contact address for Stephen, appear on the following pages.

'THE SPIRITUAL KEYS TO THE KINGDOM'
A Book of Soul-Guidance for your Life
by Stephen O'Brien

Priceless Wisdom & Guidance
to Help you Throughout your Life

- ◆ Unlock the Secrets of Eternity
- ◆ Unfold the Hidden Psychic Powers of your Soul
- ◆ Discover the Kingdom of Heaven within you
- ◆ Obtain Happiness and Peace of Mind.
- ◆ Dip into this Treasure-Chest of Guidance Each Day -
  Be Uplifted and Receive all the Inspiration you need.

You are the Traveller walking along Life's Ancient
Pathway, seeking answers to your questions and trying
to fathom the meaning of your existence. As you step
into the Mystical Valley of Wisdom, Angelic Beings of
Light speak to your mind and heart, and they hand to
you 'The Spiritual Keys to the Kingdom' which will help
you to develop your natural spiritual powers;
to generate health in your body, mind and spirit;
to increase your sense of happiness and contentment;
and to understand your life-purpose and
why you were born.
Seven years in the making, this enthralling book
contains the wisdom of some remarkable Spiritual
Voices recorded by the world-renowned visionary,
Stephen O'Brien. They will speak to you of hope and
love, and of everlasting life, and they will reveal to you
the future of your soul.

A Voices Paperback Original (384 pages)
ISBN: 0-953-6620-5-5

'VISIONS OF ANOTHER WORLD'
The Autobiography of a Medium,
by Stephen O'Brien.

Every Journey has a Beginning...

Phantom hands hammering on a door
in the dead of night:
THE SPIRIT WORLD WAS CALLING...
and Stephen O'Brien had to accept the remarkable
powers that brought him *Visions of Another World*.
Then the tragic early death of his mother broke his
life in two; but miraculously she appeared to him
from beyond the grave
and her love changed the course of his life:
he became a Medium and a Visionary.
He promised the soul of a long-dead American Indian
that he would serve the Spirit World,
and countless thousands packed out venues
to hear him relay messages of Hope,
Light and Survival
from their loved ones on the Other Side of Life.
Hundreds of thousands of the so-called 'dead' have now
communicated through Stephen O'Brien's
amazing gifts: including war heroes,
accident and murder victims,
innocent children who died too young, animals,
and even the world-famous actress, Judy Garland.

Now you can read Stephen's compelling life-story.

'Big powers in other-worldly communication
and healing' *Irish News*

A Voices Paperback (384 pages; illustrated)
ISBN: 0-953-6620-3-9

'VOICES FROM HEAVEN'
Communion with Another World
by Stephen O'Brien

Grieving parents are reunited with their children,
wives with their husbands, and even animals return
to prove what medium Stephen O'Brien affirms:
'Death is only an Illusion.'

Follow Stephen as he makes remarkable journeys
into the Realms of Light and discovers the
Eternal World of the Spirit that
awaits us all after 'death'.
In these fascinating psychic recollections
the world-renowned visionary reveals to his
countless followers many remarkable life-changing
and spiritual experiences, during which he:

❖ Crosses Time-Zones and meets people who are
  long-dead.
❖ Relays startling messages from screen goddess
  Marilyn Monroe, from Lord Olivier, and from
  Earl Mountbatten of Burma.
❖ Foresees the *Challenger* Space Shuttle disaster,
  an incredible five years before it happened.
❖ Provides irrefutable evidence of the immortality
  of the soul.

*

And the Angel's Voice said:
'The road is never spiritually lonely,
and we will not forsake you.
We will guide and bless you, for ever...'

'The epitome of mediumistic excellence'
Psychic News

A Voices Paperback (384 pages; illustrated)
ISBN: 0-953-6620-4-7

'IN TOUCH WITH ETERNITY'
Contact with Another World,
by Stephen O'Brien.

> *'As the hazy shape materialised
> there was revealed to us an Angel of Light,
> a beautiful woman with golden hair,
> whose eyes were deep blue-green like
> unfathomed ocean waters.
> "Peace," she said...'*

Make incredible journeys into the World of the Spirit
with Stephen O'Brien's remarkable
True-Life Psychic Experiences:
Go behind the scenes at Séances and discover how
Guardian Angels strive to contact us through the
Psychic Power that we unknowingly provide.
Read stunning Survival Evidence of human and
animal souls after death, including children's
messages to their parents and a communication
from Dr Martin Luther King.

◆ Unveil the truth about Reincarnation,
   Telepathy, Life Before Life,
   Out-of-the-Body Experiences,
   Soul Powers, and how to Heal with Psychic Sound.
◆ Encounter *'The Shining Ones'* deep within the
   Spiritual Spheres of Light, and learn of their
   concern for the human family and for our planet.
◆ Meet the Nature Spirits, and some amazing
   Animals that can communicate with us.

A Host of Fascinating Spiritual Experiences
from Britain's Renowned Visionary,
Medium and Healer.

A Voices Paperback (352 pages; illustrated)
ISBN: 0-953-6620-2-0